THIRD EDITION

DISCUSSION IN SMALL GROUPS:
A GUIDE TO EFFECTIVE PRACTICE

THIRD EDITION

DISCUSSION IN SMALL GROUPS:
A GUIDE TO EFFECTIVE PRACTICE

DAVID POTTER,
SOUTHERN ILLINOIS
UNIVERSITY AT CARBONDALE

MARTIN P. ANDERSEN,
CALIFORNIA STATE
UNIVERSITY, FULLERTON

WADSWORTH PUBLISHING
COMPANY, INC.
BELMONT, CALIFORNIA

Communications Editor: Rebecca Hayden
Designer: Dare Porter
Production Editor: Larry Olsen
Technical Illustrator: John Foster
Cartoonist: Tony Hall

ISBN 0–534–00426–1
L. C. Cat. Card No. 75–20733
Printed in the United States of America

2 3 4 5 6 7 8 9 10—80 79 78 77 76

Text set in 10/11 Melior

The oblong shape and three-column format of this book have been selected as the best design solution for a unique text and workbook.

The three-column format increases the amount of information per page and reduces the length of the book. The narrow columns facilitate reading and allow the student to calculate visually his or her progress. The varying column lengths increase student interest by producing a visually stimulating flow to the material, and the extended length of each tear-out analysis page allows for easy in-book work.

We believe a book designed specifically for its function stimulates the student's interest in the material, and thereby aids the teacher.

CONTENTS

TO THE INSTRUCTOR AND MEETING-PLANNER

The first and second editions of this text-workbook were designed primarily as a classroom tool—as a supplement to a theory-based discussion text or as the major teaching aid for classes where the emphasis was on *practice*. The primary function of this third edition is the same. Like its predecessors, it should prove to be a valuable planning and training aid for leaders in community organizations, businesses, church activities, and public and private agencies.

Although we consider the present organization and content to be an effective way to teach a discussion class, we frequently vary the order and selection of material depending on student background and interest. In classes where students have a wide range of experience and interests, we might start with private-discussion forms and techniques, assign subgroups to begin planning panel-forums, and then take up the special techniques noted in Chapter 10. In classes with many business majors, we might begin with an emphasis on problem-solving techniques. And in classes composed largely of education majors, we would probably focus first on participation, leadership, and role-playing.

Whatever the make-up of the class, our goal is always to develop a high degree of understanding and skill in participation, leadership, problem solving, role-playing as a tool of analysis and training, the structure and processes of small groups, and ways in which the interpersonal needs of group members can be achieved. We use the analysis forms throughout the book extensively. Although we use the longer exercises in Chapter 12 only occasionally, we believe that students should consider how private- and public-discussion forms and techniques contribute to the effectiveness of large meetings.

To give this book flexibility, we have included more exercises and activities than might ordinarily be used during a term or semester. We have also provided Analysis Forms and Planning Worksheets that focus on the content of particular chapters or theoretical material but that may easily be modified. Lastly, we have sought to make the text more useful in both campus and non-campus situations by content additions, deletions, and modifications.

Users of the second edition are asked to note the changes in Chapters 2, 6, and 7, and the addition of a new Chapter 3 on "Communication in Small Groups." To bridge the gap between practice and theory in selected chapters we have added sections in several chapters on "Implications for the Discussion Group Member." In addition, exercises have been updated; changes have been made in the content and number of various Analysis Forms; the outside reading references for each chapter have been updated and amplified; and all chapters have been revised to make them more meaningful and helpful to the students.

Many people have contributed, both directly and indirectly, to this revision. On our own campuses, students and colleagues have given much of their time to evaluating sections of the manuscript. Especially, we should like to acknowledge the contributions of Ann Ellerbrook, Randall Witte, Gretchen Jack, and Michael Agase. Further, we are grateful to those instructors who have used the text and have given suggestions for its improvement: Larry Bradford, Barton County Community College; William F. Brenner, Bucks County Community College; Ronald Burke, Syracuse University; Robert A. Dickey, Rock Valley College; Thomas C. Droessler, Owens Technical College; George Hale, Hillsdale College; Jack Holland, Orange Coast College; Pat M. Taylor, University of Alabama in Birmingham; Harold Wennstrom, El Camino College; Ralph W. Widener, Jr., University of Texas at Arlington. We have incorporated most of these helpful criticisms in this third edition. Herbert Booth, at the California State University, Fullerton, helped immensely in reviewing the entire manuscript and aided materially in the preparation of Chapter 3. We are also indebted to Gracia A. Alkema for her patient and judicious editing of this edition.

And finally, we owe continued appreciation to Rebecca Hayden, Communications Editor of Wadsworth Publishing Company, for her helpful guidance in all phases of the revision.

The purpose of this text-workbook is to help you become more effective in private and public discussion both on- and off-campus. You can use it to gain an understanding of the discussion theory, improve your skills of discussion, increase your sensitivity to yourself and others as you interact in group situations, develop problem-solving skills in all forms of confrontation situations, and increase your efficiency in related forms of communicative behavior.

This book may be used as the sole text in a discussion class or in conjunction with either a standard discussion text or a small group communication book oriented toward the behavioral sciences. In either case, the following suggestions may help you learn more during the course.

1. During the first few days of the class, fill out and turn in to the instructor the Questionnaire and Inventory sheet that follows this list. The information will enable your instructor to advise you on the basis of your personal needs. If the data are summarized for the whole class, you will know more about your classmates — knowledge that will facilitate interaction in your small groups.

2. During the first two weeks of class, glance through the entire text, noting particularly the analysis forms at the end of several chapters. When you participate in sub-group activities, try to use each of the forms at least once. Use the self-analysis forms to check on your progress.

3. Your instructor may not ask you to complete every exercise in the workbook. However, we suggest that you read and think about — and talk over with your friends — the exercises not assigned. All of the exercises focus on selected theoretical and/or practical aspects of the discussion process.

4. If this book is the only textbook used in your course, we suggest that you sample the discussion texts listed in Exercise 1 in Chapter 1 and in the "Suggested Readings" sections.

5. You will find it profitable to use as much of the material as possible outside of class — in campus committees, in your living groups, for planning longer meetings or conferences, and in confrontation situations. You will quickly learn how to adapt the theory and practical suggestions in the text to the demands of other communicative situations.

6. We have used all of the analysis forms in this workbook extensively, both in and outside of the classroom. In most instances, these analysis forms are based on research in discussion and communication. However, we realize that they may not necessarily meet the needs of every discussion class. When appropriate, therefore, we recommend that you modify our forms or develop your own.

7. Skill in discussion comes from numerous sources. Some of these are: (1) attitudes toward learning, (2) present knowledge of and opportunity to participate in problem-solving and/or confrontation situations, (3) sensitivity to others and flexibility in adjusting interpersonal behavior to meet the demands of any discussion situation, (4) knowledge of the theory of small group communicative behavior, and (5) continuous self-evaluation. Seek the reactions of your classmates to your techniques of participation or leadership in discussion. You will be working in sub-groups part of the time during the term or semester. Try to become sensitive to the workings of your group. Experiment to see what techniques work best. What method or behavior creates blocks to effective discussion? How do different communication networks affect discussion? Who are the leaders and who are the followers? What pressures are exerted on the group members? What roles do you personally play in improving the group's efficiency? Evaluate your own performance continuously.

8. Although this book emphasizes practice, we believe that theory should not be overlooked. Chapter 2, "The Small Group: Structure and Process," and Chapter 3, "Communication in Small Groups," overview significant theoretical concepts and hypotheses that are relative to practical discussion. To make this theoretical material more meaningful, ask your instructor to recommend additional sources that deal with discussion and small group theory and research. The "Implications for the Discussion Group Member" sections at the end of these and other chapters are helpful bridges between theory and practice.

PERSONAL QUESTIONNAIRE AND INVENTORY OF DISCUSSION SKILLS

Please fill out this questionnaire completely and give it to your instructor at the next class session. Your answers will help your instructor to (1) assess your needs and skills in discussion, (2) place you with compatible or challenging classmates when working in small groups, and (3) adapt the course to your specific needs as well as to the needs of the class as a whole.

1. College address: _____

_____

_____ Phone: _____

2. Age: _____ 3. Year in college: _____

4. College major: _____

minor: _____

5. High school from which you were graduated (school, city, state):

_____

_____

_____

6. Favorite high school extracurricular activities:

a. _____

b. _____

c. _____

7. Favorite college extracurricular activities:

a. _____

b. _____

c. _____

8. What high school or college debating or speaking experience have you had? (Give number of years, list specific activities or contests, and indicate if they were on local, state, or national levels.)

_____

_____

_____

_____

9. What high school and college speech communication courses have you taken? Also list courses in behavioral sciences.

_____

_____

_____

10. What public (off-campus) speech communication experiences have you had?

_____

_____

_____

11. In what full-time or part-time work are you now engaged? In what ways, if any, is speech communication or discussion involved?

_____

_____

12. What is your intended occupation? In what ways may small group discussion be involved?

_____

_____

13. In what campus and community activities do you now or have you participated? (List service organizations, student government committees, luncheon clubs, minority protest groups, political campaigns, and so on.) What leadership positions have you held?

_____

_____

_____

14. Do you like to work with other people? Under what conditions?

_____

_____

_____

15. To what radio or television programs do you listen or view? Indicate if occasionally or regularly.

_____

_____

_____

16. What books have you read recently that you would recommend to the class?

_____

_____

17. What newspapers and magazines do you read? Indicate if occasionally or regularly.

_____

_____

_____

18. Comment briefly on your communicative assets and deficiencies.

_____

_____

_____

19. What are your specific goals in taking this course?

_____

_____

_____

"The aim of the true democracy is to secure the active participation of every individual up to the limit of his capacity in the conduct of all his social, vocational, and political affairs."

Harrison S. Elliott
The Process of Group Thinking

In the days of the early New England town meeting, when democracy operated at the "grass-roots" level, discussion and debate were the essential tools with which decisions were made. Today, because American society and government have become so much more complex, there is an even greater need for effective decision-making tools. For this reason, our concern in this book is with improving discussion skills.

In the mid-1970s, men and women— whether in business, industry, labor, education, government, agriculture, the mass media, social rehabilitation, or minority group activities—are spending more time than ever before communicating in small groups. The committee meeting has become a basic ingredient in conducting government affairs at all levels. Thus, more and more people are now responsible for decision making in small groups. To ensure that their decisions are in the best interests of *all* the people, the decision makers must understand both the limitations and values of discussion, be skilled in its use, be prepared to counter its misuse, and insist on ethical standards.

A PRESCRIPTION FOR DISCUSSION

What is discussion? We define it simply and prescriptively as the *purposeful, systematic,* primarily *oral* exchange of *ideas, facts, and opinions* by a group of persons who *share in the group's leadership.* Note carefully the six different elements we stress in our prescription. Each is an essential part of the process; neglect of any one will usually result in ineffective or misused discussion.

1. *Discussion is purposeful.* Of the six elements, determining the purpose is perhaps the most important. Ideally, a group clearly defines the goals of its discussion at the outset so that group members understand them and can keep them constantly in mind during the discussion. In addition, they frequently review decisions and action resulting from discussion to ensure that they are in the best interests of the group as a whole.

2. *Discussion usually follows a systematic, logical plan.* Effective discussion results from having accurate evidence available, cultivating the knack of suspending judgment, carefully testing fact and opinion, avoiding specious reasoning, and systematically developing the topic that is being considered.

3. *Discussion is primarily an oral process and has both verbal and nonverbal aspects.* Being proficient in oral skills is as important in small group communication as in any other speaking situation. If discussion is to produce worthwhile results, voice and gesture must be used effectively, language must be meaningful, content must be relevant, listening skills must be at a high level, and the total participating group must be able to adapt to the discussion situation.

4. *Discussion requires considering all available information bearing on the specific topic: facts, opinions, reasoning, personal experiences, and expert testimony.* Study that leads to a thorough analysis of the problem, the exploration of all possible solutions, and the responsible participation of experts and laymen is essential to effective discussion.

5. *Discussion is a group process.* It takes place in small or large, formal or informal groups. The interpersonal relations of the participants should therefore be a constant concern. Although maintaining the group's morale and achieving its goals may be of primary importance, satisfying the members' ego needs must also be considered.

6. *Discussion, ideally, permits each member to share in the leadership of the group to the fullest extent of his ability.* "Leadership" may mean contributing to the group's plans, performing some task in the discussion process itself, or helping to evaluate the results of discussion. We believe that the best leadership occurs when it is a cooperative function performed by more than one member of the group.

Implied in all of these discussion elements is that the group's goal is to seek—in the best interests of the group and the circumstances—the truth, the best answer, the wisest decision, or the most practical course of action at any given point in time. This concept emphasizes that differing ideas must be considered on all substantive matters, especially in relation to facts and supported opinions. Further, to secure the best answer or solution, personality clashes should be avoided—or at least such clashes should be kept to a minimum or used as a basis for examining different viewpoints in more detail.

THE FUNCTIONS OF DISCUSSION

What are the functions of discussion in democratic decision making and in various group processes? We view discussion as a way to resolve most human problems in a rational manner. When it is possible for people to participate in decision making, they are motivated to apply the decisions that are reached, and their morale is raised or preserved. Discussion provides both the environment and the method for combining facts and ideas (input) into decisions and learnings (output) that are of greater consequence than the simple sum of the individual contributions. It aids our understanding in both learning and problem-solving situations by encouraging that we air our differences, develop agreements, plan action, and explore related facets of a topic. Membership in a functioning discussion group may encourage timid individuals to shed their shyness and join in working toward a mutual goal. Because of its social nature, discussion fosters group loyalties and offers opportunities for developing friends and achieving a sense of security. Discussion effectively trains individuals in the skills of critical thinking, communication, and interpersonal relations. Finally, it is a useful tool to use in experiments and research on group processes and human relations.

But using the tool of discussion will not further something that does not exist. If group members do not bring some knowledge and sense of responsibility to a discussion, the result is only a pooling of non-knowledge and irresponsibility. Discussion is not a substitute for individual decision and action. When time pressures make group action difficult and inadvisable, it should not be relied on. Group methods to oblige the clock can lead observers to condemn the methods rather than the abusers of those methods. Also, discussion should not be a drape to cover authoritarianism, for authoritarianism creates a deceptive situation in which individuals are suppressed. And if discussion lacks planning and guidance, it is an invitation to group frustration and anarchy.

In brief, discussion, like democracy, is no stronger than the thinking and behavior of its adherents. Only when we develop our abilities to detect problem situations, to locate pertinent information, to use approved methods of diagnosis and prognosis, and to employ sound reasoning and effective communication—practicing good human relations all the while—will we be able to increase the usefulness of discussion in American society. How do we develop these vital attitudes, skills, and abilities? This is the question this text-workbook tries to answer—at least in part. We say "in part" because much of what you learn, and how you learn it, depends upon you and your instructor.

PREPARING FOR DISCUSSION

This book consists of a carefully selected body of practical materials related to the major forms, principles, and practices of discussion. The chapter arrangement progresses from small group discussions to larger, extended meetings. You will take part in a number of different discussion activities that should make you more sensitive to interpersonal relations in discussion. In addition, these activities will help establish standards for your effective leadership and participation in group discussions, and help to improve your ability to think, communicate and evaluate.

Your effectiveness in any discussion and your improvement throughout the course will depend partly on how well prepared you are. Let's consider some steps of discussion preparation that apply equally well in both classroom and non-academic situations. You may wish to carry out these suggestions as outlined here or in a different order; under some circumstances, you may omit some of the steps altogether.

1. *Decide early on your discussion goal:* During the term or semester, you will probably participate in a number of different discussion situations: (1) as a member of a small group planning a presentation later before the entire class—a panel-forum, for example; (2) as a member of a panel discussing a topic with the rest of the class as an audience; (3) as a member of a panel-forum audience; or (4), as a participant in an off-campus discussion planned by you and other members of the class. In every instance, be sure that an early decision is made on your discussion goal, the preparation and actual discussion tasks to be performed, the purpose (for example, enlightenment, problem solving, motivation), the aspects of the topic to be covered, and whether you wish the audience to be committed to action. Specific discussion goals and tasks will be assigned to you at times by your instructor; at other times, the responsibility will be yours.

2. *Select the topic:* You will find detailed suggestions for how to select and word discussion topics in Chapter 7. We merely stress here three characteristics of every worthwhile topic: *interest, significance,* and *manageability.*

In general, discussion has two major functions: learning and problem solving. If either is to result, the participants—panel members, audience, or small group members—must have some *interest* in the topic. They must be involved intellectually in the subject of the discussion. Thus, consider your audience's interest as well as your own in picking a topic.

You must also consider the *significance* of the topic. Pick one that is of vital concern to the participants, that provides information they can use at some specific time, or that deals with some important social, economic, or political issue.

"Finally, the topic must be manageable."

Finally, the topic must be *manageable*. Don't try to decide in forty minutes on a new foreign policy. The time available for preparation and for the discussion itself, the knowledgeability of the participants, the scope of the subject, the participants' power to act on decisions made—these are some of the criteria to consider in determining whether a discussion topic is manageable.

3. *Gather the needed information:* No discussion should take place in a vacuum. Facts and well-considered opinion are as important in a discussion as in a speech. Whenever it is possible or when the nature of the discussion requires it, you should prepare in depth for your participation. You should recall and record personal experiences that bear on the subject, read widely on the topic, talk to others about it, listen to radio and television programs dealing with it, and anticipate some of the questions and issues that may arise.

4. *Determine the duties of the participants:* In this book, we view leadership in discussion not as the responsibility of one person alone but as a function shared by many. Implementing this concept requires that many persons perform tasks that contribute to the accomplishment of the group's goals. These tasks usually are determined and delegated in advance. For example, you will need to know who will act as chairperson or moderator, who will operate the audio-visual equipment, who will summarize the results, and who will distribute any written materials. In many discussions, there will be additional duties.

5. *Prepare a discussion outline:* In some discussions, it is impossible to prepare an outline in advance—for example, when a team of scientists tries to solve some highly technical problem or when a "one-shot" committee carries out some assigned task. But even in these situations, the discussion can follow a relatively orderly sequence.

In most situations, you will benefit from preparing a discussion outline. At times, you will find it sufficient to list a series of questions that show how the problem develops from definition to solution. At the other extreme, you may wish to prepare a very detailed outline dealing with every phase of the topic that might conceivably be considered.

You should not permit the outline to straitjacket the discussion. Use the outline as a guide, but let the discussants determine how closely they wish to adhere to it. Points that you have not listed may prove to be of greater significance than those included.

Additional suggestions for preparation of the discussion outline will be found in Chapter 7.

6. *Establish a time schedule:* Once you have prepared a discussion outline, make a rough schedule of how much time is to be devoted to the major points. Again, you do not need to follow this schedule to the second. Use it as a guide; do not let it rule you.

7. *Consider the physical aspects of the discussion:* Consider the acoustics of the room, the comfort of the participants, the availability of needed audio-visual equipment (be sure to examine its working condition), the lighting, the seating arrangements, and the other discussion aids. Although the physical situation is not

the most important factor in ensuring the effectiveness of a discussion, do not overlook it.

8. *Arrange for needed evaluation:* Although the major concern of participants is the content or goal of the discussion, discussants should always be aware of the process itself. Even slight sensitivity to the question "How well are we doing?" is likely to improve the discussion.

Evaluating or analyzing the process is not always possible or necessary. Some discussion groups come together for a single time, consider a problem, take action, and never meet again. On the other hand, many groups—such as classes in discussion, study clubs, or community forums—meet regularly over long periods of time. For them, evaluation should be integrated into their other activities.

If evaluation is to be effective, you should plan for it *before* the discussion takes place, be sure that the participants take part in it, keep it from overshadowing the discussion itself, and always report the results to the participants.

Throughout the book, you will find a number of analysis forms designed to help you improve your discussions. In addition, because evaluation is so important to improvement, the subject is treated in greater detail in Chapter 11.

9. *Plan how to get the discussion underway:* Assuming that you have done everything possible to prepare for a discussion, you still have to get the actual discussion started. For example, if you are the moderator of a panel-forum you must decide— together with the other panel members— how to introduce the panelists, what rules of procedure to announce, how to call attention to the significance of the topic, what background information to present, and how to direct the first question. Except in unstructured situations where no person has been designated as leader, you should always give some consideration in advance to the opening moments of a discussion.

10. *Conduct all needed planning meetings:* As you complete certain of our suggestions, you obviously will work alone. No one else can study or do research for you. However, the decisions needed to prepare for a discussion should be group decisions in most instances. In both its planning and execution stages, discussion should be a cooperative venture—its success depends on it.

As you get ready to participate in the discussion exercises presented in this text, in others recommended by your instructor, or in discussions in your community, try to carry out the steps we have suggested. Years of experience have convinced us that, almost without exception, the most effective discussions are the ones that are carefully planned.

We present these brief suggestions for preparation early in this text-workbook for two reasons: (1) to sensitize you at the outset to the need for careful preparation and (2) to improve the quality of your initial discussions. Detailed suggestions will be presented throughout the book.

A SUMMARY AND LOOK AHEAD

Discussion is the systematic, primarily oral exchange of information by persons working cooperatively toward a particular goal. In colonial times, it was a basic tool in democratic decision making, and it is even more so today. It serves individuals in learning, problem solving, and improving interpersonal relations. Using discussion effectively depends largely on the extent to which the discussants prepare for participation and on their knowledge and skill of discussion techniques.

Since much discussion occurs in small groups, a first step in learning effective discussion skills is to study the structure, processes, and dynamics of the small group—the subject of Chapter 2.

SUGGESTED READINGS

To become skillful in using discussion methods, you should study theory as well as practice. Here, and for each chapter, we list a number of selected references that are excellent supplements to the content of this book.

Andersen, Martin P., "A Model of Group Discussion," *Southern Speech Journal,* Vol. 30 (Summer 1965), pp. 279–293.

Applbaum, Ronald L., and others, *The Process of Group Communication* (Chicago: Science Research Associates, 1974), Ch. 1.

Barnlund, Dean C., and Franklyn S. **Haiman,** *The Dynamics of Discussion* (Boston: Houghton Mifflin, 1960), Chs. 15–16.

Bormann, Ernest G., *Discussion and Group Methods,* 2nd ed. (New York: Harper & Row, 1975), Ch. 1.

Chase, Stuart, and Marian **Tyler,** *Roads to Agreement* (New York: Harper & Row, 1951).

Fisher, B. Aubrey, *Small Group Decision Making* (New York: McGraw-Hill, 1974), Ch. 1.

Galvin, Kathleen, and Cassandra **Book,** *Person-to-Person: An Introduction to Speech Communication* (Skokie, Ill.: National Textbook Co., 1974), Chs. 1, 5.

Harnack, R. Victor, and Thorrel B. **Fest,** *Group Discussion: Theory and Technique* (New York: Appleton-Century-Crofts, 1964), Chs. 1–3.

Phillips, Gerald M., and Eugene C. **Erickson,** *Interpersonal Dynamics in the Small Group* (New York: McGraw-Hill, 1971).

Scheidel, Thomas M., *Speech Communication and Human Interaction* (Glenview, Ill.: Scott, Foresman, 1972), Ch. 1.

Zelko, Harold P., *The Business Conference* (New York: McGraw-Hill, 1969), Chs. 1–2.

EXERCISES

1. Below are a number of references in which the process of discussion is described, prescribed, or defined. Look up at least three of these textbooks to determine whether their definitions differ from the one given in this chapter. What are the differences, if any? Which definition do you prefer? Why? Be prepared to report on and discuss your findings in class.

Barnlund, Dean C., and Franklyn S. Haiman, *The Dynamics of Discussion* (Boston: Houghton Mifflin, 1960).

Bormann, Ernest G., *Discussion and Group Methods,* 2nd ed. (New York: Harper & Row, 1975).

Braden, Waldo W., and Earnest S. Brandenburg, *Oral Decision-Making* (New York: Harper & Row, 1955).

Brilhart, John K., *Effective Group Discussion,* 2nd ed. (Dubuque, Iowa: Wm. C. Brown, 1974).

Crowell, Laura, *Discussion: Method of Democracy* (Chicago: Scott, Foresman, 1963).

Fansler, Thomas, *Creative Power through Discussion* (New York: Harper & Row, 1950).

Fisher, B. Aubrey, *Small Group Decision Making* (New York: McGraw-Hill, 1974).

Gulley, Halbert E., *Discussion, Conference, and Group Process,* 2nd ed. (New York: Holt, Rinehart and Winston, 1968).

Hannaford, E. S., *Conference Leadership in Business and Industry* (New York: McGraw-Hill, 1945).

Harnack, R. Victor, and Thorrel B. Fest, *Group Discussion: Theory and Technique* (New York: Appleton-Century-Crofts, 1964).

Keltner, John W., *Group Discussion Processes* (New York: David McKay, 1957).

Sattler, William M., and N. Edd Miller, *Discussion and Conference,* 2nd ed. (Englewood Cliffs, N.J.: Prentice-Hall, 1968).

Smith, William S., *Group Problem-Solving Through Discussion,* rev. ed. (Indianapolis: Bobbs-Merrill, 1965).

Utterback, William E., *Group Thinking and Conference Leadership,* rev. ed. (New York: Holt, Rinehart and Winston, 1964).

Zelko, Harold P., *Successful Conference and Discussion Techniques* (New York: McGraw-Hill, 1957).

2. During the 1960s and 1970s, students have been and are continuing to be granted a greater voice in administrative and academic decision making. Perhaps you are a member of one of these joint faculty-student groups. Attend at least two or more of these group meetings and (at the discretion of your instructor) discuss in class or write a brief paper on whether or not the six elements of discussion presented in this chapter were evident in the group discussions you observed.

3. The following "radio discussion," written by Dr. Arvin L. Workman of Indiana State University, and used with his permission, focuses on various problems in discussion procedure. Although you may wish to use this scripted "role-play" later in the text in connection with such aspects as conflict resolution, styles of leadership, or role-playing in discussions, at this time produce the radio show "live," or on tape. Concentrate (1) on Dugan's concept of the role of discussion, indicating whether you agree or disagree and why; and (2) on Daniel's comment about surrendering "individuality" to the group. Try to reach a consensus among the class members as to how an individual may actively belong to, and actively participate in, a discussion group without giving up a precious part of his or her personality.

A Radio Script

MUSIC: FADE IN, UP AND UNDER

Voice I: (*deep and hollow*) Thou shalt not kill. Thou shalt not bear false witness. Thou shalt not take the name of the Lord (FADE) thy God in vain, for the Lord will not hold him guiltless that taketh his name in vain.

MUSIC: UP AND UNDER

Voice II: (*high pitched and loud*) Hear ye. Hear ye. Hear ye. Let it be known by order of the King that there will be a hanging in the village square at 4 o'clock Sunday. Hear ye. Hear ye. Hear ye. Let it be known (*fade*) by order of the King that there will be a hanging in the. . . .

MUSIC: UP AND UNDER

Voice III: (*softly, but well projected*) You will be extolled throughout all ages if you rescue your brethren from danger. To those present, in God's name I command this, to the absent I enjoin it. Let such as are going to fight for Christianity put the form of the cross upon their garments, that they may outwardly demonstrate the love arising for their inward faith. Let them enjoy, by the gift of God and the privilege of St. Peter, absolution from all crimes.

Let this in the meantime soothe the labor of their journey, satisfied that they shall obtain, after the death the advantages of blessed martyrdom. . . . (*fade*) Go and employ in noble warfare that valor and that sagacity which you used to waste in civil broils. . . .

MUSIC: UP AND UNDER

Voice IV: The proletarians have nothing to lose but their chains. They have a world to win . . . Workers of the world. . . . unite. . . .

MUSIC: UP AND UNDER

Voice V: Democracy is a kingless regime infested by many kings who are sometimes more exclusive, tyrannical, and destructive than one, if he be a tyrant.

MUSIC: UP AND UNDER

Voice VI: . . . that government of the people, by the people, and for the people shall not perish from the earth. . . .

MUSIC: UP, HOLD, BUT ABRUPTLY

Bering: (*deep, measured, and with a sense of command*) Now, panelists, we can discuss some of your impressions. First of all, did you recognize any of the ideas that you heard on the tape recorder?

Parma: Well, I guess you couldn't miss Lincoln there — the idea of democracy.

Wilson: The town crier. . . .

Bering: What would that represent? Mr. Wilson?

Wilson: Well, I suppose it could represent anything that happened in the 16th through the 19th century.

Bering: I think the important thing in this case is not who the man is but what he is saying.

Daniel: The man was crying something about a hanging by the king. . . .

Wilson: Divine rule. Is that the idea?

Bering: Good. Any more? Dugan?

Dugan: Well, I think I recognize Marx. "The proletarians have nothing to lose but their chains."

Bering: Good. What ideas do these represent?

Parma: That would be Communism and, I guess, Nazism.

Dugan: Marx would be Marxism. There's a difference.

Parma: (*defensively*) I don't see the difference. They're both rotten.

Bering: There's no need to argue. I meant to imply Marxism.

Daniel: I couldn't place the long speech, but it might have been one of the Caesars.

Parma: Probably Julius!

Bering: No, I'm afraid you're wrong on that one.

Parma: (*defensively*) Well, there were a lot of Caesars—four or five.

Bering: That is a rough one. It isn't a Caesar at all. It was Pope Urban II exhorting the Christian Knights to go and fight in the crusades. This should represent Papal Law.

Parma: By gosh, I shouldn't have missed that one.

Bering: How about "Democracy is a kingless regime infested by many kings who are sometimes more exclusive, tyrannical, and destructive. . . . ?"

Wilson: (*pondering*) That could be anybody in Europe or Asia who is against democracy.

Parma: Probably a Commie.

Bering: Well, I won't hold you up on this one, panelists. You're right, of course, about the speaker's being against democracy. It's Benito Mussolini. And by now, I hope you see the pattern. I've given you some symbols, or at least several different forms of control: divine rule, facism, democracy, papal law, mosaic law, and I could have gone to socialism, collectivism, and so on.

Parma: (*puzzled*) According to the note you sent me, Commander Bering, we were going to discuss—I have it right here—"The role of group discussion in a democratic society."

Bering: Quite true, Mr. Parma, and we will begin the discussion after I introduce everyone. On my left is Dr. Daniel, a political scientist at the University, and Ms. Dugan, of the History Department.

Daniel: Good afternoon.

Dugan: Good afternoon.

Parma: Hi.

Bering: I'm Commander Bering of the N.R.O.T.C. (*pause*) Discussants, I've sent you all a copy of the question and as a starter, I've given you some different forms of control. How would you say group discussion would function in these forms of control as compared to democratic control?

Daniel: Speaking of control, Commander, ah, wouldn't you consider "control" a rather awkward word to use in conjunction with "democratic?"

Parma: (*enthusiastically*) I'm with you on that point, Doctor. "Democratic" and "control" definitely don't go together.

Bering: Perhaps a rephrasing of the question might clarify my meaning. Actually, several methods of control were alluded to on the tape we heard, and some of them were forms of government. How does group discussion play a part in these different forms? Ms. Dugan, I see you nodding your head.

Dugan: Frankly, Commander, I think you'll find group discussion a *disruptive* force in any form of government when it is used alone. Actually, as I see it, group discussion is a method of collecting and clarifying ideas which must then be submitted to either one person, say in the case of facism, or to a group vote for a final decision as we do in our congressional system.

Wilson: (*disturbed*) Wait a minute. Do you really mean a "disruptive force," Ms. Dugan?

Dugan: (*calmly*) By itself, yes. Take this group, for instance. We will put some ideas into a common pot and that's all that will happen to them as far as this group is concerned. We're not going to vote on them, neither are we going to submit them to higher authority. So, our ideas will just be left where we put them.

Bering: You are saying then that any group discussion has no function by itself and that it's a disruptive force. I . . . .

Wilson: Excuse me, Commander, I'd like to chase this down a bit. Dugan, would you clarify what you mean by your statement that group discussion has no function alone or by itself? Then I'd like you to explain how you classify discussion as a "disruptive" force.

Dugan: Be glad to. Let's take your first question. (*pause*) In any group discussion the participants divide into two classes; those that have power or those who don't have power. Ah, in other words, you have group discussants—if that's the right word—who have what I call a power-wielding vote. In other groups the discussants do not have this vote. Therefore, if a group is a nonpower group, its members have no real function except to talk.

Daniel: (*mildly*) I can't agree to that. . . .

Parma: I'm with you, Dr. Daniel. Group discussion is vital to . . . to . . . everything!

Dugan: (*calmly*) But what end results do group discussions have, gentlemen?

Parma: How?

Wilson: (*disturbed*) Wait a minute. I still want to know what Dugan means by "no function."

Parma: Yeah. How about in business? A business conference is group discussion. (*self satisfied*) And don't tell me that conferences aren't important in business.

Dugan: All right, let's take a business conference. The discussion by itself is usually meaningless. Actually, the decision is made by the board of directors or the person in charge of operations after the talking is over. Let me modify this. If discussion accomplishes anything, it is only by collecting information and opinions and by classifying that information and opinion. Oh *perhaps* it serves as a form of mass confession.

Wilson: I can't follow you. If group discussions have no function other than seeking information and opinions and letting off steam and conscience, why would the method be relied on so heavily practically everywhere in our country?

Parma: (*triumphantly*) My point exactly!

Dugan: No, let me put it another way. (*calmly and smoothly*) The ends of discussion are usually determined ahead of time by the leaders of the groups. The participants are merely there to suggest some ways to accomplish a foregone conclusion. I don't mean that discussion performs a completely useless function as far as the group is concerned. It really serves as a pacifying function—say, in the case of business: The president decides to expand the company. He or she issues the topic for discussion—"How can we best expand our business?" The conclusion is already there. The group then works out the details and accepts the change because the discussants feel a responsibility for making the change. (*with emphasis*) In reality they're puppets!

Daniel: Aren't you exaggerating your point, Ms. Dugan? "Puppets" is a strong word. (*with emphasis*) *Inaccurate too!* People who are given the responsibility of implementing a decision *do* have a *real* and *useful* role in business or any phase of society.

Wilson: (*emphatically*) You're right. And let's go a step farther. Take the city planning groups who work out problems and recommend sweeping changes in zoning. And what about grand juries? And the boards of directors of corporations? Don't they serve a real function? (*irritated*) Puppets, my neck!

Dugan: Wait a minute. With the city planning group, if it doesn't submit its plans for a vote, a higher power makes the final decision. And there is another point that should be considered. During a discussion, the only problem is to persuade enough people to go one way or another. And. . . .

Parma: (*bursting in*) Look, I can't see. . . .

Bering: (*firmly*) Please let Ms. Dugan finish.

Dugan: Thank you. As I was saying, the board of directors is an example of uneven power. Each member has a different number of stocks that he represents, and so he has a weighted contribution. Consequently, there is little necessity for the cooperative meeting of minds. If a couple of board members have made up their minds and they have enough votes to push through their plans, that's all there is to it.

Parma: (*awed*) Ms. Dugan has something there. I'm going to have to agree.

Wilson: (*caustically*) On what?

Parma: That group discussion doesn't really accomplish anything unless the members of the group have the power to vote.

Bering: (*with authority*) Excuse me, panelists, but I think we've got ourselves up a tree and we may never get down to earth. We *were* discussing the role of group discussion in a democratic society, and I think we are quite away from that subject now. As we might say in the Navy, "We're a hundred and eighty out," or for you civilians, "We're going in the wrong direction."

Dugan: The wrong direction from what *you* planned, Commander?

Bering: (*flash of anger, replaced by sudden calmness*) Well, it's not a matter of planning, Ms. Dugan. It's more a matter of staying on the subject.

Dugan: That's just my point, Commander. *You* selected the question or problem and *you*, no doubt, have an outline of the best arguments concerning roles in group discussion. Now I've taken the stand that group discussion doesn't play any major role other than collecting and clarifying material and *you* say I'm a hundred-eighty out. As a member of this discussion group, shouldn't I have as much to say about the direction of the discussion as you?

Bering: Dr. Daniel is smiling. What do you say to Ms. Dugan's accusation?

Daniel: I say there may be an element of truth in what she says. But I think our present problem is largely one of definition. Do we all mean the same thing by "group discussion?"

Bering: That's an excellent idea, Dr. Daniel. Perhaps we should define group discussion before we go any farther. Mr. Wilson, you're a speech man.

Wilson: (*pensively*) Well, there are several pretty good definitions. Baird says discussion is the "Art of reflective thinking and communication, usually oral, by the members of a group whose aim is the cooperative solution of a problem." And . . . let me see . . . oh, yes, there's the Potter and Andersen prescription: . . . "the purposeful, systematic, primarily oral exchange of ideas, facts, and opinions by a group of persons who share in the group leadership." Essentially, I'd say that discussion involves a group of people pooling ideas and resources, more or less cooperatively, in order to clarify their thinking or to solve their individual or collective problems.

Dugan: Not bad. . . .

Bering: Then you retract your earlier statements, Dugan?

Dugan: Not at all. Mr. Wilson may be guilty of stretching the point a little when he attached discussion to the process of clarifying thinking and solving individual problems. Actually, I'm not convinced that more problems are solved than are introduced by group activity— but to return to your question, neither of the textbook definitions goes much further than to declare that discussion has only the properties of conversing together while thinking reflectively. They don't—the texts, that is—contribute much authority to the process except by relatively unsupported generalization.

Wilson: (*disturbed*) I'm afraid that Ms. Dugan is stretching her point. What generalizations must a textbook definition support? But forget that for a moment. I'd like to ask her if she has any *authority* to support her arguments.

Dugan: No, they're my own ideas.

All: (*There is a sustained silence for a few seconds*)

Bering: Let's see if I can paraphrase your ideas now, Dugan. You assert that group discussion has no function in society other than to clarify and collect information and that groups are all controlled as to their conclusions. You said, further, if I remember correctly, that the only freedom exercised in the group is in finding ways to arrive at foregone conclusions. Now, if this is true, Ms. Dugan, what do you think the foregone conclusion of this group is?

Dugan: Well, first of all, it doesn't make any difference because this is a nonvoting, or non-power group. Still, we hope to prove that group discussion has a place in our society. This is evident by the question. It doesn't ask any questions like "Are there any roles?" It merely assumes that there are roles and that we must discover what they are. The decision has been reached by you, Commander Bering, that there are roles; our job is only to discover what they are.

Bering: Well, at the risk of being called a dictator, I suggest that we leave this point. We've exhausted it anyway. Now let's move on to the question: "What effect does the discussion have on its individual members?" A possible answer was mentioned earlier—"it might pacify discussants if they think they are helping to make the decision."

Parma: (*disturbed*) Hold it, Commander. I don't know about the rest of the group, but I feel pretty upset when Ms. Dugan hinted that we in this group were only working toward a preconceived conclusion. I don't like to be called a rubber stamp.

Wilson: I don't think that Ms. Dugan intended to brand us as rubber stamps, Parma. But I'm bothered by another of her conclusions. I don't think we ought to dismiss group discussion even if its only advantage is to give members experience in clarifying and collecting facts. Why, that experience alone develops a feeling of importance . . . a feeling of belonging. And . . . .

Daniel: (*cutting in*) But that feeling of belonging to the group can result in a person surrendering his or her individuality to the group. In other words, the group is the source of importance. No, Wilson, let me explain. I think a law of physics applies here. For every action, there is an opposite and equal reaction. For instance, if you contribute to a group, you become a part of the group in equal proportion to the amount you contribute. The more you contribute, the more you become a part of the group and the less you are an individual.

Wilson: If what you say is true, Dr. Daniel, the only reward one receives from being a good member of the group is to become its slave.

Daniel: No, I don't mean that. I've overstated my position and you've caught me. What I mean is that there is a law of society which seems to say that everyone in a group has to give up something in order to belong. The catch is how much of ourselves can we retain while enjoying the benefits of belonging?

Dugan: As Whyte points out in his *Organization Man* (an acceptable authority, Mr. Wilson?), the tendency is for modern people to give up most of their individuality and to do it willingly. The very prevalence of "Group Think"— Mr. Whyte's uncomplimentary name for group discussion—seems to prove his assertion.

Bering: We have said, then, that joining the group in mind and spirit is essential if group participation is to be satisfying. We have said, also, that there's danger in becoming too involved in the group and losing one's individuality. Now in the few seconds we have left, I'd like to return to the question we left earlier in our discussion. We were questioning whether group discussion was a necessary force in our society.

Dugan: We . . . I . . . also said that most group discussions leave nothing but a lot of ideas in the melting pot.

Wilson: Exactly! And those ideas allow the leaders to make better decisions. Discussion, then, educates the leaders and voters as well as the discussants.

Bering: Perhaps *we've* reached some sort of decision here. Could we agree that group discussion is necessary as an educational factor in our society? That one of its prime functions is to teach us to focus on the problem, the issues, the facts, and the opinions *before* we are stuck with a decision?

Wilson: Nicely put. And you might add that research has indicated that when a group *must* arrive at a decision, that decision is more likely to be a good one than when one individual is solely responsible. And from my own classroom experience, I can say that practice in problem solving, examining evidence, reasoning, and searching for pertinent information helps to develop acuity and maturity in young people. And the faster we develop that acuity and maturity among the people of the world, the better our chance of surviving.

Dugan: A good speech. But if you and the social psychologists who've done the "research" you've mentioned are so right, this world should be ruled by monkeys and crows. Matter of fact, there are times when I think it is . . . .

All: (*Everyone talks at once*)

Bering: I'm sorry, panelists, but I have to cut in here because our time is up. We have come to the close of another program with some disturbing ideas having been placed before us. Just what value does group discussion have for a democratic society? How can we belong to a group without giving up a precious portion of our individuality? Are the ends of group discussion preconceived by the very topics or questions that are proposed? Just what research supports the claims that the process of group discussion is a major tool in teaching reflective thinking? We've only been able to raise these and other questions and nibble at some of the issues involved. And if Ms. Dugan is right, all our group can do is toss the ideas into the melting pot for your decision. Good afternoon.

THE STRUCTURE
OF THE SMALL GROUP

Although the emphasis in this book is on the practice of discussion, we believe you should also be conversant with its theory. In this chapter, therefore, we present an overview of hypotheses and concepts that apply to discussion practice. Specifically, we will do three things in this chapter: (1) Review currently accepted principles of small-group work. (2) Provide understanding of the parameters of interaction in small groups. (3) Establish a theoretical framework for further study of small discussion groups. We will look at the structure of the small group and the interaction processes, including selected aspects of group input and output.

The list of discussion texts and related behavioral science books following Chapter 3 provide in-depth materials on topics touched upon only briefly here. The list of "Implications for the Student" will provide a bridge between theory and practice.

Definitions of "group" are almost as varied as the number of groups that exist. Basically, however, most definitions recognize four characteristics that *all* groups share.

The first is physical and temporal. That is, a group functions within certain physical and time boundaries. Second, individuals bring to the group certain physical and psychological characteristics such as sex, age, race, language, skills, need-value systems, and mental abilities. Third, group members have a sense of shared purpose and activity—in other words, each member identifies with the group and its goals. Fourth, the individuals interact in some way. That is, the behavior of each influences the behavior of the others. Thus, a group consists of interrelations, more or less structured, though they are not always obvious.

A Definition of the Group

What is a group? We define it as *a face-to-face or co-acting system in which interactions by the members determine its structure, identity, and content and help to satisfy some of the members' needs.*

In all human society, each of the four characteristics of groups is primarily symbolic. Hence, pre-existing language and communication patterns, or ones that develop through interaction, influence the input, processes, and output of any group.

In the latter part of this chapter—in our model of the discussion process—we consider some of the implications of the symbolic nature of communication. And, in Chapter 3 on "Communication in Small Groups," we deal with some of the ways in which communication—its characteristics, factors affecting it in small groups, and the roles of listening and feedback—can determine the outcome of small group discussion. Here, let us examine some aspects of group structure.

Internal and External Systems

All groups, through interpersonal interaction, develop an *internal* pattern or system of behavior, which functions in the context of an *external* system. The external system affects and is affected by the internal system. An analogous relationship exists between individuals and their reference groups; in other words, people *are* — and function as — individuals even though their relationships with others help to define who they are.

Homans has explained the relationships between the internal and external systems of a group as consisting of two parts.[1] The first deals with three concepts that describe the behavior of people in everyday life: *activities*, *sentiments* or *feelings*, and *interaction* (behavior that goes from sender to receiver and back to sender). The second part refers to the context in which each group operates — this is the *social system*. It contains an external system of interrelationships between activity, interaction, and sentiment that

[1] George C. Homans, *The Human Group* (New York: Harcourt, Brace and World, 1950).

external forces impose on a group. And, it also includes an internal system dealing with the interrelationships among interaction, activities, and sentiment that develop over time within the group and that sometimes become guides to behavior. These systems are interdependent, and their relative dominance varies. Thus, informal and formal structures develop.[2]

For example, consider a scientific team in a large industrial plant producing hardware for some aspect of our national defense. The team must first act within the framework of the function it is performing within the plant — planning specifications,

[2] The reader should study the results of research conducted at the Western Electric Company's Hawthorne Works in Chicago and reported in F. J. Roethlisberger and W. J. Dickson, *Management and the Worker* (Cambridge: Harvard University Press, 1939).

"Role differentiation
occurs among the team members."

constructing, or testing. But the team must also operate within the contractual arrangements that the company has made with some government agency and within the larger needs of national defense. At the same time, interplay is going on *within* the team. Role differentiation occurs among the team members. Norms (a set of expectations regarding accepted behavior) are established. The roles an individual plays[3] and the norms accepted within a group strongly influence individual be-

[3] The literature on "role theory" is voluminous. For a review, see Theodore R. Sarbin and Vernon L. Allen, "Role Theory" in Gardner Lindzey and Elliot Aronson, eds., *The Handbook of Social Psychology*, 2nd ed., Vol. 1 (Reading, Mass.: Addison-Wesley, 1968), pp. 488–567. A meaningful statement of the importance of "taking the role of the other" is presented by George H. Mead in *Mind, Self and Society* (Chicago: University of Chicago Press, 1934). A comprehensive overview of "perceptual" psychology is found in Arthur W. Combs and Donald Snygg, *Individual Behavior: A Perceptual Approach to Behavior*, rev. ed. (New York: Harper & Row, 1959).

havior. In discussion groups in particular, it is important to understand how the other group members perceive the meaning and intent of interaction. And, it is also important to be able to perform many different functional roles.

The Life Cycle of Groups

Analyzing a group's life cycle — that is, the stages in its growth — also helps us to understand its structure. A group tends to develop in a certain pattern that comes from the members' nebulously defined shared characteristics and from their tenuous ties of shared purpose. The stages of growth develop from the constantly changing interrelationships within this internal system of the group. Thelen and Dickerman[4] suggest that, from first contacts to maturity, groups evolve in a four-step sequence.

[4] Herbert Thelen and Watson Dickerman, "Stereotypes and the Growth of Group," *Educational Leadership*, Vol. 6 (February 1949), pp. 309–316.

First, because individuals possess certain needs when they enter a group and because these are initially not group needs, this phase is primarily personal. It represents an effort by individuals to satisfy their needs and to establish their relationships with all others in the group. Individuals try to get the group to adopt customs with which they are comfortable; in other words, most members want the group to function according to stereotypes they hold. Stereotyped views of group operations include: a group needs a strong leader; a nonparticipating person is not a good group member; the group is wasting its time unless it is actively doing something; cohesiveness and effective functioning cannot be achieved until everyone is "acquainted" — has certain information about every other member of the group; expression of feeling is bad. Thus, in phase one, each individual acts according to his or her past understandings of how a group should function.

In the second phase, frustrations and conflicts created by the stereotyped ways of behaving show up. Individuals are frustrated because they are uncertain about their status in the group and because they have certain expectations about the group itself, especially about "leadership." In a democratic discussion group, for example, the typical American brings to it certain stereotypes about leadership; and these different views may conflict with each other. An individual may expect the leader to "take charge," yet he or she may hold only vague notions about "democratic processes." These stereotypes may lead individuals to rebel against the group and its "leaders" and encourage one or more of them to "take over" in order to "get something done." In the less democratic group, since most Westerners have ambivalent feelings about strong leadership, the rebellion may take a different turn. The response may be submission, overt hostility, or self-contained aggression and withdrawal.

In the third phase, a feeling of cohesiveness and a desire to avoid conflict "at any cost" develops. At this point, participants experience an increased sense of responsibility for satisfying group needs and those of individual members. However, if stability and harmony are achieved merely to avoid conflict, the group may become static and unable to make use of the task-oriented conflict so necessary to progress.

Fourth, the mature group maintains its sense of group-centeredness and sensitivity for the rights of others in the group, as well as for the processes of interactions. At the same time, however, it develops the sense of urgency and purpose that it needs in order to become an effective social instrument. The group becomes less process-centered and more task-centered, and its chief interest in group process is for self-analysis: "How can we do the job better?"

Thelen and Dickerman summarize their findings as follows:

Beginning with individual needs for finding security and activity in a social environment, we proceed first to emotional involvement of the individuals with each other, and second to the development of a group as a rather limited universe of interaction among individuals and as the source of individual security. We then find that security of position in the group loses its significance except that as the group attempts to solve problems it structures its activities in such a way that each individual can play a role which may be described as successful or not in terms of whether the group successfully solved the problem it had set itself.[5]

[5] Thelen and Dickerman, p. 316.

To a large extent, the Thelen and Dickerman study focused on the *emotional factor* in group growth. As students of speech communication, we must also be concerned with the nature of a group's *verbal interaction.* A pertinent study, reported by B. Aubrey Fisher in 1970, sought to discover the character of the verbal interaction over a period of time as a group sought consensus on a decision-making task. Socio-emotional factors, individual differences among the members, and the diversity of social dimension among non-classroom groups studied—all were purposely excluded.

Fisher concluded that task-oriented small groups, whose interaction is primarily verbal, will experience four phases: orientation, conflict, emergence, and reinforcement.[6] The basic research method he employed was one of content analysis (analysis of substantive comments resulting from interactions of the group members). Interaction units were classified as favorable, unfavorable, or ambiguous toward the decision proposal. The following distinctive interaction patterns describe the four phases: (1) *orientation* contained the most statements of clarification and

[6] B. Aubrey Fisher, "Decision Emergence: Phases in Group Decision-Making," *Speech Monographs,* Vol. 37 (1970), pp. 53–66.

agreement; (2) *conflict* was characterized by dispute in which the attitudes expressed were polarized; (3) *emergence* was characterized by ambiguity that served to mediate between attitudes of disfavor and favor toward the decision proposal; and (4) *reinforcement* reflected greater unity among the group members.

Group Purposes: Individual and Collective

As we look at the growth of a group and the characteristics of its interaction, we must consider the purposes for which groups are formed and the personal reasons why individuals participate in them. Elsewhere in this book, we point out that the basic purposes of the discussion group are problem solving (including decision making and resolving differences), learning, therapy, and commitment. These group goals are usually clearly stated and understood. However, in order to understand the role of the individual in the group and to evaluate group progress toward its goals, we must also understand the less obvious psychological functions of the group.

Individuals are drawn into groups, continue to function in them, and find their greatest satisfaction in them because of psychological forces. The most important of these forces may be the sense of "belonging"—being an integral part of an ongoing group activity. Riesman[7] points out that some individuals join groups because they are "outer directed." That is, they are in need of external support for their ego. It is interesting to note that Riesman is critical of the lack of "inner-directed" maturity of many or most Americans. Eric Fromm,[8] a psychiatrist also concerned with such lack of inner resources, considers dependence on others as "escape from freedom"—a psychological retreat from individual responsibility. Whyte[9] has also remarked on this tendency

[7] David Riesman, *The Lonely Crowd* (New York: Doubleday, 1950).

[8] Eric Fromm, *Escape from Freedom* (New York: Farrar & Rinehart, 1941).

[9] William H. Whyte, Jr., *The Organization Man* (New York: Simon and Schuster, 1956).

to conform, to "belong"—to find a justification and defense of the self in depending on the group, on group standards, on group membership. He slightingly describes it as the "tyranny" of the group.

Group-oriented behavior has many implications in our consideration of discussion groups. Before getting into those implications, however, we want to stress a major thesis of this book: that the seemingly contradictory needs of "belongingness" and of "individuality" can be maintained only through democratic discussion. Only in this way can the individual in a group preserve her or his integrity as a person.

Festinger[10] classifies some other significant reasons why people join groups:

1. Groups frequently serve as intermediaries to help individuals attain important goals.

2. Group activities frequently attract members.

3. People have needs that can only be satisfied by personal relationships with others.

Some personal needs that fall under the third classification have been listed by Fouriezos and others as dependency,

[10] Leon Festinger, "Architecture and Group Membership," *Journal of Social Issues,* Vol. 7 (1951), pp. 152–163.

status, dominance, aggression, and catharsis.[11] A somewhat different rundown is provided by Ardrey who states that personal needs are identity, stimulation, and security.[12] A. H. Maslow, who has undertaken some of the most significant studies of motivation, believes that an individual's needs occur at five levels. He further states that a person must partially or wholly satisfy a need on a lower level before he or she can go on to higher-level needs. His five levels are as follows:

1. *Physiological* needs—including hunger, thirst, and sex.

2. *Safety* needs—including security, self-preservation, order, and stability.

[11] Nicholas T. Fouriezos and others, "Self-oriented Needs in Discussion Groups," in Dorwin Cartwright and Alvin Zander, eds., *Group Dynamics,* 2nd ed. (New York: Harper & Row, 1960), pp. 354–360.

[12] Robert Ardrey, *The Social Contract* (New York: Atheneum, 1970), pp. 91–93.

3. *Belongingness* and *love* needs—including affection, friendship, identification, and love.

4. *Esteem* needs—including prestige, self-respect, success, and pride.

5. *Self-actualization* needs—including all forms of personal achievement.[13]

The famous studies by Roethlisberger and Dickson[14] illustrate some of these individual needs as they were met in groups in an industrial setting. They found that the group gives status to individuals, directs certain of the roles that they play, and gives them a sense of participation. In other words, the group serves their needs for security. Such personal, psychological reasons are more important than "practical" reasons. Thus, although the groups were originally formed to increase pro-

ductivity and although outward purposes included such incentives as increased pay, the chief justification for individual participation was the sense of "belonging" that resulted.

Regardless of the classification used, one or more of the personal, basic needs must be met, or the individual must think they are capable of being met, in order for him or her to remain a member of the group.

Group Dimensions as Structure

As a way of summarizing some of the concepts already considered in this chapter, let's examine the dimensions that give a group its essential character. One classification of group dimensions, devised by Hemphill and Westie, is presented below.[15] Although not all of the dimensions are equally significant, they do suggest the wide range of forces that affect individual behavior in the group and give shape to the group itself. Following each description, we ask two questions that might help you see some of the implications of these dimensions.

1. *Autonomy* refers to the degree to which a group functions independently of other groups and occupies an independent position in society. It is reflected by the extent to which a group determines its own activities, by its absence of allegiance, deference, and/or dependence in relation to other groups.

What is the relation of the group to its external system?

To what extent is any individual member's reference group a factor in shaping the group's activities?

2. *Control* refers to the degree to which a group regulates the behavior of individuals while they are functioning as group members. It is reflected by the extent to which group membership imposes restrictions on an individual's freedom of behavior and by the amount or intensity of group-derived government.

Is leadership centered in one autocratic person, or is it spread among all members?

Are the members aware of the degree to which they are free to take action in the group?

[13] A. H. Maslow, *Motivation and Personality* (New York: Harper & Row, 1954), pp. 80–92. The list is adapted from these pages. Copyright © 1954 by Harper & Row, Publishers. By permission of the publishers.

[14] See F. J. Roethlisberger and W. J. Dickson, *Management and the Worker* (Cambridge: Harvard University Press, 1939).

[15] As reported by Carroll L. Shartle, "Studies in Naval Leadership," in Harold Guetzkow, ed., *Groups, Leadership and Men* (New York: Russell & Russell, 1963), pp. 127–128.

3. *Flexibility* refers to the degree to which a group's activities are marked by informal rather than established procedures. It is reflected by the extent to which members' duties are *not* specified by custom, tradition, written rules, regulations, codes of procedure, or even unwritten but clearly prescribed rules of behavior.

Does power potentially reside in the formal or in the informal structure of the group?

Is the flexibility of the members' activities directed into productive channels?

4. *Hedonic tone* refers to the degree to which group membership is accompanied by a general feeling of pleasantness or agreeableness. It is reflected by the frequency of laughter, conviviality, pleasant anticipation of group meetings, and by the absence of griping and complaining.

In what ways do the members of the group talk in terms of "we"?

Do the members manifest their liking for others by overt acts of mutual support?

5. *Homogeneity* refers to the degree to which members of a group are similar to one another in terms of socially relevant characteristics. It is reflected by relative uniformity of the age, sex, race, socioeconomic status, interests, attitudes, and habits of the members.

Have the similarities among the members resulted in cooperation or competition?

To what extent has the homogeneity built cohesiveness?

6. *Intimacy* refers to the degree to which members of a group are mutually acquainted with one another and are familiar with the most personal details of one another's lives. It is reflected by the nature of topics discussed by members and by modes of greeting and forms of address. It is also reflected by interactions that presuppose that members know how other members will react under widely differing circumstances, as well as by the extent and type of knowledge each member has about others in the group.

In what ways has intimacy helped to satisfy the "belongingness" need of group members?

Has intimacy resulted in fight, flight, dependency, or pairing?

7. *Participation* refers to the degree to which group members spend time and effort on group activities. It is reflected by the number and kinds of duties members perform, by voluntary assumption of non-assigned duties, and by the amount of time spent on group activities.

Does the group provide participation opportunities that satisfy ego needs of the members?

Is the participation pattern both group- and task-centered?

8. *Permeability* refers to the degree to which a group permits ready access to membership. It is reflected by the absence of entrance requirements of any kind and by the degree to which membership is solicited.

Can the group readily assimilate new members?

In what ways do "new" members have to act in order to gain acceptance?

9. *Polarization* refers to the degree to which a group is oriented, and works, toward a single, clear, and specifically understood goal.

Are the goals of the group clearly defined?

Do hidden agendas of the members subvert group productivity?

10. *Potency* refers to the degree to which a group has primary significance for its members. It is reflected by the kind of needs that a group satisfies or has the potential to satisfy, by the extent of readjustment that would be required of members should the group fail, and by how relevant a group is to the central values of its members.

In what ways do group activities satisfy individual needs for affection, inclusion, and control?[16]

Are group activities relevant to both the overt and covert need-value systems of the members?

[16] These three needs will be discussed further in Chapter 3.

11. *Size* refers to the number of members in the group.

Is the group's size appropriate for effective productivity?

Is the group small enough to be functional yet large enough to include all the socialization and achievement skills needed for task accomplishment?

12. *Stability* refers to the degree to which a group persists over a period of time with essentially the same characteristics. It is reflected by the rate of membership turnover, by frequency of reorganizations, and by constancy of group size.

Is the group's stability a barrier to needed changes in procedural methods?

Do the forces that shape the internal system of the group contribute to instability? If so, in what way?

13. *Stratification* refers to the degree to which a group places its members into status hierarchies. It is reflected by the differential distribution of privileges, obligations, and duties.

Is leadership considered a functional responsibility of the total group rather than the "job" of a "leader"?

Does the "pecking order" of the group, if one exists, impede or promote productivity? Why?

14. *Viscidity* refers to the degree to which group members function as a unit. It is reflected by the absence of dissension, personal conflict, and activities that serve to advance only the interests of individual group members. It is also reflected by the group's ability to resist disrupting forces and by members' belief that the group does indeed function as a unit.

In what ways do leaders and members work together in planning and achieving group goals?

In what ways does communication within the group contribute to group unity?

Our next chapter deals specifically with the subject of communication in small groups. At this point, however, let us emphasize that each of the fourteen dimensions of group structure listed above affect or are affected by communication. For example, item 6, *intimacy*, cannot exist unless the group members have, over a period of time, developed close, permissive, and interdependent relations. The main ingredient for achieving item 7, *participation*, is communication, both verbal and nonverbal. A third dimension, *stratification*, may have either positive or negative affects on the group, but in either case, the hierarchies within a group result from the nature and frequency of communication between members.

INTERACTION PROCESSES IN THE SMALL GROUP

In this chapter, which is primarily theoretical, the ways that discussion practice can be applied are not always stated explicitly. If you wish to improve your skills in working more effectively with others, you must make a systematic study of small group processes. In the next few pages, we present selected concepts and theories that are basic to understanding group interaction.

Field Theory

One way to study group processes and interaction is by Lewin's "field theory," which is essentially a phenomenological[17] approach. The observer or student of the group directs her or his attention not to

[17] The reader is referred to Arthur W. Combs and Donald Snygg, *Individual Behavior: A Perceptual Approach to Behavior*, rev. ed. (New York: Harper & Row, 1959), pp. 16–36, for a useful explanation of the perceptual or phenomenological approach to behavior.

what she or he perceives as reality but to what each individual group member perceives as reality. The basis for Lewin's theory is a set of assumptions and concepts about the individual.[18]

1. Each person (behaving self) perceives reality (life space or psychological field) from a highly personal point of view.

2. The person's life space has distinguishable parts (regions or activities) related to the entities (objects, events, or persons) in the life space.

3. The person has attitudes of relative desirability (valence) toward the entities in his life space.

4. The person occupies varying sequential activity regions (position) in his other life space that are oriented toward goals (positive valence) and aversions (negative valence).

5. The person assumes varying positions at different times (locomotion) in his or her life space depending on the strength of his or her drives (force) toward or away from stated ends.

[18] See Kurt Lewin, *Field Theory in Social Science*, Dorwin Cartwright, ed. (New York: Harper & Row, 1951), pp. 37–41, 238–303; Gardner Lindzey and Elliot Aronson, eds., *The Handbook of Social Psychology*, Vol. 1, 2nd ed. (Reading, Mass.: Addison-Wesley, 1968), pp. 423–465; Clovis R. Shepherd, *Small Groups: Some Sociological Perspectives* (San Francisco: Chandler, 1964), pp. 23–27.

6. The person's locomotion results in variations in the relative position (cognitive structure) of different parts of his or her life space.

7. In the process of locomotion toward stated ends (goals and aversions), the person encounters difficulties (barriers) that result in his or her attitudes and behavior being modified toward the ends themselves (ends may be changed), toward the sequence of activities leading to or away from the ends, or in the total life space of the individual.

Field theorists have applied the speculations of Lewin to groups and have focused part of their attention on concepts that concern you as a student of discussion. The classic study dealing with leadership types described in Chapter 6 is one instance. Learning theory, behavior development, change and resistance to change, and motivation—all of these have been studied in relation to groups. In addition, field theory has been directly applied to the concept of cohesion in groups, concen-

trating on factors associated (1) with the *amount* of cohesion, such as methods of decision making (authoritarian edict, voting, integration, or consensus), role structure and differentiation, and norms and group pressures, and (2) with the *results* of cohesion, such as interaction patterns, influence and dependency, and productivity.

Dimensions of Small Group Processes

Interaction processes (designated as "dimensions") in small groups manifest themselves in numerous ways. Two pairs of dimensions are especially important in understanding how to contribute to the effectiveness of discussion.

Cooperation versus Competition

In a classic study, Deutsch[19] described these concepts of group interaction as follows: A *cooperative* group has "promotively

[19] See Morton Deutsch, "A Theory of Co-operation and Competition," *Human Relations,* Vol. 2 (1949), pp. 129–152; and Morton Deutsch, "An Experimental Study of the Effects of Cooperation and Competition upon Group Process," *Human Relations,* Vol. 2 (1949), pp. 199–232.

inter-goals." That is, if the goals of one individual are reached, the goals of all other members can be reached to some degree. A *competitive* group has "contriently interdependent goals." In other words, if a goal or "goal region" is reached by one individual or by a number of individuals, the other individuals will be unable to reach their respective goals. We can see the significance of this study to the small discussion group in the following review of experimental results.

Compared with cooperative groups, the competitive groups demonstrated:

1. Less intermember influence and less acceptance of others' ideas.

2. Greater communication difficulties and less attentiveness.

3. Less coordination of effort, less division of labor, and poorer productivity.

Goal, Group, or Self-Orientation

In an early article dealing with how group members function in discussion, Benne and Sheats[20] describe three types of participation. The first is goal-oriented, in which members seek primarily to accomplish the group's goals. The second is group-oriented, in which the members' first consideration is maintaining the group as an entity; members are also concerned about its morale, cohesion, and autonomy. The third pattern is ego-oriented, in which individuals seek mainly to enhance their own self-interests. This third form of participation may sometimes be valuable, as when it serves as a means of individual catharsis or provides enough ego-satisfaction to make the member's later contributions more constructive. A combination of goal- and group-centered patterns of activity would seem to be the most productive.

[20] Kenneth D. Benne and Paul H. Sheats, "Functional Roles of Group Members," *Journal of Social Issues*, Vol. 4 (Spring 1948), pp. 41–49.

Noncognitive Factors in Group Process

A fascinating account of interaction within a group, in this case a psychotherapy group, is given by Bion,[21] who concentrates on the emotional factor in group process. In his theory, Bion contends that individuals expose their own personalities in a group, that they adjust their personalities to the group culture, and that they seek to satisfy their own personal needs through a rather unique set of reactions to others. These types of reaction and interaction — which heighten as a group develops — are fight, flight, pairing, and dependency. The first three are aspects of *control* in groups, and the fourth is related to *intimacy*. All of these concepts are considered as the primary emotional factors in group process. Although these theories have mainly been applied in therapy groups, the discussion leader and participant will find it useful to study individual personality development, the ways in which individuals adjust their personalities to meet their needs, and the pressures that the group exerts on individuals.

[21] W. R. Bion, *Experiences in Groups* (New York: Basic Books, 1959).

Bales[22] has also studied the emotional dimension of group process. His system of interaction process analysis is a way to observe individual contributions in group interaction.[23] He classifies contributions as either *social-emotional* or *task oriented*. The social-emotional contributions deal with aspects of feeling and integration. They are either positive (showing solidarity, tension release, agreement) or negative (showing disagreement, tension, antagonism). The task contributions

[22] Robert F. Bales, *Interaction Process Analysis* (Reading, Mass.: Addison-Wesley, 1950).

[23] See the Analysis Form adapted from the Bales categories, p. 87.

"... individuals expose their own personalities in a group ..."

deal with adaptation to the external, and control of the internal, system. They are either direct (giving suggestions, opinion, orientation) or indirect (asking for orientation, opinion, suggestions).

There are many advantages to Bales' system: it focuses attention on the total interaction process in a group, it provides the means for describing and measuring individual contributions, and it indicates the state of the group in relation to the main problems with which it must deal. In other words, communication, evaluation, control, decision making, tension reduction, and integration are all primary concerns of the small discussion group.

A Model of Discussion in Small Groups

In presenting some theories and concepts on the structure and process of small groups, our aim has been to encourage you to become familiar with background materials. By way of summary, let's look at

the discussion group itself and the nature of its input, process, and output.[24]

Refer to the diagram. Column 1 represents the six essential components of the discussion process: *purpose, communication, leadership, group structure, thought pattern,* and *content.* These components show up before any discussion begins as either individual inputs or group characteristics. Thus, purpose is either predetermined, or it emerges through interaction. The individual brings whatever communication skills she or he may have to the discussion. Leadership is either designated or it can emerge—for each member has potential leadership skills. The group may or may not have a pre-existing internal structure, but it always has a pre-existing external system—that is, the members have convened as a group. Each individual brings to the discussion his or her systematic or unsystematic ways of thinking. Finally, each member brings to the group various facts and opinions that are related to the discussion topic.

[24] This material has been modified from Martin P. Andersen, "A Model of Group Discussion," *The Southern Speech Journal,* Vol. 30 (Summer 1965), pp. 279–293.

In the diagram, the lines connecting the five columns represent the actions of group members as they first function unilaterally and then move toward consensus in the final stages of a discussion. A number of socio-psychological processes begin as soon as the discussion starts. These processes operate in all participants—when either speaking or listening—as screens that filter all contributions. We list five of these screens: the *perceptual, semantic, internal forces, external system,* and *interaction potential.* These psychological and interrelated phenomena affect the input of discussion, its process, and output.

Column 3 indicates essential characteristics of each component that are required for maximum goal achievement. When the discussion is in progress, the contributions of the members are filtered through a second set of procedural screens, shown in Column 4. These are *physical factors, inquiry-advocacy dimension,* and *evaluation.* Physical factors are self-explanatory. The inquiry-advocacy dimension refers to the extent that the discussion seeks to answer a problem or seeks approval of some previous decision. The evaluation screen refers to ways in which the discussants seek to improve their procedures in order to improve substantive decisions.

Finally, in Column 5, we list some characteristics that are essential for the discussion to be most effective: The goal must at least have been partially achieved. Group members must have gained some ego-satisfaction. Communication must have been clear and acceptable so that some agreement will have been reached. Leadership must have been effective and shared so that group members will have developed greater understanding of, and skills in performing, leadership tasks. An effective discussion group must have some degree of maturity as demonstrated by an appropriate balance between group goal achievement and the members' ego-satisfaction. The decisions and understandings reached should reflect the best possible use of reasoning and evidence. Finally, for maximum productivity, the output should reflect a balance between the cognitive (thought involving) and affective (emotional) elements of the interaction.

You might feel that modifications could and should be made in the diagram, but this discussion model is useful in that it partially summarizes this chapter, delineates some boundaries of discussion, shows important socio-psychological processes that operate in discussion, and serves as a guide for practice and further study.

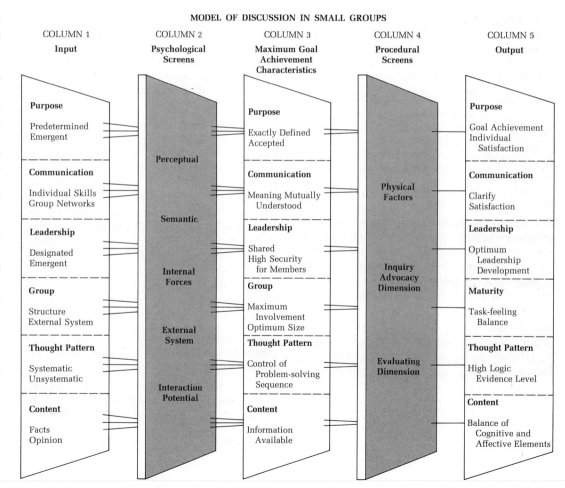

MODEL OF DISCUSSION IN SMALL GROUPS

IMPLICATIONS FOR THE
DISCUSSION GROUP MEMBER

1. Since discussion is the major tool used in democratic decision making and problem solving, understanding the theory of small group interaction will help develop skill in its practice.

2. Each small discussion group is like an island in that it has its own physical and temporal boundaries, psychological characteristics, purposes, individual goals, and interaction patterns. To be maximally effective, the individual group member must study and understand these dimensions of small groups.

3. Since each discussion group has an internal system created by the activities, sentiments or feelings, and interaction among its members, the discussant can greatly affect the output of any small group discussion, if he or she so desires.

4. The external system of a discussion group (the forces acting on it from the socio-economic milieu of which it is a part) will be taken into account by the effective discussion group member.

5. Merging the internal and external systems of a given discussion is a major factor in determining the roles a member of a group is required or permitted to play. The discussion group member must understand and develop skills in various discussion roles.

6. From the time of its first meeting, every discussion group will undergo four sequential stages in reaching maturity and effectiveness. These stages are: (1) interaction conforming to previously established stereotypes, (2) frustration resulting from uncertainty about status, (3) feelings of conflict avoidance and a desire to meet both individual and group needs, and (4) development of group- and goal-centeredness. Knowing that these stages exist in group growth will help the discussants to make appropriate contributions to their groups.

7. Conformity and belongingness are important influences on individual behavior in a group.

8. A balance between belongingness and preserving individuality can best be achieved in a democratic discussion climate.

9. Individuals join groups to achieve both personal and group goals. Many of these goals are psychological—such as esteem, belongingness, and security—and can be partially achieved by the nature of the interaction within a group.

10. All groups may be said to have both structure (dimensions) and process (interaction), both of which affect the way a group functions. Hemphill and Westie have described fourteen dimensions. The questions that follow these descriptions suggest ways in which leadership, participation, the external and internal forces acting upon and in the group, cohesiveness, goal clarity, and procedures can be modified for greater productivity.

11. Discussion procedures can be improved when group members understand that the reality of verbal and nonverbal interaction is what the participant perceives it to be, not what someone as an observer perceives it to be.

A SUMMARY AND LOOK AHEAD

12. Every contribution in discussion has both affective and cognitive characteristics. Bion, in speaking primarily of the emotional element in small group interaction, says that individuals seek their personal needs through fight, flight, pairing, and dependency reactions.

13. Bales states that interaction in discussion may be social-emotional or task oriented. Effective discussants perceive and can adapt to either type of interaction. They can also act in ways that will help to create either type of atmosphere.

14. Any member's input in small group discussion is screened by a number of both psychological and procedural filters. Knowing what these filters are, how they modify the content of a discussion, and skill in adapting to their functioning is absolutely indispensable for the effective discussion participant.

Although the primary focus of this book is on discussion practice, this chapter deals entirely with theory. It has presented a review of selected writings on the structure and processes of small group interaction.

A group is defined as a *face-to-face or co-acting system in which interactions by the members determine its structure, identity, and content and help to satisfy some of the members' needs.* A group has both an internal and an external system. Forces that affect both systems, according to Homans, are interaction, activity, and sentiment. Each group has a characteristic growth pattern that usually consists of four stages: (1) an attempt by members to get the group to function according to pre-existing stereotypes, (2) frustration resulting from conflicts among the stereotypes, (3) avoidance of conflict, and (4) task- and group-centered balance.

The group can be a means by which both individual and collective needs are satisfied.

The unique structure of any group may be described by its dimensions. Hemphill and Westie state that a group obtains its essential character from the dimensions of *autonomy, control, flexibility, hedonic tone, homogeneity, intimacy, participation, permeability, polarization, potency, size, stability, stratification,* and *viscidity.*

Lewin's field theory is useful for understanding how both individuals and groups function. Satisfaction of individual and group needs depends, in part, on effective interpersonal relations, on control of the emotional phases of interaction, and on a balance between the social-emotional and the task contributions of the members of the group.

The input and processes of a small discussion group are always filtered through socio-psychological and procedural screens that determine the productivity of the group.

The way members communicate is an integral part of small group theory. It is the subject of Chapter 3.

SUGGESTED READINGS

Andersen, Martin P., E. Ray **Nichols,** and Herbert W. **Booth,** *The Speaker and His Audience,* 2nd ed. (New York: Harper & Row, 1974), Ch. 16.

Bass, Barnard M., *Leadership, Psychology, and Organizational Behavior* (New York: Harper & Row, 1960), Chs. 3–4, 17–18.

Berkowitz, Leonard, "Group Standards, Cohesiveness, and Productivity," *Human Relations,* Vol. 7 (1954), pp. 509–519.

Bonner, Hubert, *Group Dynamics: Principles and Practice* (New York: Harper & Row, 1969), Chs. 2–3, 5, 12.

Bormann, Ernest G., *Discussion and Group Methods,* 2nd ed. (New York: Harper & Row, 1975), Chs. 7–10, 12, 14.

Cathcart, Robert S., and Larry A. **Samovar,** *Small Group Communication: A Reader,* 2nd ed. (Dubuque, Iowa: Wm. C. Brown, 1974), Chs. 1, 4.

Clevenger, Theodore, Jr., and Jack **Matthews,** *The Speech Communication Process* (Glenview, Ill.: Scott, Foresman, 1971), Chs. 2, 7.

Deutsch, Morton, "An Experimental Study of the Effects of Cooperation and Competition upon Group Process," *Human Relations,* Vol. 2, No. 3 (1949), pp. 199–231.

Deutsch, Morton, "A Theory of Cooperation and Competition," *Human Relations,* Vol. 2, No. 2 (1949), pp. 129–152.

Fausti, Remo P., and Arno H. **Luker,** "A Phenomenological Approach to Discussion," *Speech Teacher,* Vol. 14 (January 1965), pp. 19–23.

Fisher, B. Aubrey, *Small Group Decision Making* (New York: McGraw-Hill, 1974), Chs. 2–4.

Giffin, Kim, "Interpersonal Trust in Small Groups," *Quarterly Journal of Speech,* Vol. 53 (October 1967), pp. 224–234.

Goldhaber, Gerald M., *Organizational Communication* (Dubuque, Iowa: Wm. C. Brown, 1974), Ch. 7.

Gruner, Charles R., Cal M. **Logue,** Dwight L. **Freshley,** and Richard C. **Huseman,** *Speech Communication in Society* (Boston: Allyn and Bacon, 1972), Ch. 13.

Homans, George C., *The Human Group* (New York: Harcourt, Brace & World, 1950), Chs. 2, 5–6.

Luft, Joseph, *Group Processes: An Introduction to Group Dynamics,* 2nd ed. (Palo Alto, Calif.: National Press, 1970).

Phillips, Gerald M., *Communication and the Small Group,* 2nd ed. (Indianapolis: Bobbs-Merrill, 1973), Ch. 2.

Schutz, William C., *FIRO: A Three-Dimensional Theory of Interpersonal Behavior* (New York: Holt, Rinehart and Winston, 1958).

Shaw, Marvin E., *Group Dynamics* (New York: McGraw-Hill, 1971).

Thelen, Herbert A., *Dynamics of Groups at Work* (Chicago: University of Chicago Press, 1954), Chs. 7–8, 10.

EXERCISES

1. Think critically about some of the small groups of which you are or have been a member. How has discussion helped in achieving some of the goals of these groups? Make a list of factors that have blocked discussion. Be prepared to comment on your findings in class.

2. Refer to the definition we give of a group. Discuss your reaction to this definition in class. Is it adequate? Have elements been omitted? Which ones?

3. Make a drawing of the external system of some small group of which you are a member. Show by concentric circles the ever-expanding nature of the external system. You may wish to reread the comments about the external and internal systems of groups.

4. Select some famous person (a Bono, Rockefeller, Hearst, Ford, Fonda, etc.) whose family life is reasonably well known. Indicate which of the theoretical concepts presented in this chapter can be used to describe the family life of the person selected.

5. Small group discussions:

a. Break up into small groups of five to seven persons.

b. Select some current campus issue—for example, student participation in college administration, quality of minority group college courses and/or programs, teacher rating by students, and so on.

c. Conduct a twenty-minute discussion of the topic selected. Try to reach agreement on "action to be taken."

d. Then, take ten minutes to write an explanation of how the external and internal systems in which the discussion took place affected the decision-making process.

CHAPTER 3

COMMUNICATION IN SMALL GROUPS

THE NATURE OF COMMUNICATION

If individuals cannot communicate effectively, they cannot be constructive members of a small group discussion. It is as simple as that. A casual survey of significant events in the 1960s and 1970s, at all levels of government and in all walks of life, reveals the importance of communication. Depending on your viewpoint, you'll note that the results of communication have sometimes been constructive and sometimes destructive. It is impossible to deny that the effective *use,* or the *lack of, misuse,* or *abuse* of the communication process have greatly modified such events as changes in American foreign policy, the growth and effectiveness of minority groups, the emerging power of women, drastic changes in the power and political future of many public leaders, the development of group techniques in training and therapy, and the increasing influence of laypeople in religion and conservation.

"Human beings literally live in a sea of communication."

Human beings literally live in a sea of communication. They are constantly bombarded with messages from the physical world, from the world of people, and from themselves. For a typical student, a day includes some, if not all, of the following sorts of communication. She might talk to herself about what to wear; comment to her family about personal matters; on the way to school, she might be reading and thinking (a form of talking) about class assignments; at school there would be almost constant communication between her and her instructors; at mealtimes she would be communicating with herself or other students; she might attend one or more student or student-faculty committee meetings; and after returning home, she probably would be communicating continuously until bedtime, and even then she would be thinking about communicative events that might take place the next day. In all of these communicative acts, she would be *sender* part of the time and *receiver* part of the time. Hence, she must know how to make the best use of her communicative skills in both roles. In other words, she must understand the total process of communication.

No two writers use exactly the same words in their definitions of communication, although they do agree on some of its basic components.

Shrope states:[1] "Communication is deceptively simple; it is the act of sending ideas and feelings in such a way that the receiver can *recreate* those ideas and feelings for himself. This implies three essential elements: the sender, the message, and the receiver." Mortensen[2] states that "Communication occurs whenever persons attribute significance to message behavior." Goldhaber,[3] in describing the nature of communication in organizations, states merely "In order to limit the uncertainty and ambiguity attached to the abstraction 'communication,' we have adopted a very broad definition, 'the flow of messages.'" Goldhaber then develops his definition further by indicating some main traits.

[1] Wayne Austin Shrope, *Experiences in Communication* (New York: Harcourt Brace Jovanovich, 1974), p. 7.

[2] C. David Mortensen, *Communication: The Study of Human Interaction* (New York: McGraw-Hill, 1972), p. 14.

[3] Gerald M. Goldhaber, *Organizational Communication* (Dubuque, Iowa: Wm. C. Brown, 1974), pp. 96–97.

One of the authors of this text has defined communication elsewhere[4] as the *"purposeful, transactional process by which one person, through the use of audible and visible symbols, engenders meanings in the minds of his listeners."*

Another definition is that of Myers and Myers,[5] who say "Communication is a generally predictable, multilevel, continuous, and always present process of sharing meaning through symbol interaction."

Many, many more definitions are to be found, and it is difficult to pick one that includes all aspects of the process or that all readers might accept. From these definitions however, we can infer both the characteristics of and the elements in a communication system.

---

[4] Martin P. Andersen, E. Ray Nichols, and Herbert W. Booth, *The Speaker and His Audience* (New York: Harper & Row, 1974), p. 77.

[5] Gail E. Myers and Michele Tolete Myers, *The Dynamics of Human Communication* (New York: McGraw-Hill, 1973), p. 12.

First, let us consider the characteristics of the *process* of communication:

1. *Communication is purposeful.* The purpose of a given communicative event may have been determined in advance or, as in a small group, it may emerge as the discussion continues. Purpose may be ego-, group-, or goal-centered. It may be overt or covert. Always, however, communication serves as a means to an end.

2. *Communication is transactional.* This implies that the process involves a relationship among the participants, and that this relationship is flexible, everchanging, and dynamic. Communication is not a static concept.

3. *Communication is symbolic.* This means that some code is employed by the participants. For example, this code may be verbal language, nonverbal signs, vocal intonations or bodily action, mutually experienced activities, sensory perceptions of smell, taste, or touch, or some combination of these.

4. *Communication is complex.* It is an intricate yet understandable set of intra- and interpersonal relationships. A number of neuro-muscular adjustments take place within the participants as they act as senders and receivers. Memory, percep-

tion, motivation, and the cognitive skills and affective states of each individual are involved. Extrapersonal factors, such as the physical setting, external forces, and the size, make-up, and structure of the group also affect the outcome of communication.

5. *Communication is personal.* Each participant in a communicative act is a unique person, different in many respects from every other person.[6] Goldhaber[7] puts it this way: "the important point is that because people have different perceptions, their way of responding to messages will be different. If we don't account for these perceptual differences we may be assuming an attitudinal structure and a behavioral

---

[6] See Arthur W. Combs and Donald Snygg, *Individual Behavior: A Perceptual Approach to Behavior*, rev. ed. (New York: Harper & Row, 1959), pp. 16–36, for a comprehensive and basic statement as to how the "perceptual fields" (their complete but differing universes) affect communication.

[7] Goldhaber, p. 103.

response that does not exist. These assumptions may lead directly to conflict and unwarranted hostility. If we remember that communication is a personal process, that no two people are alike, we may reduce the possibility for such confrontation.''

6. *Communication is irreversible.* Communicative acts, while continuous, change from moment to moment. Although we may look back at what has happened, we can never retract what has been said; we cannot return to some previous point and "start over" again.

7. *Communication is the sharing of meanings.* In one of the definitions, the expressions *engenders meanings* and *sharing meanings* were used. In other words, when a speaker seeks to duplicate in the listener's mind the exact meaning he or she intended, that person is sharing his or her meaning with the listener. Whenever we speak, we seek the greatest amount of message duplication possible.

We have now considered the major characteristics of the communication process. Let us now briefly list the elements or components of the system in which communication occurs. Many of these components are stated explicitly in previous sections of this chapter. Elements include:

1. A meaningful stimulus to communicate.

2. A sender or group of senders.

3. The content of a message to be sent.

4. An encoding (putting ideas into words) and transmitting apparatus for the sender.

5. A channel over which the message is to be sent.

6. A receiving and decoding apparatus for the receiver.

7. A feedback system by which the receiver(s) report back to the sender the way in which the message has been perceived and will be acted on.

8. A receiver or group of receivers.

9. Noise, or any factor that interferes with message understanding.

INDIVIDUAL FACTORS AFFECTING COMMUNICATION IN SMALL GROUPS

All communicators in small groups bring with them unique sets of experiences, needs, knowledge, attitudes, beliefs, prejudices, and expectancy of results. Although people may enter the group discussion situation with open, investigative minds, their participation in the discussion and acceptance of the decisions will be influenced by the way they think and feel.

A person's attitudes are complex; they are not just a point on a continuum. According to Sherif, Sherif, and Nebergall, they consist also of latitudes of acceptance, rejection, and noncommitment.[8]

[8] C. W. Sherif, M. Sherif, and R. E. Nebergall, *Attitude and Attitude Change* (Philadelphia: Saunders, 1965), pp. 18–27.

In a small group, one would not have much chance of having a position he's advocated as being acceptable, if the group perceived the position as falling within their latitude of rejection. . . . The highly involved person tends to have a latitude of rejection that takes up most of the attitude continuum. That means it's nearly impossible to get him to accept any position other than the one he currently holds. The lowly involved group member, on the other hand, having a larger latitude of acceptance and noncommitment, is more likely to be receptive to stands discrepant from his own more acceptable one. In addition, members highly involved in their positions are not likely to work harmoniously with others espousing contrary views.[9]

When individuals enter a group, their prejudices accompany them. If the other group members support these prejudices,

[9] R. L. Applbaum and others, *The Process of Group Communication* (Chicago: Science Research Associates, 1974), p. 37.

they become more intense, and the members are more willing to express them openly. If the group rejects these prejudices, a variety of things might happen: individuals might withdraw from participation, they might modify their prejudices because of new information, or they might hold their ground despite the possibility of alienating other group members. If a substantial number of members in a group hold the same prejudices, the group bias will affect the group's capabilities for quality decisions.

An individual's attitudes toward himself will influence his or her behavior in a group. Secord and Backman[10] have grouped these self-conceptions into three components:

The *cognitive* component represents the content of the self, illustrated by such thoughts as, "I am intelligent, honest, sincere, ambitious, tall, strong, overweight, etc." The *affective* component represents one's feelings about oneself and is more difficult to illustrate,

[10] P. F. Secord and C. W. Backman, *Social Psychology* (New York: McGraw-Hill, 1964), p. 579.

because feelings toward oneself are usually not expressed in words. It would include a rather general feeling of self-worth, as well as evaluations of more specific cognitive aspects or other aspects of self. For example, a woman may dislike her nose, which is slightly crooked. The *behavioral* component is the tendency to *act* toward oneself in various ways; a person may behave in a self-depreciating or a self-indulgent manner, or he may show oversensitivity to certain of his characteristics.

"When individuals enter a group,
their prejudices accompany them."

Individuals enter a group situation with varying degrees of openness toward others, both consciously and subconsciously. Many times a discussion reaches an impasse or culminates in low-quality decisions because participants do not have a high degree of openness toward each other. Luft and Ingham[11] designed a model called the Johari Window, which illustrates four areas of openness. One of the areas represents behavior that is openly known to oneself and to others. The second area represents behaviors and motivations not known to oneself but apparent to others. The third area represents behaviors and motivations known to oneself but kept from others. The fourth and last area represents behaviors and motivations on the subconscious level, of which neither oneself nor others are aware. The four areas are indicated in the following diagram of the Johari Window:[12]

[11] For a more complete description, see Joseph Luft, *Group Processes: An Introduction to Group Dynamics*, 2nd ed. (Palo Alto, Calif.: National Press, 1970), pp. 11–20.

	Known to Self	Not Known to Self
Known to Others	1 OPEN	2 BLIND
Not Known to Others	HIDDEN 3	UNKNOWN 4

[12] Reprinted from *Of Human Interaction* by Joseph Luft by permission of Mayfield Publishing Company, formerly National Press Books.

The Johari Window is valuable to the discussant because it stimulates awareness as to *why* certain things occur in a group. This awareness may help discussion members (1) to recognize that in a new group interaction is frequently guarded and may lack spontaneity; (2) to understand that complete openness in discussion is not always desirable; (3) to reveal themselves as they really are; (4) to realize that they must spend more time on group tasks; (5) to appreciate the covert aspects of behavior and respect the rights of others not to "reveal all"; (6) to develop greater self-understanding; (7) to accept the fact that change may occur slowly if there is not mutual trust or when Areas 2 and 3 are small; and (8) to understand that discussion is affected by psychological as well as substantive factors.

When an individual joins a group, he or she brings to it certain characteristics already known to some or all of the other members, and these characteristics affect his or her credibility. Credibility is not inherent in the individual. Rather, it is the evaluative perceptions others have of the authoritativeness and trustworthiness of an individual. Known past experiences of the person, his or her reputation, personal appearance, occupation or profession, ethnic background, religious affiliation, education, even people and groups with whom he or she associates, are included in the factors that make up credibility. A person's credibility, as others perceive it, will affect his or her role in the group and the responses of the other members. In any group, however, credibility is not static. One's participation, what is said and done in the group meetings, may bring about a change in one's credibility at any time. Although perceptions of competence and trustworthiness are vastly important in bringing about the acceptance of viewpoints, they are not the sole factors. Credibility operates in conjunction with other variables such as authoritarianism and dogmatism, social sensitivity, self-reliance and dependability, emotional stability, and intelligence.

As we discussed in Chapter 2, one factor affecting the amount of productivity in group situations is the degree to which the members' needs are met. Schutz[13] states three interpersonal needs that must be met for effective group functioning.

1. *Inclusion:* the need to establish and maintain a satisfactory relation with people in terms of interaction and association. "Satisfactory relation" includes a psychologically comfortable relation with people on two dimensions. The first one ranges from originating or initiating interaction with all people to not initiating interaction with anyone. The second deals with eliciting behavior from others on a scale ranging from always initiating interaction with the self to never initiating interaction with the self.

[13] William C. Schutz, *FIRO: A Three-Dimensional Theory of Interpersonal Behavior* (New York: Holt, Rinehart and Winston, 1958), pp. 18–20.

2. *Control:* the need to establish and maintain a satisfactory relation with people in terms of control and power. "Satisfactory relation" here includes a psychologically comfortable relation with all people on two different dimensions. The first one ranges from controlling all behavior of other people to not controlling any behavior. The second deals with eliciting behavior from others on a scale ranging from always being controlled by them to never being controlled by them.

3. *Affection:* the need to establish and maintain a satisfactory relation with others with respect to love and affection. In this category, "satisfactory relation" includes a psychologically comfortable relation with all people on another two dimensions. The first one ranges from initiating close, personal relations with everyone to originating close, personal relations with no one. The second ranges from always initiating close, personal relations toward the self to never originating close personal relations toward the self.

Effective discussion leaders and participants are those who, because of their experience in relations with other groups, help group members to attain some of these personal needs.

ASPECTS OF
NONVERBAL COMMUNICATION

The primary concern in discussion is with verbal interaction. However, the verbal message cues—spoken and written words—are only *part* of the messages sent and received. Authorities in the area of nonverbal communication estimate that only about one-third of the meaning in a normal two-person conversation is carried by verbal symbols. This means that about two-thirds of the meaning is transmitted by nonverbal cues.[14] These cues, many of which we are unaware, are observed by others in the form of our apparel, a raise of the eyebrow, a shrug of the shoulders, a diploma on the wall, or any of a number of other symbols. How we behave is a constant communication device to others in our presence. Therefore, since we are always behaving in some manner, we cannot refrain from communicating.

[14] Mark L. Knapp, *Nonverbal Communication in Human Interaction* (New York: Holt, Rinehart and Winston, 1972), p. 12.

Most research in the field of nonverbal communication has been based on the classifications of Ruesch and Kees:[15] In broad terms, nonverbal forms of codification fall into three distinct categories:

Sign language includes all those forms of codification in which words, numbers, and punctuation signs have been supplanted by gestures; these vary from the "monosyllabic" gesture of the hitchhiker to such complete systems as the language of the deaf.

[15] Jurgen Ruesch and Weldon Kees, *Nonverbal Communication* (Berkeley: University of California Press, 1956), p. 189.

Action language embraces all movements that are not used exclusively as signals. Such acts as walking and drinking, for example, have a dual function. On one hand, they serve personal needs; and on the other, they constitute statements to those who may perceive them.

Object language comprises all intentional and nonintentional display of material things, such as implements, machines, art objects, architectural structures, and—last but not least—the human body and whatever clothes it. The embodiment of letters (known as *typography*) as they occur in books and on signs has a material substance, and this aspect also has to be considered as object language.

It is not surprising to learn that research in nonverbal communication indicates that a person's physical characteristics, as well as the attractiveness of attire, affects the kinds of responses he or she receives

"... about two-thirds of the meaning
is transmitted by nonverbal cues."

from others.[16] Further, most movements of the body (hand gestures, facial expressions, eye blinking, direction and length of the gaze, failure to look at the audience for long periods, and so on) are nonverbal cues that others perceive and interpret, either consciously or unconsciously, as having meaning.

[16] J. E. Singer, "The Use of Manipulative Strategies: Machiavelliansim and Attractiveness," *Sociometry*, Vol. 27 (1964), pp. 128–151; J. E. Singer and P. F. Lamb, "Social Concern, Body Size, and Birth Order," *Journal of Social Psychology*, Vol. 68 (1966), pp. 143–151; J. Mills and E. Aronson, "Opinion Change as a Function of the Communicator's Attractiveness and Desire to Influence," *Journal of Personality and Social Psychology*, Vol. 1 (1965), pp. 73–77; R. N. Widgery and B. Webster, "The Effects of Physical Attractiveness upon Perceived Initial Credibility," *Michigan Speech Journal*, Vol. 4 (1969), pp. 9–15; D. Byrne, O. London, and K. Reeves, "The Effects of Physical Attractiveness, Sex, and Attitude Similarity on Interpersonal Attraction," *Journal of Personality*, Vol. 36 (1968), pp. 359–372.

The significance of facial nonverbal communication was illustrated in one of the numerous Watergate trials when a defendant asked that his case be dismissed because the facial features of the judge had unduly influenced the jury. "Facial expressions are very complex entities to deal with. Of all the areas of the body, the face seems to elicit the best external and internal feedback which makes it easy for us to follow a variety of facial display rules. Not all facial displays represent single emotions; some are 'blends' of several emotions."[17]

Paralanguage is concerned not with what is spoken, but with *how* it is said. Paralanguage is vocal but nonverbal. Trager classifies paralanguage into four components: (1) *Voice qualities*, which include pitch, rhythm, resonance, and tempo. (2) *Vocal characterizers*, which include laughing, crying, moaning, clearing the throat, and the like. (3) *Vocal qualifiers*, including heavy inhaling and exhaling, sighing, and so on. And (4), *vocal segregates*, which include any intrusive sounds such as "uh," or "um."[18]

[17] Knapp, p. 137.

[18] G. L. Trager, "Paralanguage: A First Approximation," *Studies in Linguistics*, Vol. 13 (1958), pp. 1–12.

Of particular interest to group discussion participants is the nonverbal communication aspect of personal space. "The term 'territoriality' has been used for years in the study of animal and fowl behavior. . . . Most behavioral scientists agree that territoriality exists in human behavior, too, and that it is frequently an extremely important variable in a particular interpersonal transaction."[19] We are all familiar with daily manifestations of territoriality: "his" seat in the classroom, "the professor's" desk, "your" parking space. Invasions of one's private territory or personal space can cause a great deal of frustration, as when someone stands six inches away from you while you're talking. We read meaning into the distance between ourselves and others in conversation, and we often become uncomfortable if this personal space is invaded or expanded.

[19] Knapp, p. 37.

Considerable research has been done on the relationship of seating arrangements to the flow of communication in groups.[20] Hare and Bales have concluded that a seating arrangement determines the amount of interaction a person will give and receive. Locations at the ends of a rectangular arrangement and the middle seat of the sides are central seats, or high-talking positions. Leaders and dominant personalities tend to choose these positions of centrality.[21] Sommer concluded from his research that individuals in a discussion group prefer to sit across from others (obliquely opposite) as opposed to sitting side-by-side. When the distance across is too great for comfortable conversation, side-by-side seating is preferred.[22] Argyle and Dean suggested that side-by-side seating is not frequently chosen by those who want to communicate directly because the nonverbal cues of the eyes cannot be observed.[23] In sum, to ensure the most effective communication in group discussion, we must consider the need for maintaining comfortable social distance and the tendencies for participation according to seating arrangements. Applbaum put it like this:

Many stressful encounters could be avoided through proper spatial arrangement. Those who feel uncomfortable under the gaze of others should be seated in positions with less centrality. If a high level of interaction and participation in a group situation is desirable, it might be advantageous to have an expressive individual sit opposite a quiet person in order to encourage the quiet person to speak more. Or the leader might find it helpful to have two people who tend to monopolize a discussion sit next to each other.[24]

[20] F. Strodtbeck and L. Hook, "The Social Dimensions of a Twelve Man Jury Table," *Sociometry*, Vol. 24 (1961), pp. 297–415; N. Russo, "Connotation of Seating Arrangement," *Cornell Journal of Social Relations*, Vol. 2 (1967), pp. 37–44; Robert Sommer, "Further Studies of Small Group Ecology," *Sociometry*, Vol. 28 (1965), pp. 337–348.

[21] A. P. Hare and R. F. Bales, "Seating Position and Small Group Interaction," *Sociometry*, Vol. 26 (1963), pp. 480–486.

[22] Robert Sommer, "Leadership and Group Geography," *Sociometry*, Vol. 24 (1961), p. 106.

[23] M. Argyle and J. P. Dean, "Eye Contact, Distance, and Affiliation," *Sociometry*, Vol. 28 (1965), pp. 289–304.

[24] Applbaum, p. 88.

THE IMPORTANCE OF LISTENING IN DISCUSSION

Have you ever had any of the following experiences when participating in a small group discussion?

When someone was talking, were you spending more time thinking about what you were going to say than listening to the speaker?

Have you ever found yourself thinking about matters not related to the discussion?

Have you ever been called on in a discussion and have had to ask, "Would you please repeat that question?"

Have you ever "turned off" a speaker because of the way he spoke or what he wore?

If your answer to any of the above questions is "yes," then you know something about barriers to effective listening. The questions for you to answer are: "What is the importance of listening in communication?" and "How can I improve my own listening skills?" These questions are especially important to the student of discussion because you spend most of your time listening.

Research studies have discovered a number of amazing facts about the process of listening.

1. About one-half of a person's waking hours are spent in listening. This may be even higher in some vocations.

2. Most people lack skill in effective listening.

3. Most people are unaware of the importance of good listening in improving interpersonal relations.

4. Listening is not the same process as hearing, although many think it is.

5. There is a relatively high correlation between listening and certain other language skills.

6. People can be trained to be more effective listeners.

7. It is generally accepted that there are four functions or types of listening: appreciative, therapeutic, critical, and informative. Each requires a different approach.

8. Most speakers wrongly assume that just because a member of an audience has heard what has been said, that person will understand it.

9. The effective listener is motivated to listen.

10. Normal speech is related in some ways to normal hearing.

11. The majority of persons who have hearing defects are in the upper-age groups.

Although we will not consider each of the above findings in detail, they do suggest that listening is extremely important to effective communication in small groups. Further, speakers should give greater attention to understanding the process of listening; and, training can improve one's skills in the various functions of listening.

Listening, as with all perceptual skills, is a complex process. Many definitions of the process can be found. We suggest the following: "The perceptual process by which verbal and nonverbal communications (including mechanical sounds) from one source or sources are selectively received, and interpreted by a receiver or receivers in relation to the perceptual field of the parties in the process. Listening then becomes a part of a total communicative transaction."[25]

In relation to the question "How can I improve my own listening skills," we make these suggestions:

1. Determine in advance the purpose for which you will be listening.

2. Be motivated to listen. Think about the topic for discussion. Study it. Talk to friends about it. Be prepared.

3. Place yourself in situations demanding ever-increasing listening skills.

4. Maintain an objective attitude toward the speaker and the subject. Do not let any possible biases you may have interfere with your listening. Try to maintain emotional control.

[25] Andersen, Nichols, and Booth, pp. 230–231. See also Ralph G. Nichols, "Ten Components of Effective Listening," *Education*, Vol. 75 (1955), p. 302.

IMPLICATIONS FOR THE
DISCUSSION GROUP MEMBER

1. National and international events that have occurred in the 1960s and 1970s underline the need for effective use of the communication process. Communication can be used for good or evil.

2. Most people actively participate in small group discussions every day. The effective speaker will be in greater control over the conduct of her or his social, political, and vocational affairs than the ineffective speaker.

3. Definitions of communication suggest that both senders and receivers have a responsibility for making communication effective.

4. A study of the process of communication reveals that it (1) is functional; (2) involves a partnership between the participants; (3) has intra-, inter-, and extra-personal facets; (4) is uniquely personal; (5) is a continuous, flowing process; and (6) seeks mainly to share meanings among or between participants.

5. Because the process of communication is complex and consists of numerous stages or components, an individual needs to know as much as he or she can about the process in order to isolate communication breakdowns and then to control or eliminate them.

6. The outcome of any discussion is always affected by the inputs of the participants. These inputs reflect the entire perceptual worlds of the group members. The effective speaker realizes that when the perceptual worlds of speaker and listener coincide, the meaning of his or her message is more likely to be *shared* with the listener.

7. When discussants are open toward each other, the result is usually a positive input in discussion.

8. Credibility is necessary if one's ideas are to be accepted. Credibility reflects the evaluative perceptions others have of an individual's knowledgeability and trustworthiness. For this reason, the speaker should try to develop factors that contribute to his or her credibility.

9. Part of a listener's understanding of what a speaker says comes from the nonverbal aspects of communication including body movement and gesture, the physical aspects of the speaking situation, and member positions in the small group. Many of these factors can be controlled by the group member or the meeting planner.

10. Because communication is a transactional interaction and involves listening as well as speaking, the discussant should seek to improve his skills and eliminate his faults in listening.

A SUMMARY AND LOOK AHEAD

Chapter 2 dealt primarily with theory, and so does this chapter.

Almost all individuals engage in some form of communication during almost every waking hour. Important events of recent years bear witness to the effective use, as well as to the lack of, misuse, or abuse of communication. To be successful in relations with others, each individual must be skilled in effective communication. We define it as the "purposeful, transactional process by which one person, through the use of audible and visible symbols, engenders meanings in the minds of his listeners." From a survey of the literature and observation of the process itself, it is apparent that communication is purposeful, transactional, symbolic, complex, personal, irreversible, and seeks to share meanings.

The essential components of a communicative act include the following: a stimulus to communicate, a sender, message content, a decoding and transmitting apparatus, a channel, a receiver, a receiving and decoding apparatus, feedback, and noise, or possible interference with the process at any point in its sequence.

Because the parties involved in a communicative act have uniquely different perceptual fields, individual inputs always affect the process. Some of these individual inputs include a person's experiences, attitudes in general, beliefs, knowledge, prejudices, expectancies, and needs. The individual's attitude toward her- or himself, openness toward others, and his or her credibility are three major criteria of communicative effectiveness.

Communication is the primary tool of small group discussions, which seek to achieve both group goals and individual needs. Classifications of individual needs are numerous. One classification that is significant for small group discussion suggests that a person wants inclusion, control, and affection.

Authorities estimate that only about one-third of the meaning in a normal two-person conversation is carried by verbal symbols and that the balance is transmitted by nonverbal cues. This stresses the need for the speaker to be concerned about physical behavior, personal attire, and his or her one-to-one relationship with the members of the audience.

Paralanguage is vocal but nonverbal; it deals with *how* one speaks, and includes voice qualities, characteristics, qualifiers, and segregates.

Physical position (where one sits) and social distance (where one sits in relation to others) are important in ensuring effective communication in discussion.

Listening is a part of the total communication transaction. It may be defined as "the perceptual process by which verbal and nonverbal communications (including mechanical sounds) from one source or sources are selectively received, and interpreted by a receiver or receivers in relation to the perceptual fields of the parties in the process." Research reveals the following findings: About one-half of a person's waking hours are spent in listening. Most people lack needed listening skills. Training can improve one's listening ability. Listening is related positively to other language skills. Listening is functional. And, the effective listener is one who is motivated, deliberately determines his or her goals in listening, practices in situations demanding increasing skills, and is objective and maintains emotional control when listening.

Study of the small group and communication will aid in understanding the nature of the private, face-to-face discussion group—the subject of Chapter 4.

SUGGESTED READINGS

Applbaum, Ronald L., and others, *The Process of Group Communication* (Chicago: Science Research Associates, 1974), Chs. 2, 4, 7–8.

Bradley, Bert E., *Fundamentals of Speech Communication: The Credibility of Ideas* (Dubuque, Iowa: Wm. C. Brown, 1974), Ch. 2.

Burgoon, Michael, Judee K. **Heston,** and James **McCroskey,** *Small Group Communication: A Functional Approach* (New York: Holt, Rinehart and Winston, 1974), Chs. 2–3.

Clevenger, Theodore, Jr., and Jack **Matthews,** *The Speech Communication Process* (Glenview, Ill.: Scott, Foresman, 1971), Ch. 1.

Fisher, B. Aubrey, *Small Group Decision Making* (New York: McGraw-Hill, 1974), Ch. 3.

Goldhaber, Gerald M., *Organizational Communication* (Dubuque, Iowa: Wm. C. Brown, 1974), Chs. 4–5.

Gruner, Charles R., Cal M. **Logue,** Dwight L. **Freshley,** and Richard C. **Huseman,** *Speech Communication in Society* (Boston, Allyn and Bacon, 1972), Ch. 13.

Harrison, Randall P., "Nonverbal Communication," in *Handbook of Communication,* I. de Pool, and others, eds. (Chicago: Rand McNally, 1974), pp. 93–115.

Journal of Communication, Vol. 22 (December 1972), pp. 339–476. (Entire issue is devoted to nonverbal communication.)

Knapp, Mark L., *Nonverbal Communication in Human Interaction* (New York: Holt, Rinehart and Winston, 1972).

Mortensen, C. David, *Communication: The Study of Human Interaction* (New York: McGraw-Hill, 1972), Parts I–II.

Patton, Bobby R., and Kim **Giffin,** *Problem-Solving Group Interaction* (New York: Harper & Row, 1973), Chs. 2–5.

Phillips, Gerald M., and Eugene C. **Erickson,** *Interpersonal Dynamics in the Small Group* (New York: Random House, 1970), Ch. 2.

Richardson, Lee, ed., *Dimensions of Communication* (New York: Appleton-Century-Crofts, 1969), Ch. 1.

Rosenfeld, Lawrence B., *Human Interaction in the Small Group Setting* (Columbus, Ohio: Charles E. Merrill, 1973), Chs. 4–5, 7–9.

EXERCISES

1. Review the definitions of communication given in the text. Now write your own definition. In what ways does it differ from that of the authors'? Be prepared to defend your definition in a class discussion.

2. The authors have described seven characteristics of the communication process. How were these seven manifested in some recent small group discussion that you participated in? Write out your answer.

3. Work with four or five other members of the class on this project. Consider all of the personal factors (needs, attitudes, prejudices, expectancies) that a person brings into a communication as inputs. Now make a list of the six you consider to be most important. Check your list with those prepared by the other subgroup members. Take twenty minutes to try to reach a consensus as to the six factors your group considers most important if communication is to be effective. Report your subgroup findings to the class as a whole.

4. Assuming that you have changed or modified your position in discussions at some time or another, what inputs from others have affected you the most? Make a list and compare it with a similar list to be made at the end of the semester.

5. Think of two or three members of your class whose ethnic, cultural, educational, and work experiences differ from yours. How are these differences manifested in the way each of you speaks?

6. The following single sentences have been taken from actual discussions. What barriers to understanding do they contain, if any? How would you reword the statements?

a. "Well, I think you'd better take a stand on this, John—either capitalism or communism."

b. "That's a silly idea if I ever heard one."

c. "Just think of it—this bond issue, if passed, will cost each of us exactly one hundred thirty-nine dollars and twenty-two-and-a-half cents!"

d. "I believe this to be the only infallible method of guaranteeing proper implementation of these foreign-aid programs."

e. "Not many prophets of Lincoln's stature have had the good luck to reside in approximations of their utopias."

f. "My feelings on that point are ambivalent."

g. "Let's get back on the track; we've been wasting the last half hour."

7. Working in a subgroup of five or six, select one of the events listed below and discuss the relevance of effective communication, especially listening, to the success, failure, or general progress of the event.

Watergate

Credibility decline of politicians in America

The SALT talks

President Ford's Amnesty decisions

The Women's Liberation Movement

America's role in the Middle East

What other events, situations, or occasions demonstrate the importance of listening or other dimensions of effective communication?

Forms of discussion can be classified in many different ways. One classification is based on the goal: learning, problem solving, motivation, communication, or therapy. Another is based on the manner of exchange of ideas: round-table or informal, panel-forum, symposium-forum, or lecture-forum.[1] The size of the group, degree of formality, permanency of the group, and amount of tension are other bases for classification. Although all these classifications serve useful purposes, we believe the best division of discussion is into private and public. Here we will consider some of the forms and techniques employed in private discussions; Chapter 9 will take up public ones.

[1] These forms are described in Chapter 9.

Private discussion is any discussion that occurs without an audience. It is sometimes called the closed-group discussion. We consider this form first for several reasons:

1. Since it is the type we participate in most frequently, both on and off the campus, we need to understand it first.

2. Public discussion—in which there is an audience—often employs the forms and principles of private discussion; skill in one carries over to the other.

3. Private discussion provides the best situation for learning discussion skills—effective communication, critical thinking, leadership, good interpersonal relations, objectivity, and so forth.

Your first step in achieving proficiency in any type of discussion, therefore, is to understand the conduct of private discussion.

CHARACTERISTICS OF PRIVATE DISCUSSION

If we accept the idea that discussion involves a group of people sharing their ideas and resources in order to clarify their thinking or solve problems of mutual concern, we can recognize the basic importance of the private discussion group. Private discussion is face-to-face, informal discussion. Since ancient times, the circle has been a symbol of sharing, belonging, and uniting. Physically, circular arrangement places no person in a position more exalted than that of her or his neighbor. In a circle, everyone also has the opportunity to observe the actions and reactions of his or her peers, without employing an embarrassing scrutiny.

.........I THOUGHT THE CIRCULAR ARRANGEMENT GUARANTEED EQUALITY.....

Although forms of private discussion vary today, the basic form has the following characteristics:

1. The round table, circle, or rectangle provides the basic physical format; everyone can look at everyone else face-to-face.

2. The conduct in such a discussion is usually informal. That is, there are no spectators, and all members take an active part.

3. There may not be an assigned leader.

4. There are no set speeches—each person participates when and how he or she sees fit.

5. Leadership, if there is no assigned chairperson, usually rotates.

6. Rules of procedure are determined by the group.

7. There is usually a high degree of homogeneity among the members in knowledge of and interest in the topic.

On both the physical and interpersonal levels, the keynotes are informality, permissiveness, and a sharing of responsibility for the functioning of the group.

The size of this private, informal, face-to-face discussion group can vary greatly. But size does impose certain limitations that affect the use and abuse of this form in all situations. Let us consider some of these limitations and their implications.

Generally speaking, one might surmise that in smaller groups there's more time for responsible speaking and that less time is required for making a decision. Conversely, it would appear that the larger the group is—up to the point where distance turns discussion into public speaking—the more time is required to achieve decisive action. Further, we might assume that there's greater opportunity for a wide range of contributions. But we should remember that a small group does not guarantee well-informed and responsible participants. And, on the other hand, a large number of discussants does not guarantee that a wide variety of opinions will not be stifled by group pressures.

It is our belief that groups of three to twelve persons can deal effectively with such tasks as determining policy, exploring and evaluating ideas, planning programs and performances, and completing the steps involved in the problem-solving sequence. (Of course, we must always consider the size of the meeting room, the ability and preparation of the participants, the demands of the objective, and the emotional interests and stability of the members and leaders.) Generally, we can say that groups should be small when there is a great demand for speed, more knowledgeable members, and more readily accessible facts and opinions. On the other hand, where the exchange of information is largely for personal gratification and learning and where the expression of opinion is not of stock-tumbling import, the group may be larger and still function admirably—especially if there is adequate time and if effective small group techniques are employed.

In all discussion, but particularly in private groups, a number of conditions are necessary for maximum productivity:

1. The group members should be somewhat homogeneous as to status, knowledge of the topic, and willingness to contribute to the discussion's progress.

2. The atmosphere in the group should be informal and should contribute as much as possible to the permissiveness and security of the members.

3. The goals must be understood by all group members or determined by them early in the discussion.

4. The group must make—and be aware of making—conscious progress toward its goal.

5. The group should have within its membership—or readily available—the information needed for achieving its goals.

6. All group members should contribute to goal-achievement. In other words, the productivity of the group should not depend on any one individual, and there should be no spectators.

7. Group members must have the desire and authority to make decisions that contribute to improving group performance.

8. The size and the seating arrangement of the group should be based on maintaining effective intercommunication among all members. Splinter discussions and hidden agendas should be kept to a minimum. There should be no blind spots where members cannot see or be seen. Everyone should speak loudly enough to be heard.

9. The size must be small enough for optimum participation by all.

10. The members should have a high degree of interpersonal trust, compatibility, and mutual respect.

11. The leadership should be primarily functional, mutually shared, and group- and task-oriented.

12. The members should have an understanding of, and skill in, the essentials of effective communication, including both its verbal and nonverbal aspects.

EFFECTIVE QUESTIONING IN DISCUSSION

A basic assumption about the private, small group discussion is that the participants are selected for, join, or belong to the group because they have experiences, information, or skills that the group needs in order to achieve its goal. What is necessary, then, is to ensure that each individual makes an optimum contribution to the discussion. The person who is involved intellectually in a discussion—follows what is being said, thinks about it, and even phrases questions or comments—but remains withdrawn must be encouraged to participate by the leader or by other members of the group. Some people may not be accustomed to speaking even in small groups. Some may be shy or timid. Some may be afraid of ridicule.

Others may not understand what is being said. We need some technique, therefore, that will tap the resource potential of each discussion group member. The skillful use of questions is one method by which members' contributions can be improved and increased. Barriers can be reduced by this technique, but discussion leaders too frequently overlook it. Questioning is useful in controlling discussion, testing for consensus, revealing needed and latent resources, uncovering feelings, resolving differences, and insuring the thorough exploration of a topic.

Effective questioning depends partly on knowing the different types of questions, their specific functions, their effect on attitudes, and cautions to be observed in their use. Because questioning is almost a lost art and because it is so important in discussion, we look briefly at four ways questions can improve the functioning of small groups.

Types of Questions

Questions are usually classified according to whether they are (1) closed-end, (2) directive, or (3) open-end. A closed-end question is one to which the respondent must select a single, brief answer from two or more specific options. Examples are questions that require a "yes" or "no" answer, a selection from a number of options (multiple-choice), or the statement of a single fact (true-false). The closed-end question gives the respondent no opportunity to amplify his answer. The directive question asks the respondent to reply by stating facts and/or opinions that relate to one or more options presented. Some limitations are still placed on the respondent. The open-end question is one to which the respondent may give any answer that he or she believes is pertinent. No direction or restriction is placed on the reply.

A second way to classify questions is by noting the designees. A group or *overhead* question does not designate any particular person but rather the group as a whole, as "What is the group's thinking on this point?" A *directed* or referred question includes the name of the intended respondent. Finally, a "reverse" question is one referred back to the asker.

Thirdly, questions may be classified according to intent. When, for example, the questioner's unethical purpose is to unlock biases or prejudices, he or she frequently employs the *loaded* question. An instructor may put down a student who challenges him by asking: "Haven't you listened to a thing I've been saying? Don't you ever get the facts before you mouth off?" The consequence, usually, is a strong emotional reaction—or withdrawal—that makes logical response next to impossible. It precludes the reasonable exchange of information and ideas.

Less frequently employed than the loaded question is the *hypothetical* one. This is a "what if" or "supposing you were" idea primer. This type of question can help the process of brainstorming and elicit the hidden values, sentiments, and aspirations of the respondents. The hypothetical question is particularly useful when discussants are not open to alternative modes of acting or thinking because of practical reasons. But there is always the danger of tangential wandering. The questioner must keep in mind the major purpose of the discussion and introduce and phrase her or his hypothetical question accordingly. Thus, if major disagreement stalls group progress, a member might help bypass an emotional or mental road block by asking: "Supposing that we forget for a moment the difficulty of obtaining the money—if we had the two hundred dollars for publicity, what benefits might be gained by spending the money?" Occasionally, appealing ideas can be suggested that will help the group to surmount its problems.

Specific Functions of Questioning

Skill in questioning comes from practice in specific situations. The following illustrations indicate some of the specific functions of questioning.[2]

1. *To draw out a silent member:*

   "Does anyone else care to comment on this topic?"

   "John, from your experience in local government, would you . . . ?"

2. *To suggest the need for sharing personal experiences:*

   "Does anyone know of times when this has worked?"

   "Since I will want to call on each of you later, will you think about your own experiences in this matter?"

3. *To call attention to points that have not been considered:*

   "Does anyone have any information on the student protests at Columbia?"

[2] Adapted from "A Guide to Successful Conference Leadership," *Personnel*, Vol. 25 (July 1948), pp. 33–34. By permission of the American Management Association and *Personnel*.

"What has been your thinking on this point?"

"Before we continue, would it be profitable for us to explore this angle?"

4. *To keep the discussion focused on the subject:*

   "That's interesting—but how does it fit in with the issue being considered?"

   "I must have missed something you said. Will you please explain the connection between your suggestion and the point we were talking about?

   "Does the group feel that this point bears directly on the issue at hand? How?"

5. *To use conflict constructively:*

   "Since we do not seem to be able to resolve this issue now, could we move on to the next point? Perhaps further discussion will reveal additional information."

6. *To suggest that additional information is needed:*

   "Do we have enough information on the teacher's point-of-view to decide now?"

"Is it agreeable to the group if we ask a subcommittee to bring back the needed information to our next session?"

7. *To call attention to the source of information:*

"Where did this information originate?"

"Since the facts presented seem to be in conflict, perhaps considering their source will help us to determine their reliability."

8. *To test the strength of a particular viewpoint:*

"Is this position held by a majority of our group? May we have a show of hands?"

"How much importance should we attach to this point?"

"The newspapers have recently expressed considerable opposition to this point. Do we agree with the media or not?"

9. *To focus attention on issues rather than personalities:*

"Which seems to be more important, the facts in the case or the supporters of the different viewpoints?"

"Would we make more progress if we confined our discussion only to the subject and to the people involved?"

"Are we placing too much importance on the source of the information and not enough on the content?"

10. *To focus attention on the need for objectivity:*

"Are personal interests causing us to overlook the general interests of the group?"

"Would it be best to hold off making a decision until more information is available?"

11. *To prevent a few from monopolizing the discussion:*

"Excuse me, Janet. Before you continue, may I ask if anyone has a comment on the point you have just made?"

"May we hear now from some who haven't expressed an opinion?"

"Jim, since we have only a few minutes left, could you summarize your remarks so we may hear what the others think?"

12. *To suggest the need for closing the discussion:*

"May we have two or three final comments before we close?"

"According to my watch, we're scheduled to finish discussion in about five minutes. Is there a final comment?"

13. *To indicate the need for procedural decisions:*

"In view of the limited time we have, may we decide now on the phases of the topic we should try to consider before we adjourn?"

"How much more time do you think we should spend on this point?"

14. *To focus attention on needed follow-up:*

"Who will accept responsibility for carrying out the action we've decided on?"

"When should we hold our next meeting?"

"Mary, will you take responsibility for making the opening statement at our next meeting?"

15. *To ventilate feelings:*

"Fred, I know you have some strong feelings about this—will you share them with us?"

"Could some feelings be expressed on the decision so we know the extent of our commitment?"

You will be able to improve and add to these questions as you participate in more and more discussions. Remember, whether you are the leader or a member of a discussion group, you need questioning skills. Asking questions keeps the lines of communication open; too frequently, a declarative statement closes them.

The Effects of Questioning

Any question—an input into discussion—is filtered through the perceptual screen of each hearer before it is answered. Whenever a question is asked, the potential or designated respondent reacts to both the cognitive and affective aspects of the question. He or she tries to determine the intent of the question and the attitude of the questioner. The effective questioner, therefore, considers the impressions that may be conveyed by the questions she or he asks. Here are some of the possible impressions that a respondent may get from a question:

1.   There is opportunity for free and complete response.

2.   A "yes" or "no" answer is desired.

3.   The respondent perceives her- or himself as an authority.

4.   The respondent is requested to contrast two or more alternatives.

5.   The respondent perceives him- or herself as being put on the spot.

6.   Some censure of the respondent is implied.

7.   The impression is conveyed that no answer is desired.

8.   Some form of reaction to a procedural decision is sought.

9.   Support of the questioner's viewpoint is sought.

10.   The impression is given that the respondent should consider her- or himself as a "devil's advocate."

11.   Factual clarification only is sought; opinion is not sought.

To improve your effectiveness in discussion, give some thought to the impressions that your questions convey.

Cautions in Questioning

Although questioning can be an effective tool in discussion, some cautions must be observed. Poor questioning techniques, as we have suggested above, can frequently create barriers to sound group decision making. It's unwise, for example, to ask for information that the respondent does not have. Questions that are *obviously* leading, misleading, or inaccurate should not be asked. Questions should be as clear as the questioner can make them. Further, they should not divert the discussion but should direct the flow of ideas toward the group's goals. Personal questions should be kept to a minimum. Finally, questions should reflect the inquirer's attitudes and not those of the advocate.

Your question-asking skills can be improved with practice. In addition, the more you practice questioning, the better able you will be to build sound interpersonal relations and contribute positively to the achievement of a group's goals.

BRAINSTORMING

No matter what kind of work or leisure activities we engage in, there is a need for creativity. In particular, individual and group creativity are highly valued in industrial and scientific research. Unfortunately, many factors tend to cramp creative efforts: lack of previous experience in creative thinking, little self-confidence, discouragement by others, timidity in a group, lack of opportunity to be creative, and the absence of imagination. Few of these inhibiting factors, however, affect creative ideation, or *brainstorming*.[3]

Brainstorming is essentially a discussion situation where the keynote is creative or imaginative thinking rather than judicious or critical thinking. Primarily a private discussion method, it can be employed effectively in groups with as many as twenty persons—although half that number or less is better. Brainstorming can be combined with other discussion techniques, especially when you want to produce a large number of ideas, such as

[3] Alex F. Osborn, *Applied Imagination*, rev. ed. (New York: Scribner's, 1957).

collecting suggestions for a discussion topic, outlining different aspects of a topic, suggesting solutions to a problem, or obtaining brief answers to some questions. Let's examine the format that brainstormers all over the country employ.

1. When possible, and before the actual brainstorming session, the group receives a memorandum stating the problem to be considered. The memorandum contains background material, the "why" of the problem, several samples of ideas that could result, and sometimes a request that each participant prepare three to five ideas as possible discussion "starters." The problem itself should be a simple rather than a multiple one, and it should be stated clearly and briefly.

2. When the participants gather for the beginning of the session, the leader may start with a few ideas of his or her own if it seems advisable.

3. The aim of a brainstorming session is to amass a large number of ideas. The brainstormer is asked to assume that the more ideas there are, the more likelihood there is of "winners."

4. Unlike ordinary problem-solving discussions, brainstorming does not permit critical evaluation at the beginning, or ideation, level. Evaluations and adverse judgments are withheld until later.

5. Freewheeling is welcome. As Osborn puts it, "The wilder the idea, the better; it is easier to tame down than to think up."[4]

6. In addition to contributing his own ideas, the brainstormer tries to add to, subtract from, divide, combine, and otherwise modify and improve the ideas of others (without critical judgment).

[4] Osborn, p. 84.

"The aim of a brainstorming session is to amass a large number of ideas."

7. All ideas are recorded as they bubble forth. Some groups employ two secretaries, in order to keep up with the "ideation gusher."

8. A member of the brainstorming group, usually the secretary, checks with each participant the day after the session in case a person has had some afterthoughts. As one might expect, ideas that have been slept on often turn out to be very valuable.

9. A list of all suggested ideas is typed and submitted to the group chairperson for editing and classifying according to logical categories.

10. The executive, group chairperson, or individual concerned with the problem that gave rise to the brainstorming session screens the ideas in collaboration with selected associates.

11. The screened ideas are passed on to the individual or group that has responsibility for implementing the accepted ideas.

12. The action of the implementing group is reported back to the original brainstormers, thus completing the cycle of communication.

When the technique just described is used in industry, business research, or education, it also includes the final implementation steps. In the classroom, where the method is used primarily for training purposes, the final steps may be omitted. In relation to discussion, the characteristics of brainstorming are: (1) the desire for quantity, (2) the outlawing of criticism, (3) the encouragement of freewheeling, and (4) the search for combination and improvement.

As with all discussion techniques, we must watch out for pitfalls if we are to use this method effectively. Even when the leader and participants understand the rules, the net result of a brainstorming session can sometimes be mediocre. To extract ideas from nonthinkers is a monumental task. It helps if some of the participants are self-starters and if all of them have the "right" attitude. If there are no controls, the eager beavers may often keep the more timid members from participating. Even more disastrous is when the group's creativity stems mainly from the lone thinkers who insist on getting credit for their ideas. The storm will subside after the first few gusts.

When brainstorming is used in industry, the process may break down as ideas are passed from chairperson to implementer. Unwise exclusion, dilution, and lack of understanding may negate the effectiveness of the best brainstorming sessions. But these possibilities of failure do not constitute a valid reason for ignoring or castigating the entire process. When the personnel is select, brainstorming can unleash an amazing torrent of ideas. And when the brakes of good judgment are applied after the ideation stage, much time and energy can be saved. Even when few usable ideas are contributed, another worthwhile by-product can result: the gates that man frequently erects around his store of creativity may be unlocked.

THE PROBLEM-CENSUS

Another technique used extensively in private, small discussion groups is the problem-census. It is a way to take a quick poll of the problems, or aspects, of a topic that a group wants to discuss. Used at the opening of a discussion, it serves to outline what the participants consider the main issue to be.

The problem-census moves one step beyond brainstorming. Besides seeking numerous ideas, it also provides the opportunity for enough discussion on each problem or suggestion to ensure that everything is clearly understood. Here are the steps in conducting a problem-census.

1. Present a single, direct question to all discussion group members. The group may act as a full committee or in subgroups. The question should call for relatively simple, short answers or statements that can be clearly phrased in a few minutes of discussion.

2. Secure one answer from every person before letting anyone give a second. When the group acts in subgroups, each subgroup gives only one answer at a time.

3. Continue this procedure, letting all members of the group (or all subgroups) give second, third, and fourth answers in turn.

4. Write the answers on a blackboard. (You will discover that, after the first or second round, many answers are duplicates.) Keeping all suggestions directly before the participants in this way makes the sixth step in the process somewhat easier.

5. Group all the answers in larger classifications, if possible.

6. By means of a show of hands, determine which problems or topics most of the members would like to discuss first, second, and so forth, until you have established a priority listing of all topics.

7. Recognizing the time limits for the meeting, determine the number of topics that might possibly be considered and how much time to spend on each.

8. Discuss each topic in the order determined by the group.

9. If not all the topics can be discussed by the end of the meeting, call this to the attention of the group sometime before adjournment, so they can decide whether to continue with a certain topic or go on to another.

It is obvious that establishing the problem-census includes only Steps 1 through 7. However, the reason for using the process is to reach Step 8—the actual discussion.

With this technique, as with others considered thus far, there are a number of cautions to keep in mind. It is important to avoid extended discussion on any problem put forth until you have secured all possible suggestions from the group. You should accept every suggestion as a usable one. To do otherwise may earn you the label of "biased chairperson."

As in the brainstorming technique, no suggestion should be evaluated until priorities have been set up. You should try to keep a few individuals from stealing the show by limiting the number of their suggestions. Encourage everyone to submit suggestions, but do not press any individual to the point of embarrassing him. Accept every idea as presented.

You will find the problem-census a useful tool in selecting topics for class discussion, in determining class procedures, and in reaching agreement on general and specific aspects of discussion theory and practice to be considered during the term. Since the problem-census may permit complete anonymity, it may also prevent embarrassment or possible discrimination. A questioner asks a group for a list of problems, answers, issues, causes, or viewpoints. The questioner assures the group that he or she desires honest reactions and does not want to know who is responsible for a particular answer—indeed, the method of questioning makes it impossible for him or her to find out. The questioner then hands out identical cards or sheets of paper that contain a question or an incomplete sentence and tells the participants what they are to do. The instructions may be to list objections to a proposed policy, note difficulties in the production of a certain item, or complete a sentence such as "The major cause of difficulty on our project is . . . ." No individuals are to sign their cards, and individuals may print or disguise their handwriting if they wish. The questioner then collects the cards or sheets, shuffles them, and redistributes them so that no member will have his or her own. Finally, a composite list of problems or questions is compiled by means of buzz groups or any method devised by the chairperson. Depending on the time available, the questions may be used for immediate discussion or arranged in order for future consideration.

SELECTING MEMBERS OF SMALL GROUPS: SOCIOMETRICS

A person may become a member of a private discussion group in many different ways. Both the individual and the group benefit the most, however, when each person has some freedom to choose the groups in which he or she participates. In this section, we deal with a useful and important method of indicating and utilizing individual preferences in group selection.

Sociometric refers primarily to measuring the attraction between group members *in relation to a specific event*. Its distinguishing feature is that it asks the individuals to choose colleagues for a specific activity situation. Thus, it is a way to set up a working group. We recommend its use both in and out of the classroom when the following ideas are accepted: an individual will work or interact more effectively with persons he or she (1) respects, (2) likes, (3) perceives as being capable of accomplishing a given task, or (4) perceives as supportive rather than threatening.

Sociometrics is a method originated by an Austrian-born psychiatrist, J. L. Moreno, as a tool to examine the mental health of a group by mapping lines of attraction and rejection. If we regard the present status of any group as largely the product of past communication, we may consider the test as a rough measure of how effective the communication has been.

The sociometric test or questionnaire usually has an oral or written introduction that starts, "We are going to work in committees of four or five persons on this next project." Next, the project is sufficiently described so that each member of the group or class can visualize the types of activities and responsibilities that will be required for him or her to work closely with others. Then the introduction may continue, "You probably know certain of your classmates well enough to judge which ones you would enjoy working with on this project. In order that you may be grouped with some of them, I am going to ask you to list their names for me in order of preference. You may, if you wish, make a second list of those you hope will not be included in your group. Feel perfectly free in making these choices, because you are not judging your classmates, nor will anyone besides me ever know whom you chose or rejected."

Sometimes, members of a group may choose as many colleagues as they wish; at other times, the instructor or supervisor limits the choices to three or four. In general, out of a group of thirty, the average number of choices, when unlimited, will be six or seven (although a few individuals will list up to half of the entire group). Informal experiments indicate that when free choices are allowed, the distribution of choices will approach a normal distribution if the communication opportunities in the group have been adequate.[5] Sociometric data are collected for many purposes, including research, counseling, and grouping.

[5] Seth A. Fessenden, "An Index of Cohesiveness–Morale Based on the Analysis of Sociometric Choice Distribution," *Sociometry,* Vol. 16 (November 1953), pp. 321–326. See also: Lawrence B. Rosenfeld, *Human Interaction in the Small Group Setting* (Columbus, Ohio: Charles E. Merrill, 1973), pp. 173–179.

The most common method of recording the data is the *sociogram*, which is a plot of lines to represent the choices, with circles and triangles or some other code to represent classifications, meaningful for analyzing the group: boys–girls, married men–unmarried men, undergraduates–graduates, employees–supervisors, pilots–crew members, and so on. The advantage of the sociogram is that it gives a quick picture of interpersonal relationships, and this makes the formation of groups relatively simple. The disadvantage is that the lines can form a very complicated pattern when the group is large, thus making data analysis difficult.

The sociogram on page 59 shows the choices made by a subgroup of five persons formed from a class of twenty-two. Every class member had been given an alphabetical list of the class roster and asked to indicate, in order of preference, eight persons within the class with whom he or she would like to work on a proposed class project. Each was told to mark a first choice with a (1), a second choice with a (2), a third choice with a (3), and so on. Four subgroups were formed (the others consisted of five, six, and six members). The members of the group shown in this sociogram were chosen because of the strong lines of communication among them.

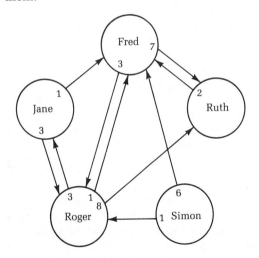

Fred was among the first eight people chosen by all other members of the subgroup. Simon was included because the group included his first choice. Jane, Roger, and Ruth had reciprocated choices. Thus, there were direct ties between all members except Simon and Ruth.

The numbers within the circles indicate the choices made by that person. For example, Fred got his third and seventh choice but was chosen by all other members of the group. Simon, who was not chosen, got his first choice (Roger) as well as Fred. Finally, the group included three reciprocated choices. Simon and Ruth were the only persons between whom there was no connection (based on eight choices) but both of them would be supported by other group members. This subgroup worked well together on the class project!

For discussion classes, subgrouping is important on many occasions. The instructor usually finds it advantageous to be able to identify the members of the class who are unchosen or infrequently chosen, as well as those who are highly chosen. Research seems to suggest that sociometrically high individuals are generally most superior to sociometrically low ones in the following kinds of behavior: extroverted interests, friendly contacts with others, positive self-regarding attitudes, cooperative behavior, cheerfulness and buoyancy of mood, and sensitivity to the responses of others.

Instructors will often find sociometric data valuable when working with their classes. As they examine the data, they will ask such questions as: Does the unchosen individual have ample opportunity to mix and to work with others? Can he or she be aided in establishing relationships? From whom and through whom can messages best reach and influence that person? Are there any apparent reasons—race, religion, and the like—which cause him or her to be unchosen? Does the individual seek security by trying to relate himself closely with the instructor or with students of high status or popularity? Have the highly chosen usurped the center of attention? Is there disrupting competition among the highly chosen? Has there been opportunity for division of leadership among members of the group?

When you use sociometric data for forming groups—and this is essential if the promise of grouping was the basis for gathering the information of choices from the class members—there are certain suggestions you should follow. These will serve to give individuals maximum satisfaction.

1. Give any person who is unchosen his first choice.

2. Give any person who is mutually chosen his or her highest reciprocated choice—that is, the first choice if it is reciprocated, the second choice if that is reciprocated and the first is not, and the third choice if that is reciprocated and the first and second choices are not.

3. Give any person who is chosen, but chooses none who have chosen him or her, first choice.

4. If there have been rejections, check to be sure that no individual is grouped with those who rejected him or her.

5. Check the placement arrangement to be sure that every person has at least one of her or his choices fulfilled, and if possible more than one.

6. Arrange subgroups so that there are as many mutual choices in each subgroup as possible.

7. Avoid having an excessive number of stars (those who have many people choose them) or isolates in any single grouping.

It is obvious that placement in subgroups according to sociometric choice is only the means to an end—namely, the accomplishment of some group task. Therefore, after forming the groups, you should also consider the following: Does each group have members with skill for dealing with the task to be done? Do the members complement one another in temperament and skill? Does the job require working together in small groups? Is the job to be done acceptable to the members? When you can answer these questions in the affirmative, you can be sure of greater productivity.

A SUMMARY AND LOOK AHEAD

Private discussion takes place when there is no audience and when all persons participate on an equal basis. It usually occurs in small, informal, face-to-face groups. As the group becomes larger than ten or twelve, its effectiveness tends to decrease. Rules of procedure are at a minimum in a private discussion. Leadership may be shared.

Tapping the resource potential of the members of a group is essential to the success of discussion. Skill in questioning aids in this respect.

Two techniques for getting lists of topics are brainstorming and the problem-census. Both are ideally suited for establishing boundaries for later discussion. Brainstorming seeks quantity of ideas without evaluation; the problem-census seeks a priority listing of ideas for later consideration.

The use of sociometrics in selecting the members for small private discussion groups usually increases the effectiveness of those groups.

In the next chapter, we consider ways of making participation in discussion more effective.

SUGGESTED READINGS

Applbaum, Ronald L., and others, *The Process of Group Communication* (Chicago: Science Research Associates, 1974), Ch. 10.

Arnold, John K., "Useful Creative Techniques," in Sidney J. Parnes and Harold F. Harding, eds., *A Source Book for Creative Thinking* (New York: Scribner's, 1962), pp. 251–268.

Better Boards and Committees (Chicago: Adult Education Association of the U.S.A., 1960).

Braden, Waldo W., and Earnest S. **Brandenburg,** *Oral Decision-Making* (New York: Harper & Row, 1955), Ch. 9.

Clark, Charles H., *Brainstorming* (Garden City, N.Y.: Doubleday, 1958), Ch. 3.

Fisher, B. Aubrey, *Small Group Decision-Making,* (New York: McGraw-Hill, 1974), Ch. 4.

Goldner, Bernard B., *The Strategy of Creative Thinking* (Englewood Cliffs, N.J.: Prentice-Hall, 1962), Ch. 16.

Harnack, R. Victor, and Thorrel B. **Fest,** *Group Discussion: Theory and Technique* (New York: Appleton-Century-Crofts, 1964), Chs. 1, 7.

Levy, Ronald B., *Human Relations: A Conceptual Approach* (Scranton, Pa.: International Textbook, 1969), Ch. 9.

Osborn, Alex, *Applied Imagination,* 3rd ed. (New York: Scribner's, 1963).

Parnes, Sidney J., "Do You Really Understand Brainstorming?" in Sidney J. Parnes and Harold F. Harding, eds., *A Source Book for Creative Thinking* (New York: Scribner's, 1962), pp. 283–290.

Phillips, Gerald M., *Communication and the Small Group* (Indianapolis: Bobs-Merrill, 1973), Chs. 1–3, 5).

Phillips, J. Donald, "Report on Discussion 66," *Adult Education Journal,* Vol. 7 (October 1948), pp. 181–182.

Sattler, William M., and N. Edd **Miller,** *Discussion and Conference,* 2nd ed., (Englewood Cliffs, N.J.: Prentice-Hall, 1968), Ch. 3.

Scheidel, Thomas M., *Speech Communication and Human Interaction* (Glenview, Ill.: Scott, Foresman, 1972), Ch. 9.

Snell, Frank, *How to Hold a Better Meeting* (New York: Harper & Row, 1958).

Trecker, Audrey R., and Harleigh B. **Trecker,** *Committee Common Sense* (New York: Association Press, 1954), Chs. 1–3, 5–9.

EXERCISES

1. Select eight of the fifteen specific functions of questioning outlined in this chapter in which you believe you need practice. Write out two actual questions that would perform the functions listed. Practice using the questions in subsequent class discussions.

2. Arrange with your instructor to divide the class into groups of five or six. In each group, select some problems on which the members of the group could take action, such as campus or community problems. Spend about an hour in your subgroup discussing one problem, with the aim of agreeing on a number of possible solutions. Present your solutions in writing to your instructor. As an individual, try to carry out as many of the suggestions as you can. As you participate in this discussion, make a mental note of how well your group works together. Then answer the questions in writing on Analysis Form 1 at the end of the chapter and submit it to your instructor.

3. In section A, we have listed the fourteen dimensions of groups presented in Chapter 2. In section B are five groups that are primarily private discussion groups. After each of the five private groups in section B, list the five dimensions that have the greatest effect on the group's goal-oriented behavior.

A. Group Dimensions

1. Autonomy (independent functioning)

2. Control (amount of control exerted over members)

3. Flexibility (degree of informality in procedures)

4. Hedonic tone (feeling of pleasantness in the group)

5. Homogeneity (similarity in characteristics)

6. Intimacy (degree of mutual acquaintance)

7. Participation (time and effort devoted to group activities)

8. Permeability (degree of ready access to others)

9. Polarization (orientation toward a single goal)

10. Potency (amount of significance to members)

11. Size (number of members)

12. Stability (persistence of group over time)

13. Stratifications (existence of status hierarchies)

14. Viscidity (degree to which group functions as a unit)

B. Private Groups

1. Golf foursome playing together once a week

2. Family group of five

3. College newspaper staff

4. A ghetto "gang"

5. A debate team

4. Assume that you are participating in a private discussion group composed of eight persons. The members are all students and you have been meeting twice a week over a two-month period to consider some campus project. Would each of the following factors (A) contribute to, (B) detract from, or (C) have no effect on the productivity of the group? In the blank at the left, indicate by A, B, or C.

a. ___ Lack of blackboards

b. ___ Unavailability of needed facts

c. ___ Presence of a "playboy"

d. ___ Occasional visits by a faculty advisor

e. ___ Aside conversations by two minority group members

f. ___ General agreement on goals

g. ___ Existence of pressures within the group to get the job done

h. ___ Group members meet frequently for social activities outside of the group's meetings

i. ___ Open communication channels

j. ___ Occasional changes in the membership of the group

k. — Group has never decided on rules of procedure

l. — Lack of a fixed meeting time

5. A group of six students in a discussion class has been asked to prepare for a panel-forum* discussion to be presented before the class in three weeks' time. The group met once, with one member absent, at which time they selected a topic, phrased a discussion question, assigned phases of the question to members for further study, and picked one member to serve as moderator. At the second meeting of the group, held again outside of class, the person absent at the first meeting was again missing, even though he had been informed of the meeting time and place and had said he would attend. The instructor has stated that both individual and group grades will be given. Anxious to do the best job possible, the five "regulars" meet to determine what to do about the absent member.

a. Is the discussion of the five a private discussion? What characteristics of a private group does it have?

b. What interpersonal relations and communication problems does the above incident create?

* Please read the description of a panel-forum given in Chapter 9.

c. As a member of the group of five regulars, what action would you propose?

6. *Practice in brainstorming:* Following is a list of topics that might be suitable for brainstorming in your class. You may add others if you and your instructor wish. At the beginning of a class session, select four of the topics. Divide the class into subgroups of five or six and have each subgroup brainstorm on each of the four topics for ten minutes. Each group should follow the same sequence of topics and start and stop at the same time for each brainstorming session.

At the same or the following class session,* brainstorm on another sequence of four topics but with the following modification in group size: (1) Let two subgroups remain at the same size (five or six) and with the same membership for the sequence of four topics. (2) For the first two brainstorming topics, combine the remaining two groups so that there is one subgroup of about ten or twelve persons. (3) For the last two topics, make one subgroup of eight and one subgroup of two and have three individuals work separately.

* Your instructor may wish to have you do Exercise 7 instead of the second half of this exercise.

Now, at a third class session (after your instructor has tabulated the total number of suggestions created by each subgroup under each of the various group sizes), answer or discuss the following questions:

a. Did your group "ideate" more suggestions on the fourth topic than on the first? Was the difference great or small? What was the difference? What reasons do you think there are for any increase between the first and fourth sessions?

b. Was it easier for you as an individual to make suggestions after practice on two or three topics?

c. Were there differences in the number of suggestions created between the large and small groups or among individuals?

d. Were there differences among the groups in the number of suggestions made on the first four sessions? If so, how do you account for this?

e. Did some individuals make more suggestions than others? If so, why?

f. What barriers seemed to hinder productivity in brainstorming?

Suggested Topics for Brainstorming

a. Campus-Related Topics

1. What can be done to develop better understanding between students and teachers?

2. On some campuses, students are asked or required to evaluate the quality of teaching by rating their instructors. However, the instructors frequently oppose the policy. Why? What barriers stand in the way of implementing such evaluation on our campus?

3. What can be done to improve school spirit on our campus?

4. What can be done to promote the participation of women in all campus sports?

5. What roles should the students play in the administration of our campus?

6. What can be done on our campus to promote better interpersonal relations between whites and minority groups?

7. How can we better utilize the physical plant at our college?

8. What can be done to develop closer relations and understanding between students and the administrative officers?

9. What can be done to promote the women's liberation movement on the campus?

10. What courses or activities should be developed on our campus to prepare students for post-graduation adjustments?

b. Off-Campus Topics

1. What can be done to help eliminate economic discrimination against minority groups?

2. What can be done to help students become more actively engaged in off-campus community affairs?

3. In what ways can college students participate more meaningfully in political campaigns?

4. What can students do to bridge the generation gap in their own homes?

5. What can be done to decrease air and water pollution?

6. What can be done to improve the lot of our senior citizens?

7. What can be done to raise the ethical level of all politicians?

8. What can be done to alert young people to the effects of drug-use?

9. What can be done to save the vanishing American wilderness?

10. What can be done to give the citizens of this country greater control over their own lives?

11. What should be done to promote better understanding and relations between the public and all law enforcement officers?

7. *More practice in brainstorming:* It has been said that brainstorming, in some instances, is not as effective a situation for creating ideas as individuals working alone. In order to test this generalization, use the problem-census technique to draw up a large list of topics suitable for brainstorming in class. From this list, select one in which most of the students are interested. Divide the class, selecting three or more brainstorming groups of five members each and letting the rest of the class work as individuals. Let the subgroups brainstorm and the individuals work separately (they may have to work in the corridor or in another room) on the selected topic for fifteen minutes. Determine the total number of different ideas suggested by each of the subgroups. Next, take any five of the individuals and do the same. Compare the totals for five persons working individually with the totals for five persons working as a group. Does your finding support the contention about individuals being superior to brainstorming groups?

You might have three individuals left over (not enough to make up a total of five), who form a smaller subgroup. After following the above procedure, you can determine approximately how many ideas might have been suggested if there had been two other persons working at the same rate as the three by: (a) finding the total number of ideas suggested by the three, (b) dividing this by three, and (c) multiplying that quotient by five.

**EFFECTIVENESS
OF PRIVATE DISCUSSION**

1. How well did you feel your group worked together? (Place a check mark on the line below to indicate your estimate.)

1	2	3	4	5	6	7
Outstandingly						Poorly

3. Did your group move in orderly steps toward your goal? What were the barriers to progress in your discussion, if any?

5. What comments or suggestions for improvement do you have for the individual members of your group? (Include yourself.)

4. In what specific ways could your group improve its functioning in another similar discussion?

2. Did everyone share about equally in the discussion? If not, why not?

(Use the reverse side of this paper if necessary in completing your answers. Hand in your reactions on the class day following your discussion.)

EFFECTIVENESS
OF PRIVATE DISCUSSION

1. How well did you feel your group worked together? (Place a check mark on the line below to indicate your estimate.)

1	2	3	4	5	6	7
Outstandingly						Poorly

2. Did everyone share about equally in the discussion? If not, why not?

3. Did your group move in orderly steps toward your goal? What were the barriers to progress in your discussion, if any?

4. In what specific ways could your group improve its functioning in another similar discussion?

5. What comments or suggestions for improvement do you have for the individual members of your group? (Include yourself.)

(Use the reverse side of this paper if necessary in completing your answers. Hand in your reactions on the class day following your discussion.)

PREREQUISITES FOR
EFFECTIVE DISCUSSION

The end product of discussion can never be better than the skills, understanding, and sensitivities of the individual participants permit. This chapter suggests ways of improving individual participation in discussion.

Your effectiveness in discussion depends on several factors, including the following: (1) your understanding of *reflective thinking* (in which you start with a problem and seek the best possible solution), and your willingness to put such thinking into practice; (2) your sensitivity to others and *flexibility in interpersonal relations;* (3) your desire and ability to *communicate effectively;* and (4) your knowledge of, and skill in, practicing a few simple *procedural rules.*

The first factor means that you approach a problem by seeking and considering all possible facts before making a decision. Reflective thinking is the direct opposite of *intentional thinking,* when a person feels that he or she already knows the answer and seeks support for that viewpoint by any means possible. In discussion, it is possible to accept another's viewpoint and combine it with your own to form a solution that may be better than either of the original ideas.

Of course, conflict and differences of opinion may still be present in a discussion, provided that conflict is used constructively to find an integrated solution. Serious discussants, however, must enter a discussion with flexible notions as to what the best solution might be. Even when they have ideas about a solution, they must be willing to listen objectively to the other side before reaching a final decision. In other words, effective discussants are much like effective scientists: they have hunches about what the answer might be, but they explore every possible angle before making a final conclusion. Even then, they realize that their conclusions may be tentative. We consider some related aspects of the reflective-thinking process in Chapter 6.

Flexibility in interpersonal relations is also a distinct asset in discussion. Flexibility means that you accept and adjust to the personalities of the other discussants. You try to understand the others' frame of reference. If you disagree with their viewpoints, you focus on the ideas, not on personalities. You try to avoid becoming defensive when your ideas are under fire. You carry out your responsibilities in helping the group achieve its goal. Flexibility also implies that you play different roles, as necessary. You may have to become a moderator, conciliator, critic, summarizer, reducer of tension, or take on any number of group- or goal-centered roles listed later in this chapter. Flexibility requires one to meet the demands of a constantly changing situation!

Your skill in *effective communication* is a third asset in all types of discussion. You are aware of the fact that each individual views the discussion process through his or her own perceptual field, which differs from yours and from all other members of the group. You understand that communication is purposeful, transactional, complex, personal, irreversible, and has shared meanings as its goal. You also understand and can adapt to the nonverbal aspects of discussion. You are first a good listener and observer, then you become a good speaker.

A willingness to engage in reflective thinking, good interpersonal relations, and meaningful communication are certainly three important requisites for effective discussion, but there are others as well. Together they form a configuration that is perhaps never achieved but always desired. Talking about these requisites or conditions will give us a model to follow when we seek to improve our own participation in discussion.

If discussion is to be effective, the *participation pattern* must:

Be cooperative *rather than* competitive.

Make constructive use of conflict *rather than* let conflict divide the group.

Be distributed among many members *rather than* limited to a few members.

Make optimum use of all resources *rather than* make limited use of resources.

Encourage freedom of expression *rather than* inhibit expression of ideas.

Follow an orderly problem-solving sequence to the greatest extent possible *rather than* reflect disorderly, nonlogical thinking.

Move away from dependency on one leader *rather than* increase the dependency on a single leader.

Reflect everyone's willingness to accept responsibility for accomplishing group tasks *rather than* develop a disregard for individual responsibility toward the group's goals.

Enable the group to make decisions affecting its progress *rather than* leave all decisions affecting the group's progress to a few.

Provide maximum opportunity for developing feelings of security *rather than* increase feelings of threat and defense.

Informal *rather than* formal.

Reflect active emotional and intellectual involvement in the subject *rather than* reflect disinterest and a noncommittal attitude toward the subject.

When practicing other discussion suggestions in this chapter, try to function as if some of the conditions listed above are reflected in the participation pattern. Awareness of what is desirable is a step toward improvement.

We have just taken a very general look at the overall requisites for effective discussion. Now we can be somewhat more specific. Let's consider briefly the roles that individuals may play in discussion and then talk about still more specific ways to contribute to discussions more effectively.

ROLES OF
DISCUSSION GROUP MEMBERS

Every discussion group, regardless of its nature, has three primary concerns: (1) *accomplishing its goals,* usually stated publicly but sometimes hidden; (2) *maintaining the group* as an identity, including concern about its morale, cohesion, autonomy, and the like; and (3) *satisfying the group members' ego needs.* For the most effective functioning of each group, the participants must be sensitive to these concerns and must contribute in every way possible to achieving them.

The role you play in discussion, therefore, should fall into one of the three categories mentioned above. You may act in a way that helps to achieve the group's goal or goals, in a way that builds group unity and morale, or in a way that gives you and other members of the group some personal satisfaction. Let us look briefly at each of these categories of roles.[1]

[1] In writing this section the authors have been influenced by several articles: Kenneth D. Benne and Paul H. Sheats, "Functional Roles of Group Members," *Journal of Social Issues,* Vol. 4 (Spring 1948), pp. 41–49; Robert F. Bales, "A Set of Categories for the Analysis of Small Group Interaction," *American Sociological Review,* Vol. 15 (April 1950), pp. 257–263; and Edgar F. Borgatta, Leonard S. Cottrell, and Henry J. Meyer, "On the Dimensions of Group Behavior," *Sociometry,* Vol. 19 (December 1956), pp. 223–240; and by related articles in Gardner Lindzey and Elliot Aronson, eds., *The Handbook of Social Psychology,* 2nd ed., Vol. 5 (Reading, Mass.: Addison-Wesley, 1969).

Goal-Oriented Roles and Behavior

What are the things a discussion group must do if it is to achieve some goal, whether or not it is clearly defined? It would probably have to do at least the following: (1) define the goal clearly so that it is understood by all; (2) determine the steps to take, blocks to overcome, or criteria to apply in achieving the goal; (3) agree on some priority to follow in carrying out stage two; (4) suggest a number of possible ways to achieve the goal and explore the ramifications of each; and (5) reach a consensus as to the best means of achieving the goal. In addition to these sequential steps, the group would need to know what facts and opinions were needed and where to get them. It would also need to distinguish between relevant and irrelevant matters, and to know and be able to chart its position in the problem-solving sequence at any given time. Finally, a group should be able to perceive and test the practicality of generalizations made or action proposed. In other words, any contribution that is related to any of these tasks would be considered as a goal-oriented or group-task role. Here are some of these roles.

1. *Goal-setting activity:* proposing goals; asking for clarification of goals; seeking agreement on goals; pointing out the significance of goals.

2. *Process-related activity:* suggesting procedures, asking for procedural suggestions; suggesting time schedules; asking for summaries or progress statements; seeking consensus on procedures.

3. *Seeking information and opinion:* requesting needed facts or opinions; asking for clarification of opinions; testing the intensity and nature of members' feelings; seeking reasons for value judgments.

4. *Giving information and opinion:* offering facts, opinions, generalizations, or specific illustrations; reporting related personal experience; giving other forms of evidence.

5. *Reasoning activity:* testing evidence and opinions; revealing fallacies in reasoning; drawing inferences; showing causes, effects, and analogies; arguing.

6. *Elaborating and exploring implications:* clarifying words or concepts, giving examples or illustrations; suggesting implications of proposals, applying proposals to real situations to test their practicality; showing relationships.

7. *Evaluating activity:* proposing group standards; measuring decisions against norms; measuring accomplishments against group goals; calling attention to blocks to progress.

8. *Synthesizing activity:* summarizing, pulling together related ideas for group consideration; testing for consensus on decisions, making compromise suggestions.

Group-Oriented Roles

In discussion, as in every other human endeavor, there are crests of success and progress and troughs of failure and retrogression. To get over the troughs, a group, like an individual, sometimes needs to have its morale boosted. Internal and external pressures sometimes integrate or disintegrate groups, and it is often necessary to strengthen or counter these pressures. Because the personalities of the members of a discussion group differ, it will also be necessary at times to resolve personality conflicts. At times, a group needs to bring these conflicts out in the open, to express its feelings or the feelings of individuals, so that all may experience a sense of catharsis. And, at some time, every group will need assistance in determining the next steps toward its goal. Any contribution that relates to any of these needs or that helps build group unity,

cohesion, morale, and dedication to achievement of goals would be considered as a group-oriented role. Here are some of these roles.

1. *Encouraging activity:* praising others and their contributions, building the status of others; calling attention to progress made; showing friendliness to others; comparing the group's progress to that of other similar groups.

2. *Compromising and mediating activity:* suggesting compromises between conflicting viewpoints; directing the emphasis toward issues and away from personalities; harmonizing, focusing attention on areas of agreement and away from areas of disagreement; modifying one's own stand in line with that of others.

3. *Improving communication patterns:* encouraging reticent members to participate; making it possible for others to contribute; clarifying, repeating, or restating; suggesting time limits on contributions; counteracting the development of hidden communication networks.

4. *Tension-reducing activity:* joking to draw attention away from conflicts; suggesting the need for expressing feelings as a catharsis and as essential for progress; showing a willingness to accept criticism without rancor.

5.   *Follower activity:* serving as an audience to individuals or the group, accepting group decisions; encouraging others to accept group decisions; concurring in and accepting passively the ideas of others.

6.   *Cathartic activity:* giving expression to the group's feelings; summarizing group feelings; serving as devil's advocate; supporting the cathartic activity of others; giving emotional expression to the group's attitudes toward its task, other groups, and itself.

7.   *Reality-testing activity:* suggesting standards for choosing content and procedures or in evaluating decisions; making tentative tests of possible group consensus; suggesting the practical implications of the group's decisions; calling attention to decisions and actions that violate group standards.

Self-Oriented Roles

One of the reasons people join groups is the personal satisfaction they derive from participating in the group's activities. And, because people are human beings, they act the way human beings do—praising, blaming, building personal status and deflating the status of others, defending, being friendly or cold, and doing other things that develop a feeling of personal adequacy and security. These self-oriented roles are not always negative, nor do they always block progress in a discussion. Indeed, even negative roles may serve to call the group's attention to the need for individual and group self-evaluation or for a critical examination of the group's progress. Frequently, the competition engendered by self-oriented roles may result in greater productivity, more creative ideas, or forced scrutiny of accepted ideas. Any contribution—whether for the benefit or harm of the group—that relates to any of these kinds of behaviors would be considered the performance of a self-oriented role. Here are some of these roles.

1.   *Aggressive activity:* acting in ways that lower the status of others, building personal status by criticizing or attacking others, showing ill will toward others.

2.   *Obstructing activity:* blocking progress by irrelevant digressions or personal anecdotes, sticking to a point for too long, being too greatly concerned with details, rejecting ideas without adequate consideration, questioning agreed-upon decisions on content or procedure.

3.   *Recognition-seeking activity:* claiming credit for ideas presented by others or by oneself through excessive and immoderate behavior; demanding to be heard on all points being considered.

4.   *Withdrawal activity:* remaining silent; engaging in side conversations; constantly asking what point is being discussed; presenting tangential ideas; acting bored; doodling.

5.   *Competitive activity:* trying to produce the best or most ideas; arguing and pointing out the logic of one's arguments; seeking the favor of the leaders; insisting on "equal time on the air" with all others.

6.   *Playboy activity:* joking, clowning; distracting the attention of the group; disrupting the work of the group.

7.   *Special-interest solicitation:* introducing and supporting personal projects and ideas; supporting the vested interests of others; pressuring others to accept these pet projects.

SUGGESTIONS FOR GROUP MEMBERS

It is obvious that no discussion takes place without some self-oriented activity. But we must stress that although some of this activity can serve a useful purpose (for catharsis, or for calling attention to the need for examination of progress), it should not be permitted to get out of hand. Because people join groups to accomplish some task, maintaining the group's identity and accomplishing its goal must take precedence over satisfying individual ego needs. At the same time, these needs cannot be disregarded. We recommend emphasizing each of the three types of roles in degrees consistent with getting the group's job done.

The analysis sheets at the end of the chapter will help the discussion planner recognize the skills discussants may have in each of these three role areas.

As we have stressed before, effective participation in discussion involves more than just talking. To implement reflective-thinking processes and demonstrate interpersonal flexibility in discussion, you must do certain things in specific ways at appropriate times. That is, there are times for assertions and times for questions, for facts and for personal experiences or opinions, for probing, criticizing, disagreeing, supporting, or explaining. Your participation in discussion will improve if you follow these suggestions:

1. *Listen critically and thoughtfully to others:* Seek the other person's viewpoint by the judicious use of questioning; probe for new information and opinion. But don't accept unsupported generalizations. Remember: Use your critical faculties when listening.

2. *Be sure you know the group's goal before, or soon after, the discussion begins:* Ask for definitions of terms, basic issues of the problem, and important background material. Remember: If you do not know where you are going, you may never get there.

3. *Speak your mind freely:* Discussion is based on exchanging ideas. No one else has your specific background of knowledge and experience. You help by sharing your ideas. Remember: You have a responsibility besides that of listening.

4. *Strike while the iron is hot:* Don't wait to speak until you are called on. You may forget your point or miss the best time to present it. Besides, the moderator may not know your name. Remember: If you wait too long, the point may be lost.

5. *Let the other person talk too:* Don't speak for more than a minute or two at a time. Make your point in as few words as possible. Remember: It makes little difference who carries the ball as long as it's carried.

6. *Develop your awareness and perception of nonverbal communication:* Study how you and others communicate nonverbally. Observe changes in seating arrangements, differences in distances among the members, varying intonation patterns, styles of dress, and gestures. Remember: These nonverbal forms of behavior reflect, though sometimes erroneously, attitudes and behavior.

7. *Don't let the discussion get away from you:* If you do not understand, say so tactfully. Ask questions until you do understand. Other members of the group may also feel that a point is unclear and be grateful for your initiative. Remember: You cannot make wise decisions later if they are based on misunderstanding.

8. *Don't fight over the ownership of ideas:* Once you have given an idea to the group, let it become the group's property. Don't feel that you must defend it just because it was yours. Remember: The aim of discussion is to explore ideas, not to win your point.

"Don't fight over the ownership of ideas."

9. *Indulge in friendly disagreement:* When you disagree with a point that is made, say so, and tell why. But do it in a friendly way. It is not necessary to "clobber" the individual and his ideas. Remember: Raw emotion always hinders sound thinking.

10. *Stay on the beam:* Since digressions usually hinder progress, keep your remarks relevant. Show how your points are related to the discussion. Don't repeat what has already been covered. Remember: You should not ride personal hobby horses in discussion.

11. *Try to maintain an open mind:* Discussion is not debate. You do not have to commit yourself irrevocably to a case or idea. Seek facts and the factual basis for opinions. Try to be unprejudiced and objective. Remember: The other side also uses facts and logic.

12. *Come to the discussion prepared to participate:* Before the discussion, think through the issues involved in a topic. Consider what facts may be needed. Study the topic. Make a list of questions you would like to have answered. Remember: Advance preparation is a necessary condition for successful discussion.

13. *Try to make the discussion a pleasant experience for all:* Don't take yourself too seriously in discussion. Try to get some fun out of it and make it pleasant for others too. A laugh or pointed joke can dispel glumness, hostility, and boredom. Remember: A smile may do more to further the discussion than your best argument.

14. *Help others to participate:* There may be some in the group who would like to participate but are too timid. Help the leader draw them out. Their knowledge and opinions are important. Call them by name, refer questions to them, or point out the need for hearing from everyone. Remember: The resources in a discussion group cannot be used unless they are tapped.

15. *Chart the progress of the discussion:* Ask for occasional summaries or give them yourself. Call attention to the group's goals and the progress made toward those goals. Point out the ground yet to be covered. Remember: The capable mariner frequently checks to see where he is.

16. *Avoid interrupting the progress of the discussion:* Try to do only those things that expedite—not block—the discussion. Avoid loud and lengthy side conversations with your neighbors, withdrawing from the discussion, excessive action, dogmatic statements, or annoying physical activities. Remember: You should be a booster, not a blocker.

17. *Keep the communication channels open:* Be sure you listen to what is being said. Don't direct your remarks only to the chairman or a few members; include the entire group. Try to make your language clear and temperate. Check to see that you have been understood. Ask others to clarify unclear points. Remember: In discussions you should beam the message so that your meaning is interpreted as you meant it to be.

A SUMMARY AND LOOK AHEAD

Skill in reflective-thinking processes and flexibility in interpersonal relations are basic to effective participation patterns in discussion groups. Individuals may participate in ways that are goal-centered, group-centered, or ego-centered. The way each of these functional roles is performed helps to determine the success of discussion. Following basic but simple rules of procedure also contributes to more effective discussion. Participation improves when the discussants continuously examine their own performance.

The suggestions in this chapter for improving one's participation apply to leaders as well as to members. In the same way, the suggestions in the next chapter for improving leadership apply to members, as well as to leaders.

SUGGESTED READINGS

Barnlund, Dean C., and Franklyn S. **Haiman,** *The Dynamics of Discussion* (Boston: Houghton Mifflin, 1960), Chs. 9–12.

Bormann, Ernest G., *Discussion and Group Methods,* 2nd ed. (New York: Harper & Row, 1975), Chs. 7–10, 12.

Bosmajian, Haig, *The Rhetoric of Nonverbal Communication: Readings* (Glenview, Ill.: Scott, Foresman, 1971).

Bradford, Leland P., ed., *Group Development* (Washington, D.C.: National Training Laboratories, 1961).

Brilhart, John K., *Effective Group Discussion* (Dubuque, Iowa: Wm. C. Brown, 1967), Chs. 4, 6–7.

Burgoon, Michael, Judee K. **Heston,** and James **McCroskey,** *Small Group Communication: A Functional Approach* (New York: Holt, Rinehart and Winston, 1974), Ch. 11.

Cathcart, Robert S., and Larry A. **Samovar,** *Small Group Communication: A Reader,* 2nd ed. (Dubuque, Iowa: Wm. C. Brown, 1974), Chs. 6–7.

Cortright, Rupert L., and George L. **Hinds,** *Creative Discussion* (New York: Macmillan, 1959), Chs. 5–8.

Crowell, Laura, *Discussion: Method of Democracy* (Chicago: Scott, Foresman, 1963), Chs. 8–10.

Egan, Gerard, *Face to Face* (Monterey, Calif: Brooks/Cole, 1973), Ch. 7.

Ellis, William D., and Frank **Siedel,** *How to Win the Conference* (Englewood Cliffs, N.J.: Prentice-Hall, 1955).

Gordon, Thomas, *Group-Centered Leadership* (Boston: Houghton Mifflin, 1955), Chs. 3–4, 7–8.

Gouran, Dennis S., *The Process of Group Decision-Making* (New York: Harper & Row, 1974), Ch. 9.

Haiman, Franklyn S., "The Specialization of Roles and Functions in a Group," *Quarterly Journal of Speech,* Vol. 43 (April 1957), pp. 165–173.

Harnack, R. Victor, and Thorrel B. **Fest,** *Group Discussion: Theory and Technique* (New York: Appleton-Century-Crofts, 1964), Chs. 11, 13–14.

Keltner, John W., *Group Discussion Process* (New York: David McKay, 1957), Ch. 21.

Knapp, Mark L., *Nonverbal Communication in Human Interaction* (New York: Holt, Rinehart and Winston, 1970).

Larson, Carl E., "Speech Communication Research of Small Groups," *The Speech Teacher,* Vol. 20 (March 1971), pp. 89–107.

Mehrabian, Albert, *Silent Messages* (Belmont, Calif.: Wadsworth, 1971).

Mortensen, C. David, *Communication: The Study of Human Interaction* (New York: McGraw-Hill, 1972), Part III.

Paulson, Stanley F., "Pressures toward Conformity in Group Discussion," *Quarterly Journal of Speech,* Vol. 4 (February 1958), pp. 50–55.

Sattler, William M., and N. Edd **Miller,** *Discussion and Conference,* 2nd ed. (Englewood Cliffs, N.J.: Prentice-Hall, 1968), Chs. 15–19.

Schuyler, Dean Hoslett, "Barriers to Communication," *Personnel,* Vol. 28 (September 1951), pp. 108–114.

Thayer, Lee O., *Administrative Communication* (Homewood, Ill.: Irwin, 1961), Ch. 6.

Weaver, Carl H., *Human Listening* (Indianapolis: Bobbs-Merrill, 1972).

Zelko, Harold P., *The Business Conference: Leadership and Participation* (New York: McGraw-Hill, 1969), Ch. 7.

EXERCISES

1. There are many reasons why individual participation in discussion is not always as effective as we expect. Under five headings below, we have listed a few of the reasons why it is ineffective or limited to only a few members of the group. Under each heading, add two more reasons. Base your reasons on your own experience, as well as on the content of previous chapters.

a. *Factors related to leadership:*

1. Issues poorly defined or unspecific.

2. Opening statement not challenging.

3. Leaders stifle discussion.

4.

5.

b. *Factors related to the members:*

1. Members do not see general purpose of discussion.

2. Too much egotism displayed by a few.

3. Members do not feel their contributions are worthwhile.

4.

5.

c. *Factors related to planning:*

1. Discussion agenda not prepared.

2. Poor topic selected.

3. Topic too broad for adequate coverage in the time available.

4.

5.

d. *Factors related to the physical situation:*

1. Too many distractions.

2. Atmosphere and seating too formal.

3. Needed equipment not available.

4.

5.

e. *Factors related to procedure:*

1. Rules not mentioned in advance.

2. Members unsure of responsibilities.

3. Leader pushes discussion too fast.

4.

5.

2. A list of seventeen "Suggestions for Group Members" is given in this chapter. Restudy these suggestions and rate yourself on each. A rating of "5" is outstanding; "1" is poor. If you rate 45 or lower you should try to improve your participation effectiveness through practice. Show your "participation profile" to your instructor and talk about ways you can improve your skills.

3. Make a list of the different kinds of "content" a person can contribute to discussion. Here are a few examples:

Statement of facts

Expression of opinions

Quotations from authorities

Analogies

4. Make arrangements to sit in on a discussion of some campus committee or board. Use Analysis Form 4 to check the types of contributions made by the various participants. It is not necessary to make a continuous record; for example, you can record the contributions for four-minute periods at intervals of ten minutes. Four such periods during an hour's discussion will give you a reasonably accurate picture of the total discussion pattern. After you have recorded your data, answer the following questions.

a. Do you begin to see role patterns developing in the way the participants contribute? Comment on this.

b. Was the chairperson's contribution pattern different from that of the other group members? Explain.

c. Were there types of contributions not made by any members of the group? Which types? How do you account for this?

d. Do you feel that some modification of the types of contributions would have made the discussion more effective? Explain.

5. At the end of this chapter are five different analysis forms. Plan to use each form for self-analysis or in analyzing at least one discussion that you observe or participate in during the semester. Submit reports to your instructor on the data you have obtained through using the forms. In addition, comment on how the forms might be improved to reveal meaningful data about participation.

6. Work in groups of five or six in completing this exercise. Assume that you are members of a minority group on campus and have decided that you want to achieve greater recognition and involvement in administrative decisions dealing with student–faculty relations. In your small group try to develop a three-step program to achieve the desired recognition and involvement. Select one member of the group to act as a procedural observer. Assume that you will have forty minutes for your discussion. Then give the observer several minutes at the mid-point and again at the close of the discussion to comment on your procedural effectiveness. The observer may wish to read Chapter 11 before starting this exercise.

7. Complete this exercise individually and submit a two- or three-page analysis to your instructor. Pick four organizations or groups on- or off-campus with whose goals you are familiar. Make a list of the needs, desires, or other motivating forces that have caused the groups to adopt their goals. Add a paragraph in your analysis in which you comment on any common factors in goal causation.

WHAT ROLES DO
I TAKE IN A GROUP?

Following three separate discussions, rate your own role performance as objectively as you can. For each type of role in the first column, place a check mark under one or more of the vertical categories. Use the columns marked "1" for the first discussion, "2" for the second, "3" for the third. Confer with your instructor on ways to improve your role contributions.

	My Role Contributions														
	Roles I filled today			Roles I should like to fill			Roles I filled least well			Roles I should like to practice			Roles I should avoid		
Goal-oriented Roles	1	2	3	1	2	3	1	2	3	1	2	3	1	2	3
1. Goal setting															
2. Process related															
3. Seeking information and opinion															
4. Giving information and opinion															
5. Reasoning															
6. Elaborating															
7. Evaluating															
8. Synthesizing															
Group-oriented Roles															
1. Encouraging															
2. Mediating															
3. Improving communication															
4. Tension reduction															
5. Following															
6. Cathartic															
7. Reality testing															

	My Role Contributions														
	Roles I filled today			Roles I should like to fill			Roles I filled least well			Roles I should like to practice			Roles I should avoid		
Self-oriented Roles	1	2	3	1	2	3	1	2	3	1	2	3	1	2	3
1. Aggressive															
2. Obstructing															
3. Recognition seeking															
4. Withdrawal															
5. Competitive															
6. Playboy															
7. Special interest pleading															

THE ROLES WE PLAY
AS OTHERS SEE THEM*

Here is a list of roles that may be performed by members of a discussion group. After the number corresponding to each role, write the name(s) of the one, or at the most two, persons — you may include yourself — who performed this role most consistently and/or noticeably in the group today. The same may be written after several roles. If you did not observe anyone in the group taking some of the roles listed, leave the space blank. Use last names only, unless two persons have the same last name.

* This checksheet was adapted from material prepared by the National Training Laboratory in Group Development, Bethel, Maine, during the summer of 1952.

Roles

1. Goal-setter (defines or proposes goals)
2. Information-seeker
3. Opinion-seeker
4. Information-giver
5. Opinion-giver
6. Logical-reasoner
7. Elaborator (clarifies)
8. Evaluator (measures progress against goals and standards)
9. Synthesizer (summarizes, suggests compromises)
10. Recorder (keeps record of group actions)
11. Encourager (praises, builds status of others)
12. Mediator (harmonizes, focuses attention on issues)
13. Communication expediter
14. Tension-reliever
15. Follower (serves as audience for others)
16. Group-observer (focuses on process to help group progress)
17. Cathartic agent (gives expression to group's feelings)
18. Reality-tester (tests group's decisions against practical results)
19. Aggressor (builds own and minimizes others' status)

Group Members

1. _____
2. _____
3. _____
4. _____
5. _____
6. _____
7. _____
8. _____

9. _____

10. _____
11. _____
12. _____

13. _____
14. _____
15. _____
16. _____

17. _____

18. _____

19. _____

20. Obstructor (blocks progress)   20. _____

21. Recognition-seeker (seeks personal atten-   21. _____
    tion)

22. Withdrawer (avoids meaningful participa-   22. _____
    tion in group activities)

23. Competitor (tries to outdo others)   23. _____

24. Playboy (avoids all serious activity)   24. _____

CONTRIBUTION RECORDS*

By placing a mark (/) in the appropriate box, indicate the number of times each participant makes the type of contribution listed. Turn in these forms at the end of the discussion.

* Adapted from the Bales interaction categories. See Robert F. Bales, *Interaction Process Analysis* (Cambridge, Mass.: Addison-Wesley, 1950), p. 9.

	Names of Participants							
Type of Contribution Made	**Number of Contributions**							
Gives information								
Asks for information								
Gives an opinion								
Asks for opinions								
Defines, clarifies, or shows relationships								
Asks for definition, clarification, or relationships								
Argues or refutes (supported)								
Argues or refutes (unsupported)								
Supports others, praises, defends								
Releases tension, jokes, shows satisfaction								
Shows tension, withdraws, blocks, attacks others								

PARTICIPATION FLOW CHART

The purpose of this diagram is to help you record the number and direction of contributions in discussion. Use it in today's discussion in the following manner:

Insert the names of the participants in the circles, using only as many circles as there are participants. Add circles for more participants as needed. The instrument becomes unwieldy when a record is kept for more than nine persons.

The directional arrows indicate the person to whom a given contribution is directed. Since the leader will usually address remarks to all group members, arrows are already drawn from the leader to each participant. Arrows ending near the center of the area indicate remarks made to the entire group. Add arrows as any one individual talks directly to another.

As the discussion flows, number the contributions consecutively 1, 2, 3, 4, etc., placing the number for a given remark close to the circle of the person making the remark and on the line indicating the person to whom the remark was made.

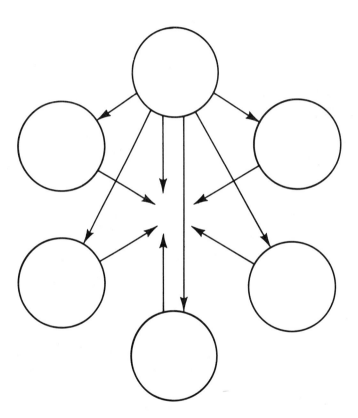

EFFECTIVENESS OF INDIVIDUAL PARTICIPANTS

Name of person evaluated _____

Date _____

1. How well prepared did the discussant appear to be? In what ways might he or she have been better prepared?

2. What analytical skills did the individual demonstrate during the course of the discussion?

3. How well did the person communicate with the other discussants? In what ways did she or he aid communication within the group?

4. What appeared to be the person's major contributions (giving and testing information and ideas, clarifying or seeking clarification, mediating disputes, relieving tension, and so on) to the functioning of the discussion?

5. In what ways did the individual aid in building a permissive atmosphere for discussion (accept ideas, complement, resolve tensions, contribute to group morale and progress, and so on)?

6. What skills, changes in attitude, and assumption of membership or leadership skills would have enhanced the person's value to the group? Give examples.

EFFECTIVENESS OF INDIVIDUAL PARTICIPANTS

Name of person evaluated _____

Date _____

1. How well prepared did the discussant appear to be? In what ways might he or she have been better prepared?

2. What analytical skills did the individual demonstrate during the course of the discussion?

3. How well did the person communicate with the other discussants? In what ways did she or he aid communication within the group?

4. What appeared to be the person's major contributions (giving and testing information and ideas, clarifying or seeking clarification, mediating disputes, relieving tension, and so on) to the functioning of the discussion?

5. In what ways did the individual aid in building a permissive atmosphere for discussion (accept ideas, complement, resolve tensions, contribute to group morale and progress, and so on)?

6. What skills, changes in attitude, and assumption of membership or leadership skills would have enhanced the person's value to the group? Give examples.

Since the early 1940s, many changes have occurred in the meaning of the concept "leadership," especially as it applies to a discussion situation. In contrast to the pre-1940 period, it is now believed that people can be trained in leadership skills, that they do not have to be born with generic traits that make them leaders in any given situation. It is now believed that effective leadership in discussion should be shared by many rather than exercised by a single person.[1] It is believed that leadership in a group should build security and self-reliance—independence of the leader—rather than uncertainty and dependence. It is thought that leadership should be goal- and group-centered rather than leader-centered. That is, leadership tasks should be carried out on the basis of what the group needs for doing its job rather than in terms of what the leader thinks should be done. Finally, there is a much less clear-cut distinction today between "leader" and "follower." Research and empirical evidence support the belief that the currently held concept of shared leadership is psychologically sound and pragmatically useful. This concept of leadership is our concern in this chapter.

[1] The authors recognize that in newly formed groups, either in or outside the classroom, the functions of leadership may need to be carried out at first by a designated leader or chairperson. As the group develops, the members should take on more and more responsibilities until leadership does in fact become shared.

CONDITIONS FOR EFFECTIVE LEADERSHIP

In this chapter and throughout the book, we use the terms "leadership," "leaders," and "leader-team" more than the term "leader." We prefer to think of leadership in discussion as the responsibility of many rather than of one. In most instances, we view all the things a group member may do to help achieve the group's goal as contributing to the leadership of that group. We call this concept *functional leadership.*

We feel that all the things that were once considered only the discussion leader's responsibility—introducing a topic, guiding, controlling, probing, clarifying, resolving differences, recording, summarizing—can partly be carried out by members of the group. Thus, there may be many persons who perform leadership tasks in discussion. Besides the moderator or chairperson, there may be a clarifier, recorder, process observer, summarizer, audio-visual aide, and resource person. In effect, we have a leader-team rather than a leader. We call this situation *team leadership.*

When we talk about leadership in discussion, we're talking about who performs the tasks necessary to reach some goal. To say that different persons may perform these tasks does not imply that there cannot be a *designated* leader. In most discussions there must be and is. (The one exception would be when there is no appointed leader, and a member of the group emerges to take over the leader's job.) The point is simply that the appointed leader will do a better overall job and the leadership function will be performed more effectively if he lets others do some of these tasks for him.

Leadership skills needed in discussion will vary somewhat from one situation to another. Hence, we also view leadership as *situational*, as something that must be adapted to the demands of a particular topic, group, purpose, or discussion form.

Because we believe that the best leadership is functional, situational, and team-oriented, we expect that new avenues for developing leadership will emerge from within the group and that there is a strong likelihood that leaders will also emerge. When leadership is considered functional, and when major responsibilities rotate among the group members, the designated leader does not have to be skilled in every facet of procedure and content. On the other hand, functional leadership gives all group members the opportunity to practice various leadership tasks, in addition to those in which they are already proficient.

Leadership in discussion should therefore be functional, the responsibility of many, and situational. It should be goal-centered. It should reflect democratic control of the group by its members. What, then, are the conditions necessary if this type of leadership is to be carried out in a group? We believe the following are the most important.

If a discussion is to be effective the *leadership pattern* must be:

Acceptive *rather than* rejective.

Nonevaluative *rather than* evaluative.

Friendly *rather than* unfriendly.

Flexible *rather than* rigid.

Permissive *rather than* restrictive or autocratic.

Supportive to members *rather than* a threat to the members.

The joint responsibility of many *rather than* the sole responsibility of one.

Seen as a service to the group *rather than* dedicated to the self-glorification of one.

Sensitive to the ego needs of the members *rather than* insensitive to the needs of each individual.

Aware of both process and goals *rather than* concerned primarily with goals and oblivious of process.

Directed toward achieving the will of the group *rather than* directed toward achieving the goal of the leader.

Perceived as skills in which all members can be trained *rather than* perceived as traits acquired only through birth.

Willing to let the group make decisions affecting its progress *rather than* insisting that the leader make most decisions about the group's progress.

Willing to let the members replace the leaders *rather than* afraid to let the members replace the leaders.

Insistent that the group's successes be viewed as a group triumph *rather than* perceiving successes as personal triumphs for the leader.

Later in this chapter we consider some of the specific ways in which a leader-team can implement these conditions.

TYPES OF LEADERSHIP CLIMATES

Under Kurt Lewin's direction, Lippitt and White carried out two investigations[2] that have become classic studies on democratic, autocratic, and unorganized (laissez-faire) social situations. The aim of both experiments was to determine the effects of the three types of group atmosphere.

[2] See R. Lippitt, "An Experimental Study of the Effect of Democratic and Authoritarian Group Atmospheres," *University of Iowa Studies in Child Welfare*, Vol. 16, No. 3 (Iowa City: University of Iowa Press, 1940), pp. 43–195; Ralph K. White and Ronald O. Lippitt, *Autocracy and Democracy* (New York: Harper & Row, 1960); and Ronald Lippitt and Ralph K. White, "An Experimental Study of Leadership and Group Life," in G. E. Swanson, T. M. Newcomb, and E. L. Hartley, eds., *Readings in Social Psychology*, rev. ed. (New York: Holt, Rinehart and Winston, 1952), pp. 340–355.

In the first experiment, two groups of five eleven-year-olds met to carry out certain activities. The groups were led by the same person, who played a democratic role with one group and an autocratic role with the other. Each group met eleven times. Observers took continuous notes on the behavior of the leader and children. A second experiment, more extensive and better controlled, was conducted later. This time each of four groups had three series of meetings under three different leaders. One group experienced a democratic form of leadership twice (under two different leaders) and autocracy only once; a second group experienced autocracy twice (under two different leaders) and democracy only once. The other two groups experienced autocracy, democracy, and laissez-faire once each. A detailed record was kept.

In understanding the results of the studies, it will help to know the nature of the three types of leadership behavior. White and Lippitt describe them briefly as follows:

"Autocracy" here implies a high degree of control by the leader without much freedom by the members or participation by them in group decisions, while both "democracy" and "laissez-faire" imply a low degree of control by the leader. "Democracy" is distinguished from "laissez-faire," however, by the fact that in it the leader is very active in stimulating group discussion and group decisions, while in laissez-faire he plays a passive, hands-off role.[3]

The following descriptive lists include most of the significant interpretations of the results of the studies as reported by White and Lippitt.

The Autocratic Climate

The following statements reflect the attitudes and behavior in groups with autocratic leaders:

1. Little discontent develops when the leaders hold high standards.

2. Much discontent develops when the leaders seem to enjoy dominance for its own sake.

3. The productive level stays high when the group is satisfied with its efforts.

[3] White and Lippitt, *Autocracy and Democracy*, p. 12. We have used this source primarily for describing the effects of the three types of leadership.

4. Negative reaction develops when the group is under constant pressure to produce.

5. The leader's positive methods make high productivity possible.

6. Greater productivity provides personal satisfactions.

7. Work effort tends to slacken when the leader is absent.

8. Clearness of roles results in greater member satisfaction.

9. The members satisfy their need for order.

10. The members satisfy their need for dependency.

11. Aggressive status-seeking activities develop among members who have a strong need for status.

12. Members may conceal their explosive tendencies.

13. High demands for status develop, since the members cannot obtain status satisfaction from the leader.

14. Hero worship of the leader frequently immobilizes the group.

15. The members accept the condition of autocracy if they see it as the only alternative.

16. Resignation to the inevitable may reduce tensions within the group.

The Democratic Climate

Democratic leadership results in these feelings, attitudes, and actions:

1. Members gain satisfaction in making their own decisions.

2. Individual self-confidence results from the success of the group's achievement.

3. The members grow in self-acceptance and self-confidence.

4. The members become more willing to listen to the ideas of others and to promote listening.

5. The members become more willing to accept the ideas of others.

6. A greater emphasis on *we* develops.

7. Respect for the personalities of other members develops.

8. Status-mindedness decreases.

9. Leaders and members function more as peers.

10. Good work becomes the criterion for gaining status within the group.

11. Status-mindedness disappears amid the genuine friendliness of the members.

12. Members begin to insist on equality of rights and opportunities for all.

13. The group develops a greater sense of reality-orientation—testing reality and adjusting to it.

14. Apathy and remoteness from the group exist for some members.

15. Group pressures frequently result in overconformity.

The Laissez-Faire Climate

Apparently this is the least effective of the three leadership styles, in terms of how it affects member satisfactions and group productivity. The following conditions manifest themselves:

1. Members have little sense of accomplishment.

2. There is a lack of clear goals.

3. There is a lack of clarity on how to achieve goals.

4. The members do not understand what is expected of them.

5. Little friendship for the leader develops.

6. The group does not develop a sense of unity.

7. The members tend toward idleness when direction from the leader is absent.

8. The members do not develop self-confidence.

9. Status-mindedness develops.

10. Competitive hostility develops among the members.

11. The members develop self-assertiveness, without regard to the effect on others.

Developing an effective personal leadership pattern results only from study and much practice. The particular pattern you develop will be related to your own personality and flexibility in interpersonal relations, your personal skills in communication and critical thinking, and your own concept of what constitutes a desirable environment in which to operate. You should not overlook the results of these studies of social climate in developing your own leadership skills.

LEADERSHIP TASKS IN DISCUSSION

Thus far in this chapter, we have given a frame of reference within which leadership can operate most effectively. We now consider some of the specific tasks that are essential to effective, functional team leadership in discussion.

If a discussion group is to be productive —that is, accomplish its goal efficiently before, during, and after the discussion— its members must perform a large number of detailed tasks. In some situations, a designated leader will perform most of these tasks; in others, the entire membership will share equally in their performance. In either event, it is important that everyone in the group understand what the tasks are. The following statement could well serve as a checklist of these discussion-leadership tasks.

1. Make an effective beginning: We commented briefly in the first chapter on the need for preparing for discussion. Discussants will participate more freely and meaningfully if they feel a meeting has been carefully planned in advance and is getting off to a good start. Therefore, don't leave anything to chance.

Advance preparation is necessary:

1. Make careful selection and/or analysis of the group members. Try to discover the participants' viewpoints, their knowledge of the subject, and the probable extent of their participation, and try to foresee possible personality clashes.

2. Be sure that all persons who need to study the topic have done so. Make needed reference materials available or suggest where the participants can find them.

3. Arrange for pre-discussion planning meetings, if needed. Plan a topic outline, assign areas for study prior to the discussion, and agree on all procedural matters. Be sure that all the leaders, panel members or symposium speakers, and, if possible, the audience members, are acquainted with one another before the discussion begins.

4. Plan for observers, technicians, resource persons, or any other special help needed.

Take care of all pre-meeting arrangements:

1. Consider the physical setup—seating, ventilation, audio-visual needs, and lighting. Arrange for coffee breaks.

2. Consider your responsibility for publicity and promotion. There will be no discussion if people do not show up.

3. Be sure that discussion outlines, handouts, and the like are ready for distribution. Assign someone to this task.

4. Try to anticipate and avoid possible distraction. Be sure the public-address system works. Avoid (if possible) holding a meeting where outside noises will distract. Plan to control the lighting and heating.

Make the start of the discussion appropriate and effective:

1. Always be brief.

2. Adapt your opening remarks to the local situation.

3. Announce any rules of procedure.

4. Announce the topic, point out its timeliness and importance, and suggest possible approaches. Indicate the goal of the discussion.

5. Make your opening statement thought-provoking. Give some suggestions for how members can begin to think through the problem.

6. Try to develop an atmosphere in which participation is easy and in which the members feel secure, responsible for participation, and satisfied that the topic is not over their heads.

7. Help the group members to get acquainted.

8. Prime someone to lead off the discussion, if necessary.

2. Aim for maximum participation: Involvement and participation are essentials for any discussion. In addition to the techniques suggested in Chapters 3 and 4, the following are useful guides for leaders:

Try to increase the extent of participation:

1. Give everyone a chance to participate unless the size of the audience prevents it. In that case, seek the maximum participation possible.

2. Recognize the person who has not talked in preference to one who has.

3. Don't talk every time a group member does. Refer questions to the group unless you are the only one who can answer.

4. Don't worry too much about silence; you cannot rush the thinking process.

5. Avoid leader-member participation only. Encourage interaction among the group members.

6. Guard against too lengthy contributions by members.

Try to improve the quality of participation:

1. When stimulating discussion, try to avoid questions that can be answered by a simple "yes" or "no."

2. Test the information and evidence presented; test the reasoning.

3. Don't push the discussion too fast, yet try to keep it orderly.

4. Help the members to improve the quality of communication, but don't embarrass them in the process.

5. Try to keep the discussion from becoming just a series of questions and answers.

6. Have the group members clarify unclear points.

7. Know enough about the subject so that you are in a position to help others.

3. Encourage democratic progress: Progress is always an aim in discussion, but it should be democratic. Leaders and participants, rather than a leader or leaders, should make decisions on content and procedure jointly.

Keep the discussion orderly and logical:

1. Point out the significance of the topic early in the discussion.

2. Be sure the problem or goal is clearly defined.

3. Suggest and explore all possible solutions.

4. Insist on testing the facts, evidence, and reasoning.

5. Chart the progress of the discussion.

6. Call attention to fallacies in reasoning.

Keep the discussion on the track:

1. Permit occasional sidetracks only as a means of relieving tension. Let the group members decide what they wish to do about digressions.

2. Provide frequent summaries to show progress in the discussion. Be sure the summaries are accurate and reflect the thinking of the group.

3. Restate the main problem occasionally.

Keep the discussion moving toward the goal:

1. Be sure the goal is understood by all.

2. Make clear transitions from one point to another.

3. Don't permit items to be considered past the point of interest.

4. Use frequent summaries to indicate the progress made.

5. Point out areas of agreement and disagreement.

6. Don't belabor a point when needed information is missing.

7. Obtain early decisions on procedural matters and stick to them.

Keep the discussion inclusive:

1. Be sure all phases of a topic are considered. Point out neglected ones.

2. Don't take sides in the discussion. A person, or persons, in the minority loses security whenever the leader is on the other side.

3. Try to delay decisions that may be based on incomplete or inaccurate facts.

4. Try to get optimum expression from everyone.

4. Create a permissive atmosphere: The resource potential of any discussion group cannot be utilized unless the members feel that their contributions are wanted. The atmosphere of a discussion group should be conducive to free, cooperative, and critical interaction.

Protect the rights of the individuals in the group:

1. Protect the right of all individuals to express their own opinions.

2. Keep conflicts focused on issues, not on personalities.

3. Don't force people to talk if they don't want to.

4. Even if you think an expressed opinion is wrong, let the group correct it. Don't set yourself up as the final arbiter.

5. Don't push the group too fast; individual security may be lost and progress slowed.

6. Try to be accepting or nonevaluative in reacting to comments by the group members.

Maintain informality as the keynote of discussion:

1. If the group is not too large, be sure that the discussants are acquainted with each other.

2. Be patient, considerate, and friendly.

3. Keep the discussion from becoming too "serious."

4. Keep the use of status symbols to a minimum.

5. Avoid keeping the group under constant pressures for decision and action.

6. Do all you can to create a comfortable and informal physical atmosphere.

5. Maintain necessary control: Control of discussion does not mean that the moderator or leader alone determines what is said or decided, but rather that the members of the group follow their own rules. Control means that the leader acts so as to enable the group to achieve its goal quickly and efficiently.

Utilize the element of psychological control:

1. Try to maintain the position of a referee. Do not dominate action; direct attention. You will "control" the group more easily if they perceive you as a neutral referee.

2. Do not exercise control over the decisions of the group, but call their attention to the ramifications of those decisions.

3. Abide by predetermined rules of procedure so that decisions will be democratically made by all.

4. Do not avoid conflict, but keep it focused on issues. Point out the value of conflict in suggesting possible alternative viewpoints.

5. Try to keep the discussants from idea-possessiveness, from feeling that they must defend the points they make.

6. Take positive and decisive action when action is in the interest of the group. This will develop confidence in you as a leader.

7. Emphasize *we*, not *I*.

8. Employ observers for evaluation and control.

9. Maintain the physical appearance of being interested in what is taking place.

Utilize the element of physical control:

1. Do not permit conversational asides by a few to disturb the progress of the discussion.

2. Avoid letting a few talk at length.

3. Be sure that everyone hears all comments. Do not hesitate to ask group members to speak up. Control is easily lost when members do not hear.

4. The comfort of the group members is important. Watch lighting, room temperature, and seating arrangements.

5. Announce rules of procedure before a discussion starts; later it will be easier to enforce these rules.

6. Be sure to make all audio-visual arrangements in advance. Few audiences like to wait—nor should they be asked to do so—while someone repairs or locates a projection machine.

7. Use the blackboard as much as possible. When members of the audience see an outline of the discussion, or a record of the decisions they have made, they are less apt to lose interest in the discussion.

6. Close the discussion effectively: Too frequently, the close of a discussion leaves much to be desired. The conclusion of a discussion is no less important than the conclusion of a speech. Plan it carefully, do not hurry it, provide a meaningful summary, indicate the next steps to be taken if any, and give proper credits.

Make the ending definite from the point of view of content:

1. The final summary should indicate progress made, differences resolved and unresolved, and possible avenues of future action, and should review recommendations and decisions made.

2. Indicate how reports of the discussion are to be distributed or made available to the discussants.

"Maintain the physical appearance of being interested . . ."

3.   Secure a consensus of future plans, dates for meetings, and other follow-ups.

4.   Suggest reference materials for future meetings.

Make the ending definite from the viewpoint of procedure:

1.   Faithfully observe the time limits. End the discussion before everyone is talked out, and leave enough time for a final summary.

2.   Involve group members in making the final summary, if possible.

3.   Be sure to make assignments for follow-up.

4.   Give proper credit to the leaders and participants.

5.   Provide for a method of post-meeting evaluation. Allow time for a quick analysis and report of the evaluation.

We do not intend the above list of leadership tasks to be complete. The suggestions do, however, provide a guide for each leader to use in patterning her or his own leadership style. The suggestions made are calculated to contribute to the functional team leadership we advocated earlier in this chapter. We believe that democratic, diffused, yet dynamic leadership contributes most to the success of discussion, even as it contributes most to the development of the discussants' skills.

LEADERSHIP AND PRODUCTIVITY

From the earlier section in this chapter on "Types of Leadership Climates," it could be inferred that the output of any group—whatever its nature—is closely related to the existing leadership styles. What gets done in a group depends on the way the leader behaves. Thus, leadership may be appropriately defined as *the influence or behavior that moves a group toward its goals.* It should be noted that these goals may be agreed on prior to discussion or may emerge. They may be clearly or not so clearly understood, immediate or delayed. They may be limited to the members of the discussion group or may have broader social ramifications. Or, they may have other variable characteristics.

It becomes apparent that leadership is a function not only of the personality, skills, and knowledge of the group members who demonstrate goal-oriented behaviors during the discussion, but is also inextricably related to the variables that constitute group process. Some of these variables include the internal dynamics of the group, its structure and organization, the external situation, the roles and inputs of the members, the communication networks, and the interactions among these variables. One writer states this succinctly: "Leadership is a dynamic relationship between personality and group situation variables."[4] In other words, when we are concerned with the relationship between leadership and a group's productivity—its output— leadership must be studied in terms of the group's organization, inputs, and processes. Thus, in addition to performing certain leadership tasks outlined earlier in this chapter, the leadership of groups must create conditions that are conducive to the most productive interaction of group-process variables. By drawing upon research findings and theoretical conceptualizations, we get an indication of what these conditions should be.

Many of these conditions or guidelines for maximum productivity seem to be common sense, yet they are frequently unknown or ignored. These necessary conditions for productivity will not occur by chance. The leader (or leaders) of the group must consciously strive to achieve a positive pattern of interaction among the factors of group structure, input, and process so that productivity is high.

[4] Cecil A. Gibb, "The Principles and Traits of Leadership," in C. G. Browne and Thomas S. Cohn, *The Study of Leadership* (Danville, Ill.: Interstate, 1958), p. 67.

The set of "necessary conditions for productivity" described below, although perhaps a little simplified, is generally accepted. When leadership seeks to implant these conditions, we can expect the output of a discussion group to improve. While most of the conditions stated are drawn from the study of small groups, most have considerable applicability in large groups as well.

1. *Size:*

   Size should be limited to the minimum number required to provide for both the task and social-emotional needs of the group.

   Leadership is more effective in small (five) than in large (twelve) groups.

2. *Member characteristics:*

   The membership of the group should include all the persons needed to perform the tasks essential for goal accomplishment.

   Status imbalances should be kept to a minimum.

   A group in which the members are low in status consensus will provide greater opportunities for all members to perform leadership functions.

3. *Communication:*

   Channels of communication must always be kept open.

   Frequent "soundings" of members should be taken to ensure maximum understanding.

4. *Interaction:*

   Productivity will be greatest in groups with a high interaction potential (in other words, the degree to which members feel free to discuss any aspect of a given topic).

   Cooperative interaction is superior to competitive interaction.

   Opportunity must be provided for the free expression of both task and social-emotional contributions. Threats and feelings of defense should be minimized.

5. *Goals and goal achievement:*

   The goals and criteria for goal achievement must be clear and must be set by the leader *with* the members.

   When goals are realistic, members have greater motivation to perform.

   Goal achievement tends to increase when systematic problem-solving methods are employed.

   Progress toward goals should be noted frequently.

Opportunity must be provided for the group members to make procedural decisions relating to their progress toward goals.

6. *Internal forces:*

   Individuals in groups tend to conform (a) to accepted group norms, (b) to the opinion of an expert, and (c) when the rewards are greater than the penalties.

   Groups will function most effectively when cohesion is high and when the rewards of membership satisfy the need-value systems of the members.

Although the responsibility for implementing the above conditions falls on all group members, it is the leader—whether appointed or emergent—who must take the initial steps and work on a peer level with the members in follow-through. Finally, a warning: Leadership effectiveness is always situational; implementing all of the conditions does not always ensure maximum productivity.

IMPLICATIONS FOR THE DISCUSSION GROUP MEMBER

1. The feeling has almost been discarded in recent years that discussion group leadership should be the responsibility of a single person. Leadership is now regarded as the function of a number of persons who perform tasks needed by the group to achieve its goal. In small groups, all members might be perceived as leaders at different times during a discussion.

2. The most effective discussion leadership is that which is functional, the responsibility of many, situational, primarily goal-centered, and democratically controlled by the members.

3. Persons who participate frequently in discussion should be aware of the characteristics of the three basic leadership climates: autocratic, democratic, and laissez-faire. Although the climate in a discussion group will be established largely by what the leader does, it is also greatly affected by leader-member relations.

4. The text outlines in some detail six important leadership tasks in discussion. It is desirable to achieve a balance of these tasks. To focus on just one—let us say, "creating a permissive atmosphere"—might keep the group from achieving its goal.

5. Productivity in discussion can be affected by these factors: size, member characteristics, communication, interaction, the nature of the group's goals, and the internal forces operating within the group. Continuous study of how these factors operate will pay off in increased discussion skills.

A SUMMARY AND LOOK AHEAD

Ideally, leadership in discussion should involve many persons, each performing tasks that contribute to group goals. We call this activity *functional team leadership.* Leadership in discussion should also be democratic; in other words, the guidance of the discussion should be under the control of the participants as well as the leader. The most important leadership functions deal with the start of the discussion, its guidance, its progress, the extent and nature of participation, the atmosphere within the group, and the closing. Research findings support the conclusion that effective leadership can help to create conditions that allow for maximum productivity. These conditions relate to the group's structure, inputs, and processes.

In Chapter 7, we see how members can use their skills in problem-solving situations.

SUGGESTED READINGS

Barnlund, Dean C., "Consistency of Emergent Leadership in Groups with Changing Tasks and Members," *Speech Monographs,* Vol. 29 (1962), pp. 45–52.

Barnlund, Dean C., and Franklyn S. **Haiman,** *The Dynamics of Discussion* (Boston: Houghton Mifflin, 1960), Chs. 13–14.

Bass, Bernard M., *Leadership, Psychology, and Organizational Behavior* (New York: Harper & Row, 1960), Chs. 5–8, 12–16.

Bonner, Hubert, *Group Dynamics: Principles and Applications* (New York: Ronald Press, 1959), Ch. 6.

Browne, C. G., and Thomas S. **Cohn,** *The Study of Leadership* (Danville, Ill.: Interstate, 1958), Chs. 1, 3, 5, 7.

Cathcart, Robert L., and Larry A. **Samovar,** *Small Group Communication: A Reader,* 2nd ed. (Dubuque, Iowa: Wm. C. Brown, 1974), Chs. 8–9.

Cattell, Raymond B., "New Concepts for Measuring Leadership in Terms of Group Syntality," *Human Relations,* Vol. 4, No. 2 (1951), pp. 115–184.

Crowell, Laura, *Discussion: Method of Democracy* (Chicago: Scott, Foresman, 1963), Ch. 11–12.

Davis, Keith, *Human Relations at Work,* 2nd ed. (New York: McGraw-Hill, 1962), Ch. 6.

Gibb, Cecil A., "Leadership," in Gardner Lindzey and Elliot Aronson, eds., *Handbook of Social Psychology,* 2nd ed., Vol. 4 (Reading, Mass.: Addison-Wesley, 1969), Ch. 31.

Guetzkow, Harold, and John **Gyr,** "An Analysis of Conflict in Decision-Making Groups," *Human Relations,* Vol. 7, No. 3 (1954), pp. 367–382.

Gulley, Halbert E., *Discussion, Conference, and Group Process,* 2nd ed. (New York: Holt, Rinehart and Winston, 1968), Chs. 10–11, 13.

Haiman, Franklyn S., *Group Leadership and Democratic Action* (Boston: Houghton Mifflin, 1951), Chs. 1–3, 5–6, 8.

Harnack, R. Victor, and Thorrel B. **Fest,** *Group Discussion: Theory and Technique* (New York: Appleton-Century-Crofts, 1964), Chs. 7–10, 12.

Hunt, James G., and Lars L. **Larson,** *Contingency Approaches to Leadership* (Carbondale: Southern Illinois University Press, 1974).

Jones, Manley Howe, *Executive Decision Making,* rev. ed. (Homewood, Ill.: Irwin, 1962), Ch. 7.

Larson, Carl E., "Speech Communication Research of Small Groups," *The Speech Teacher,* Vol. 20 (March 1971), pp. 89–107.

Lippitt, Gordon, ed., *Leadership in Action* (Washington, D.C.: National Training Laboratories, 1961).

Miles, Matthew B., *Learning to Work in Groups* (New York: Bureau of Publications, Teachers College, Columbia University, 1959), Ch. 2.

Petrullo, Luigi, and Bernard M. **Bass,** eds., *Leadership and Interpersonal Behavior* (New York: Holt, Rinehart and Winston, 1961).

Ross, Murray G., and Charles E. **Hendry,** *New Understandings of Leadership* (New York: Association Press, 1957).

Sattler, William M., and N. Edd **Miller,** *Discussion and Conference,* 2nd ed. (Englewood Cliffs, N.J.: Prentice-Hall, 1968), Chs. 11–14.

Scott, William G., *Human Relations in Management* (Homewood, Ill.: Irwin, 1962), Ch. 18.

Stogdill, Ralph M., *Handbook of Leadership: A Survey of Research and Theory* (New York: The Free Press, 1974).

EXERCISES

1. Assume that you are a member of a newly formed discussion group and are serving as leader for the first few discussions. How would you go about getting the group to accept the idea of functional team leadership? What would you do to persuade the group members to accept their responsibilities as members of a discussion leadership team?

Compare your proposed actions with those of one or two of your classmates. Be prepared to support your conclusions in a general class discussion.

2. In small groups of not over four persons, write out what each of these leadership concepts means:

Team leadership

Functional leadership

Democratic leadership

Autocratic leadership

Situational leadership

Emergent leadership

Leadershipless discussion

Leaderless discussion

Laissez-faire leadership

Task-centered leadership

Group-centered leadership

Process-oriented leadership

Next, set up a role-playing situation in which you demonstrate how two contrasting types of leadership function in an actual discussion. A careful reading of Chapter 7 will help you to prepare for this exercise.

3. *Principles of effective discussion leadership.* Effective discussion depends on many factors, and usually these are related to the extent that democratic principles are followed, that the total resource potential of the group is used, and that group members concern themselves with the discussion process itself and continuously evaluate their own progress.

Following are thirteen principles of effective discussion leadership. (Undoubtedly, you could add many more.) Select any five of the statements below and write a single paragraph on each, indicating the specific things you as a leader would do to put the principle into practice.

a. No gains toward discussion goals are made where security for anyone is lost.

b. The best gains are made when everyone has a part in the decision making, when there is no feeling that the group members have chosen up sides, and when the members agree to support the decisions they make.

c. In discussion, it is necessary to start where the participants are. Hence, although progress is as slow as necessary, it must also be as fast as possible.

d. Although sometimes there is a designated leader, leadership in discussion should pass around the group and utilize the resources of every member.

e. Leaders in discussion are made and not born; you can teach individuals to improve their leadership skills and understanding.

f. Group discussion is not a panacea for problems. It has limitations of time, subject matter, and personnel. However, effective leadership can minimize these limitations.

g. In every discussion, there is a place for lay opinion, expert opinion, factual information, and documentary evidence. One function of the leader is to ensure that a discussion includes all four aspects of content and that each remains in its proper place.

h. If each person will do a better than fifty-fifty job of seeing the other person's viewpoint, the leader can help resolve conflicts in attitudes and values creatively.

i. Productivity in discussion depends largely on following an orderly sequence from problem definition to final decision making.

j. One aspect of effective leadership is the way it maintains a balance between emphasizing tasks and methods.

k. Satisfying the ego needs of the group members is as important in discussion as accomplishing the group's task.

l. When group members agree on who the status figures are, it is difficult for persons perceived as not having status to assume leadership roles.

m. The best group leadership is that which, after a task is accomplished, causes the members to say, "We did it ourselves."

4. Following are four different analysis forms. Plan to use each form for self-analysis, or to analyze at least one discussion that you participate in or observe during the semester. In addition to the reports you submit to your instructor on the data secured through use of the forms, comment on how the forms might be improved to reveal meaningful data about leadership.

LEADERSHIP CHARACTERISTICS

Research in recent years has shown that effective leaders have the characteristics listed below. In the columns to the right check the appropriate box indicating if you have the characteristic mentioned, do not have it, or have it to a limited degree.

	Have It	In Some Degree	Do Not Have It
1. Have the ability to make needed adjustments.			
2. Frequently come to the support of others.			
3. Rarely clash with others.			
4. Am rarely perceived as a threat to the security of others.			
5. Help to increase the opportunities for others to participate.			
6. Have the ability to identify with others and act on their behalf.			
7. Internalize private worries and make public display of high "esprit de corps."			
8. Provide opportunities for the review and revision of decisions.			
9. View leadership as the responsibility of the group.			
10. Place some leadership responsibility on all.			
11. Provide an atmosphere for a dignified minority and a friendly majority.			
12. Provide opportunities for group members to gain leadership training.			
13. Try to keep all communication channels open.			
14. Utilize effective problem-solving skills.			

	Have It	In Some Degree	Do Not Have It
15. Am more concerned with getting things done than with putting things over.			
16. Point out evidences of progress.			
17. Avoid idea-possessiveness.			
18. Focus on the issue, not the fight.			
19. Help the group formulate its aims and make its own decisions.			
20. Make positive use of conflict and differences.			
21. Concentrate on the expression of the will and decisions of the group.			
22. Am objective; do not act until all facts are considered, but will act decisively when necessary.			

LEADER EFFECTIVENESS

Name of leader _____

Discussion topic _____

Date _____

Rate the designated discussion leader by circling the number that most closely represents your appraisal of his performance. The descriptions in the left-hand column are supposed to reflect the most desirable practices; those in the right-hand, the least desirable.

The leader's attitudes toward the subject, participants, and audience:

Cordial	5	4	3	2	1	Unfriendly
Open-minded	5	4	3	2	1	Inflexible
Concerned	5	4	3	2	1	Indifferent

The leader's effectiveness in performing leadership tasks:

Introduces problems fairly and clearly	5	4	3	2	1	Fails to stimulate discussion at outset
Keeps discussion on the track	5	4	3	2	1	Lets discussion wander
Speaks only when necessary	5	4	3	2	1	Monopolizes the discussion
Is informed on the topic	5	4	3	2	1	Is uninformed
Adapts to the group's desires	5	4	3	2	1	Sticks to preplanned outline at all costs
Uses humor to lighten the atmosphere	5	4	3	2	1	Lacks humor
Acts democratically	5	4	3	2	1	Dictates procedures
Handles interpersonal conflicts diplomatically	5	4	3	2	1	Ignores or overrides interpersonal conflicts
Summarizes frequently and accurately	5	4	3	2	1	Does not summarize or summarizes inaccurately

The leader's language:

Clear	5	4	3	2	1	Unclear
Fluent	5	4	3	2	1	Hesitant
Fits the occasion	5	4	3	2	1	Inappropriate
Temperate	5	4	3	2	1	Emotionally loaded

ANALYSIS FORM 9

THE RESULTS OF LEADERSHIP*

This form may be used to check on the results of leadership at any two time-points in the life of a discussion group. Use column A for the first checking and B for the second.

* Adapted from a checklist by Franklyn S. Haiman, ''The Leader's Role,'' in *How to Lead Discussions* (Chicago: Adult Education Association of the U.S.A., 1955), p. 13.

A | B

1. ____ Group starts itself at the beginning of each meeting.

2. ____ Members seem to know what goals they seek.

3. ____ Members seem able to decide quickly on their goals.

4. ____ Members do not seem to make hasty or ill-considered decisions.

5. ____ Members draw out and question one another to understand their contributions better.

6. ____ Members seem to be aware of the progress they are making.

7. ____ Members seem willing to challenge the facts and opinions of others.

8. ____ The group makes decisions without depending on me as the final judge.

9. ____ Members do not count on me alone to handle problem situations.

10. ____ Different members frequently lead the group's thinking, discussion, and procedures.

11. ____ Members often accept insights and information from other members.

12. ____ When conflicts arise, they seem focused on issues rather than on personalities.

13. ____ New ideas originate with an increasing number of group members.

14. ____ Members seem to recognize the need for sound facts and opinions on which to base their discussion.

15. ____ Members seem to listen to one another without interrupting.

16. ____ Members seem willing to give others a chance to participate.

17. ____ Members get off the track infrequently.

18.   ———   Members seem sensitive to feelings of others.

19.   ———   Members address their remarks to one another rather than to me.

20.   ———   Members sometimes disagree openly with me.

21.   ———   Members seem to rely infrequently on my decisions.

22.   ———   Members frequently express their real feelings.

23.   ———   Members assume responsibility for procedural policing.

24.   ———   Members do not seem to feel they must defend ideas that they personally suggest.

25.   ———   The group has a tendency to want to remain after the time limit has passed.

GROUP CLIMATE

Each of the statements below refers to a different aspect of a discussion group's climate. In one of the five spaces at the right of each statement, place a check mark to indicate how you rate that aspect of climate.

	Outstand-ing	Superior	Average	Poor	Unsatis-factory
Aspects of Group Climate					
1. Pleasantness: everyone seems to enjoy the discussion.					
2. Security: members feel safe in speaking; neither ideas nor people are ridiculed.					
3. Cohesion: members support one another, stick up for the group, resist outside disruptive forces.					
4. Purposefulness: goals are understood at start and kept in mind throughout.					
5. Objectivity: members are critical of prejudice and avoid it, seek the best solutions to a problem.					
6. Involvement: members are eager to participate and do so.					
7. Cooperativeness: members contribute to the best of their ability; there is little fighting for status and personal goals.					
8. Communicativeness: remarks seem addressed to everyone; no communication cliques develop; chairman does not talk only to a few.					
9. Permissiveness: members and leader are not autocratic; group makes most decisions; atmosphere relaxed, accepting, informal.					

	Outstanding	Superior	Average	Poor	Unsatisfactory
Aspects of Group Climate					
10. Productivity: members keep at the job, produce effectively.					
11. Flexibility: group adjusts to changing needs, profits from mistakes.					
12. Integrativeness: group involves new members readily, utilizes resources of all rather than relying on a few.					

Discussion situations can generally be divided into four rather different types: (1) therapeutic, (2) commitment, (3) learning, and (4) problem solving. In the first, the goal is to help individuals gain insights into their mental and personality states so that desirable behavioral change may later result. In commitment groups, the aim is to secure support of some action that the group has already approved. In learning groups, sometimes called training groups,[1] the goal is to increase understanding, improve old or develop new skills, discover relationships, or explore applications. In the fourth, the aim is to resolve differences, determine policies, make decisions, or seek consensus.

[1] An explanation of the differences between therapy and learning or training groups can be found in Andersen, Nichols, and Booth, pp. 515–519.

Obviously, the four situations are not mutually exclusive. Some learning must occur before commitment, personality change, or the solving of a problem takes place. All four may seek immediate or delayed change. They all take place most frequently in relatively small groups. All may have predetermined or emergent goals. With problem solving, however, both the content and process have unique characteristics. In this chapter, we describe these characteristics and consider some attitudes that may help to improve your effectiveness in problem-solving discussion.

THE SUBJECT MATTER OF DISCUSSION

We have to face and resolve a large number of problems every day. For example: A family owns only one car. The father must get to and from work, the mother needs to drive to a church meeting, the son wishes to go to the beach, and the younger child wants to be driven to a friend's house. What sort of schedule can satisfy everyone's needs? Or, consider a plant where piecework production has been slowing down. Is it because of new help, failure of the management to install safety devices, home problems of the work force, or a breakdown of the presses? What can be done to step up production and still satisfy everyone involved? In another example, a candidate for the doctoral degree has not done well in a final oral examination but has written a brilliant dissertation. What action should his or her doctoral committee take? These problems are representative of those that confront many of us almost every day.

Characteristics of Problems

In each of the above problems, we note certain similarities. First, there is an *awareness* of a problem. Some people perceive that something is wrong and feel that something should be done about it, although at the moment they may not know just what. In the problem of the family car, the awareness did not appear until all four members of the family wanted to use the car at the same time. In the illustration of the doctoral committee, awareness came after the candidate had failed several questions in a row.

Once the awareness has developed to a conclusion level, a *goal* emerges. This goal may be solving a problem, removing an obstacle, reaching an agreement, or preventing something from happening. In the case of production slowdown, the goal simply might be to stop further decreases. Of course, we must remember that the goal may be different for each of the persons involved—as in the case of the family car.

A third characteristic is that in each sample problem there are *barriers* to the goals — barriers inherent in the problem situation. How can four people go in four different directions at the same time in only one car? Alternate transportation may not be available.

In every problem, all of these characteristics exist. If there is no awareness of a difficulty, there is no problem, for something becomes a problem only when we perceive it as one. If the goal is absent, no problem exists. We may be aware of a disaster in a nearby town, but that awareness does not create a problem for us until we feel that we must do something about it. Finally, if no barrier exists, there is no problem. We simply act.

Whenever a problem has these three characteristics and affects more than one person (personal problems have these qualities but may frequently be solved by the individual alone), problem-solving discussion is in order.

Kinds of Problems

There are three different kinds of problems that lend themselves to problem-solving discussion: (1) policy, (2) value, and (3) fact.

Problems of *policy* are concerned with matters requiring decisions and action. The following are typical: What should be done to beautify our city? What can be done to control air traffic? What steps should be taken to reduce teenage drug use? How can college administrators and students work together to build college programs that are relevant to the problems and needs of young people?

Problems of *value* call for value judgments and the application of accepted standards in determining the goodness, rightness, or effectiveness of an object, concept, or person. Some typical illustrations are: What are the relative values of the fire-prevention measures for hillside homes suggested by our city council? What factors account for the greatest amount of worker motivation?

Problems of *fact* are concerned with the discovery of factual information. Included would be such questions as: What was the sequence of events leading to the crime? How did the accident actually happen? What were the effects of adopting a particular soil-erosion-control practice? What is the cost of a three-month tour of Europe?

In resolving any of these problems, the approach would have to be that of *inquiry*—in contrast to *advocacy,* which is the approach in debate. The discussant seeks to find answers; the debater seeks to gain support. This difference is crucial when we engage in a problem-solving discussion.

Finally, all of our illustrations either state explicitly or suggest the problem that is to be resolved. In other words, this is the essence of problem-solving discussion: there is the *need* for a number of persons to reach some agreement about some action, value, or fact.

Selecting and Phrasing the Problem

In classroom situations, the participants usually choose the topics for discussion. Although this is often true in other situations as well, participants may frequently have a topic or problem given to them. Or, the nature of their work may force them to take an active part in discussion. Thus, what we have to say about selecting a topic for discussion may not apply in all instances. In giving the major criteria for selecting a topic, we recognize that applications will vary.

Selecting the Problem

1. *The problem should be significant:* Meaningful problem-solving discussion topics are those that materially affect the lives of the discussants at the time of the discussion. Problems of government, social institutions, family matters, intergroup and interpersonal relations, or health and welfare would certainly be important enough to talk about.

2. *The problem should be suited to the group:* Age, sex, educational level, experience, training, and avocational interests are a few of the factors to consider in determining if a topic is suited to a group. A topic suitable for women might have little appeal for men. A group of doctoral candidates in chemistry might not be interested in the problem facing a junior high school administrator.

3. *The problem should be adaptable to reflective thinking:* If there is no need to explore possible solutions, if the discussants cannot summon even a modicum of objectivity, or if other methods of arriving at a decision are more suitable, discussion will accomplish little. Thus, you should avoid the occasional problem that has only one solution or problems that experimentation or some authority can resolve. It might be better for a group to wait until it can control prejudices or acquire the necessary perspective before attacking certain difficulties.

4. *The problem should be limited to the discussion situation:* In addition to being suited to the interests of the discussion group, the problem should be tailored to the time available. For example, the question, "How can we improve our foreign policy?" could occupy a long series of meetings attended by specialists in political science. But even the most dedicated and competent would find the topic ill-suited for a single two-hour session. However, they could make some progress in finding suitable answers to the question, "What changes could be made in our relations with Peru?"

The Wording of the Problem

The way a problem is worded is of particular importance to good discussion. A well-phrased problem will make it easier to arrive at an acceptable solution within the time specified. A poorly stated problem erects the most irritating barriers to even minimal group accomplishment. The following guidelines should prove helpful to those who enjoy the responsibility of selecting and phrasing discussion problems.

1. *The problem should be in the form of a question:* A general advertisement in the mass media is often sufficient to attract an audience when a discussion is public in nature and when the topic, or general area for discussion, is one calculated to appeal to certain people. Hence, one could simply advertise that certain authorities will discuss progressive jazz. But once the actual discussion is introduced, the moderator will proceed from the general topic to the specific problem to be considered. And in order to activate and direct the attention of the discussants and the audience to that specific problem or goal, he or she will generally state the problem as a question: "What musicians have made the greatest contributions to progressive jazz?" In private discussion groups, phrasing the problem in question form is similarly important in indicating what goal the discussants must reach or what difficulty they must face and overcome. Although phrasing the problem as a statement or debate proposition appeals to some groups, the outcome is that discussants frequently become advocates. When that happens, reflective thinking disappears.

2. *The problem-question should be probative:* A problem-question that tends to encourage exploratory thinking is better than one that places immediate limitations on thinking. A question like, "Should we stop giving aid to a certain country of the Afro-Asian bloc?" calls for choosing sides immediately. Similar reactions occur when the problem is phrased in proposition or resolution form. A better question might be, "What would be the results of stopping aid to Country X?" This question requires that we continue our thinking until we have analyzed the results of the proposed action.

3. *The problem-question should state a limited aspect of a subject:* As we have already pointed out, one major fault of many discussions is that they try to cover too much territory. Wise discussants will limit the scope of the topic to the time allowed. But such wisdom is slow in arriving! Beginners usually misjudge the time it takes to explore even the most limited problems, even if they are well-prepared.

4. *The problem should not be stated ambiguously:* Although most discussion groups will attempt to clarify terms early in the discussion, they can save considerable time if the problem is stated as clearly as possible. Many discussions have never progressed beyond a quibbling over definitions, and nothing kills discussion more rapidly than quibbling. Notice, for example, the opportunities for illogical meandering in the following problem-question:

"How can we control television broadcasting?" What, for example, is meant by *we*? Does it refer to the general public, some government agency, or the industry itself? And what about the term "control"? What type of control do we mean? Do we intend to apply it to all forms of broadcasting?

5. *The problem-question should be impartially phrased:* Most of us have an all-too-natural tendency to reflect our prejudices and emotions in our language. When emotionally loaded language creeps into the phrasing of a discussion question, emotional flare-ups are inevitable and problem solving is impossible. We should, therefore, avoid phrasing a question in a way that indicates partiality. Certainly we should not turn out such questions as, "How can we impress upon the Republican apologists for the American Medical Association the necessity for taking a more humanitarian attitude toward medical care for the aged?"

6. *The problem-question should be as brief as possible:* Long, involved sentences further long, involved discussion or keep discussion from getting started. Scholars often resort to carefully qualified statements to protect themselves from misinterpretation. This kind of qualifying is usually unnecessary in wording questions for discussion. Most problems, when clearly conceived, can be stated clearly. When confronted by an occasional complex or multiple problem, the framers of the question might attempt to break down the problem into its components, phrasing each component as an individual problem-question.

"The problem–question
should be as brief as possible."

PREPARATION FOR DISCUSSION

Many discussions fail simply because of inadequate preparation on the part of the discussants.[2] How much work you will have to do to help make discussion valuable to your group and yourself will depend, of course, upon the problem and upon your own background. In general, however, thorough preparation encompasses the following procedure: (1) Survey what you already know about the subject. (2) Plan carefully what further exploration is necessary. (3) Seek information from all available sources, including interviewing authorities; listening to speeches and to radio and television programs; and reading pertinent books, periodicals, and newspapers. (4) Organize your material into a readily available and usable form. (5) Critically examine your hypothesis and the conclusions as you have listed them, keeping in mind that the information and arguments put forward by the other discussants may well alter your conclusions.

[2] The reader should review the material in Chapter 1 on preparation.

In preparing for discussion, students often use analytical question sheets. A sample sheet, contributed by Larry Bradford, professor of speech at Barton County Community College, Great Bend, Kansas, follows. Its purpose is to help those of you who are to participate in the discussion to think ahead and to prepare yourselves for intelligent group consideration of an important problem. Use it as a guide to your research. Let it help you decide what you will need to study and find out about.

What Effect Will the Equal Rights Amendment Have on American Social Structure?

I.   Awareness of the problem-question.
   A.   What are the key terms that must be defined?
      1.   What does "effect" mean?
      2.   What does "Equal Rights Amendment" mean?
      3.   What is meant by "American social structure?"
   B.   What information must be processed to discuss the problem-question?
      1.   How is the ERA worded?
      2.   Who will enact the ERA?
      3.   When will the ERA take effect?
      4.   What is required for ratification of the ERA?

II.   Identifying the key issues of the problem-question.
   A.   What are the legal implications of the Equal Rights Amendment?
      1.   Will the ERA affect private business or personal relationships between men and women?
      2.   Will women lose child support rights?
      3.   How would the ERA affect alimony laws?
   B.   How will the American social structure be affected by the ERA?
      1.   Will the ERA require that women be drafted and serve in combat?
      2.   Will a state be able to prohibit homosexual marriages?
      3.   Will the ERA mean an end to separate restrooms?

III.   Expansion and Exploration of the problem-question.
   A.   Who supports the ERA?
      1.   What is the position of the National Women's Political Caucus?
      2.   What is the position of the AFL-CIO?
   B.   Who opposes the ERA?
      1.   Why did the Florida legislature defeat the ERA?
      2.   What is the position of Senator Samuel Ervin?
   C.   What is the report of the Citizen's Advisory Council on the Status of Women?

IV.   Conclusions relative to the problem-question.
   A.   How might the courts interpret the amendment?
   B.   How will controversial questions be answered?

Obviously, discussants will alter the line of questioning to suit their topic and their particular responsibility in preparing for the discussion (frequently this includes a research assignment in a particular area). But most discussants can easily adapt the general format of the outline above to most topics, whether in surveying their knowledge of the field or in examining their possible solutions to the problem. And, if they use the questions as guidelines for organizing and listing their material, discussants will also be able to locate pertinent data easily during the discussion.

STEPS IN PROBLEM-SOLVING DISCUSSION

Problem-solving discussion is a form of group thinking. When the thinking is sound and based on careful analysis, thorough preparation, and logical inference, the resultant discussion may bear a striking resemblance in format to the discussion outlined above. The resemblance is not accidental. Both are based on a sequence in scientific procedure observed by Dewey[3] and advocated by many teachers of discussion. The sequence consists of the following steps: (1) There is an awareness of a problem. (2) The problem is located and defined. (3) Possible solutions to the problem are suggested. (4) The ramifications of these solutions are considered. (5) Each solution is rejected or accepted only after further observation, experimentation, and/or discussion. (6) The solution accepted as the best one is subject to further testing.

Let us examine this sequence in some detail in order to discover how it may be used in problem solving and why it has been so widely adopted.

[3] John Dewey, *How We Think* (Boston: Heath, 1933), p. 107.

Developing an Awareness of the Problem

Too frequently we assume that the presence of a person in a discussion group is *prima facie* evidence that he or she is aware of the problem involved. Actually, as we have noted previously, many individuals may not sense the difficulty at all or may not recognize that they are in any way affected. Because sensitivity to difficulty heightens interest in the problem, motivates greater effort during the preparation and participation stages, and ensures greater commitment to whatever decisions are made, it is the essential first step in problem solving.

In this stage of problem solving, the members of the group consider the significance and immediacy of the problem, its possible effect on individual members, its broader implications for the group, and the need for decision or action. In essence, this awareness prepares the discussants mentally and emotionally for further exploration of the problem.

Defining and Exploring the Problem

This step develops an understanding of the exact nature of the problem. Here the group members define or clarify unclear terms, recognize possible limitations, establish the nature and extent of the problem, propose and adopt criteria for evaluating possible solutions, suggest immediate causes for the problem, and determine main issues.

How this step develops will vary from problem to problem. In some problems, the terms will be clear. In others, limitations beyond those suggested in the statement of the problem may be necessary. In still others, there may be no need to explore issues because only a single issue is involved.

Perhaps the two most important aspects at this stage are to be sure (1) that you have isolated the exact problem and (2) that you have determined what the criteria are for its solution or what barriers stand in the way of solution. Too frequently, discussants are unsure of what problem it is that they are discussing. Consequently, they have not established criteria for evaluating its solution. When you know the conditions a solution must meet to be acceptable, it is easier to suggest and determine possible solutions.

Suggesting Possible Solutions

Here the group suggests those solutions that have some feasibility. The solutions should reflect thoughtful, realistic, and representative proposals for decision or action. When the brainstorming technique is used to carry out this step, all solutions should be recorded regardless of their apparent impracticality.

Exploring the Possible Solutions

In this step, the discussants explore the ramifications of each possible solution. They consider such questions as these: "Does it conform to the criteria for an acceptable solution?" "Is the solution practical?" "Will it cost too much?" "Will the proposed solution actually better conditions?" "Will the people who are empowered to act actually implement the proposed solution?"

Sometimes suggestion and exploration of solutions are combined. That is, the participants explore each solution as it is suggested. The danger with this technique, however, is that frequently the considera-

tion of the first few proposed solutions takes up so much time that none is left for consideration of those listed last. Thus, a best solution is sometimes overlooked. We recommend that you first list the possible solutions and then consider their respective merits.

Selecting the Best Solution

In most discussion situations steps 5 and 6 of Dewey's steps in thinking are combined.[4] By the time the discussants have considered several solutions to a problem, a consensus begins to develop as to which is the best. At most, only a few solutions remain for final consideration. The discussion group must then subject these to a rigid examination, again considering their ramifications, testing each by the criteria established above (under Defining and Exploring), and contrasting and comparing each with the remaining possible solutions. Unfortunately, because of the limitations of the classroom situation, student discussants will seldom have the opportunity to test favored solutions under conditions approximating reality.

[4] For some problems, role-playing can be used to test which solution is the best.

VARIATIONS OF THE PROBLEM-SOLVING SEQUENCE

There is nothing sacred about the Dewey-inspired sequence even though some partisans would have each discussion, regardless of its purpose and its participants, follow every step in exact order. Yet most good problem-solving discussions do seem to incorporate the steps, usually in the order we have listed. Most discussants find the sequence admirable for studying and exploring a problem during the preparatory stage. And many teachers find that following the sequence seems to encourage reflectiveness on the part of the student-discussants. However, the sequence is the result of careful observation; it is not an unalterable prescription. Rigid adherence to the steps in the order listed can prevent creativity—especially in a non problem-solving discussion and even in a classroom problem-solving situation. Frequently, for example, the topic is so broad or involved that a single period will not permit consideration of more than the initial stages—

perhaps up to the introduction of various solutions to the problem. In such a case, it might be wise for the discussants to word the question so that the group is directed toward discovering possible solutions rather than reaching an agreement on one solution. Sometimes a group will continue the discussion at its next meeting or meetings and follow through the remaining stages, modifying the phrasing of each problem-question in order to focus on the scope of each discussion session.

There are times, of course, when the group will discover that the definition stage in problem-solving is most unsatisfactory. This discovery is to be expected. In preparation for discussion, it is often impossible to examine the problem and its phrasing sufficiently. Even after the discussion has progressed—jerkily—to the examination of various solutions, the group may find it necessary to return to the first two steps before continuing in a logical pattern.

On other occasions, the discussants may consider the first step so important that they will want to discuss it for thirty or forty minutes. Pushing the group on to other stages may only annoy some sincere individuals who want to get something off their chests. Hopefully, the leader will throw out questions that, if pursued, will lead the group to the next stage. If, despite this tactful effort, there is no progress, a brief coffee or cigarette break will often give the discussants enough chance to air their feelings.

Sometimes a group will divide the definition and the exploration of the problem into two steps, each a unit in itself. This procedure may include determining the barriers to a successful solution and deciding on the order in which they are to be considered.

On occasion, the moderator will sense that his or her group is so split or so antagonistic to the introduction of certain vital issues or possible solutions that a change in procedural tactics is indicated. The leader might adapt a variation of a format we found helpful when a women's club broke into political factions during a discussion of a proposed school bond issue. Disregarding the sequence of defini-

tion of terms followed by the suggestion of possible solutions, we advised the moderator to try starting the women out on, "If we didn't have to worry about practicality, finances, or politics, what might our *ideal* school system resemble?" After some priming by the moderator, the women came to an amazingly rapid agreement as to an ideal, if admittedly impractical, goal. Then the moderator asked them to consider what obstacles existed to achievement of *their* goal. After much reflection, they agreed upon a number of major barriers. "Well, then," continued the moderator, "how might we overcome these barriers?" When an impasse developed, the moderator asked the women to think of how they might have to change their goal to allow for obstacles they could not circumvent. Finally, he led the group to a consideration of how they might put into effect their solution. Like all other discussion techniques, the problem-solving sequence must never be considered infallible or inflexible.

Frequently, modifications in the Dewey sequence are required because of the nature of the problem, the knowledge and skills of the group members, or the situation in which the problem has arisen. Numerous writers have suggested different patterns of discussion that allow for such variables. We believe a brief reference to several of these patterns will broaden our understanding of how problems can be solved.

First, we must consider a related factor touched upon in Chapter 2. Remember that, in any problem-solving discussion, all inputs have two dimensions: the affective and the cognitive—the feeling content and the intellectual content. The existence of emotions or feelings will frequently determine the nature of the intellectual contributions made in discussion. Because of this effect, one writer[5] suggests that the first step in conducting a discussion is to

[5] Norman R. F. Maier, *Problem-Solving Discussions and Conferences* (New York: McGraw-Hill, 1963), p. 99.

determine the discussants' state of mind. When negative emotional states exist, they must be dealt with appropriately, early in the discussion. Failure to recognize and deal with the feelings of the group members by decreasing or removing threats, building a sense of security, and providing opportunity for airing feelings can frequently create almost insurmountable barriers to effective problem-solving. In employing any problem-solving pattern of discussion, the importance of the members' emotional attitudes must be kept in mind.

Some writers explicitly state that implementing a solution is an essential part of the problem-solving process. This view is held by Smith, who lists the steps in the "pattern of constructive thinking" as follows: (1) identifying the goal, (2) analyzing the relationship between the goal and the barriers to it, (3) considering possible solutions, (4) selecting the solution that appears to be most satisfactory, and (5) considering ways in which the solution might be put into effect.[6] When a discussion group stops at step 4, it may later discover that what was thought to be the best solution cannot be easily implemented.

[6] William S. Smith, *Group Problem-Solving through Discussion* (Indianapolis: Bobbs-Merrill, 1963), p. 33.

A second writer[7] who is also concerned with output or with a program to implement the solution suggests a "standard agenda" as the pattern to follow in problem solving. The steps are essentially these:

1. Specifying and defining the problem
   a. Does the problem fall within the purview of the group?
   b. Is the problem pertinent?
   c. Does the problem refer to something about which data can be gathered?
   d. Does the wording of the question allow the widest possible latitude for investigation?
2. Gathering facts
   a. Do the facts and evidence conform to logical tests?
   b. On the basis of data secured, how should the problem be redefined?
3. Discovering the cause
4. Assessing the authority and restrictions on the problem-solving group
   a. Does the group have the authority to act?
   b. Within what restrictions can the group act?
5. Developing solutions

[7] Gerald M. Phillips, *Communication and the Small Group* (Indianapolis: Bobbs-Merrill, 1966), pp. 72–108.

A third writer[8] develops a viewpoint about the Dewey model which provides needed insights into problem-solving discussions. He states that, except under unusual circumstances, groups do not proceed rationally and in a step-by-step manner toward the solution of a problem. Rather, participants frequently attack the entire problem at a relatively superficial level, returning again and again to the problem, exploring deeper into its ramifications with each successive approach. There appears to be no clear-cut differentiation between solution and problem definition. At some point during this process, the group will discover a decision (or a series of decisions) to which they are committed and which they are willing to implement.

This author is essentially describing the way decisions are frequently reached in discussion groups. In some discussions, there does not appear to be a systemized approach. The final decision appears to emerge after successive trials. In some situations, an opportunity for tension release may be needed. In others, different members may try out their "plans" on the group. Or, there may not seem to be a clear differentiation between problem definition, exploration, and solution. Some groups may be characterized by a rotation of leadership. Further, areas of consensus and disagreement may be successively reached as the participants probe deeper into the problem. Between one successive decision and the next, the criteria that appeared applicable earlier may no longer apply. Establishing new criteria often promotes creativity and free interchange of ideas. Ways of looking at a problem, like the prediscussion conclusions of a participant, must be open to change if a group is to retain its capacity for growth and effectiveness in problem solving. It is important to recognize that some groups function in a "stop and go" manner, yet still produce worthwhile decisions to which the group members are committed.

A study by Larson[9] sought to "discover whether variations in forms of analysis would produce associated variations in the accuracy of small group problem solving." In his discussion of the results of the study, Larson states that "The most interesting observation which emerges is that more recently developed patterns appear to be more productive than the traditional reflective thinking pattern."

Although these studies do suggest that we should not rely too much on the Dewey pattern, the accumulated findings do not warrant dismissing systematic analyses of problems.

One final caution: Even when a group believes it is following a logical pattern of problem solving, it may discover from a tape recording of the discussion that it has been guilty of many obvious repetitions and false starts. To a large extent, the redundant nature of oral communication is responsible. We customarily take many mental short cuts. Because it takes individuals different amounts of time to absorb information, we may often fail to tune in to the contributions of other discussants. Thus, repetition is frequently necessary, even though it slows down group thinking and action. But we can avoid much of our repetition in speaking, just as we can in reading. The conscious application of the Dewey pattern of thinking would help most of us.

[8] Ernest G. Bormann, *Discussion and Group Methods*, 2nd ed. (New York: Harper & Row, 1975), pp. 286–287.

[9] Carl E. Larson, "Forms of Analysis and Small Group Problem-Solving," *Speech Monographs*, Vol. 36 (November 1969), pp. 452–455.

ATTITUDES VITAL
TO PROBLEM SOLVING

As we have stated before, an effective discussion must stem from an honest attempt to seek the best solution to a vexing problem, to discover or verify facts, or to determine the best of several possible value judgments.

Developing and
Maintaining a Reflective Approach

One characteristic of reflective thinking is its *inclusiveness.* In other words, discussants give equal hearing to all viewpoints regardless of their prejudices. Closely related to this desirable attitude of objectivity is a willingness to consider and even accept a solution that may counter or compromise an idea originally considered valid. However, discussants should not disregard their own opinions just because someone else disagrees, even though superior argument should supersede personal prejudice. Whenever possible, discussants should avoid defensiveness. They should treat ideas as the property of the group rather than of the individual who proposed them. Thus, an appraisal of an idea or argument will not necessarily involve loss of face and consequent displays of emotion. Thoroughness, an insistence upon accuracy, skepticism based upon considered judgment, a lively imagination, sensitivity to the feelings of others, patience, and, above all, a willingness to hold decisions in abeyance until all solutions have been explored—all of these should characterize both the participants and their performance in discussion.

Awareness of and Desire to
Satisfy the Needs of Other Discussants

In varying degrees, every group has four types of problems that it faces at all times: (1) the problem that is the basis for the group's existence, (2) the problem of dealing with the hidden, unformulated anxieties related to the announced goals, (3) the efforts of the individuals to contribute to the publicly stated goals, and (4) the individuals' efforts to satisfy their own unstated and sometimes unconscious needs. Although the first type of problem is most important to consider, often a group cannot achieve its publicly stated goal until it does something about the second, third, and fourth types of problems.

In discussion, it is important to be concerned about satisfying individual needs at the same time that progress is being made toward group goals. There are many ways in which both factors can be taken care of. Some people are shy but want to talk; they just need to be asked. Some fear to speak up; they must be placed in a position where it is easy to speak and where they feel secure while speaking. Some must be given encouragement; still others need to be challenged, given status, or just listened to. Here are three individual needs that should be satisfied.

"... they must be placed in a position where it is easy to speak ..."

1. *Self-respect:* Each of us has a self-image—of which we may or may not be aware—that guides us in all our feelings and behavior. It serves as a yardstick that tells whether we are successes, failures, or just so-so. When we are not perfectly satisfied with ourselves, we seek ways of restoring the balance between our self-image and what we perceive ourselves to be at any moment. Our actions in such a situation may not always be acceptable to the groups we belong to. In discussion, for example, we may seek to dominate, withdraw, reject new ideas, or engage in personal attacks. At such times, we need understanding, acceptance, support, respect, and the assurance that we do have an important role in the group's activities.

2. *The need to belong:* People who feel they belong to a group will talk about "Our group," or say, "When we do this," and, "It was good for us." The person who feels he or she does not belong to a group will place him- or herself in opposition to the rest. Such a person will say: "It's your decision," or, "If you folks really want my opinion," or, "After all, you're the ones to be affected." People who feel they do not belong but who want to belong are the ones who need help if they are to contribute maximally in discussion. They may not talk and hence need encouragement; they may resist and must be shown that the group wants to include their ideas; they may withdraw and will need to be given a significant task to do. Developing a feeling at the outset of a discussion that everyone is wanted, encouraging the growth of team spirit during the discussion, and showing how the results of a discussion will benefit all are three ways to instill a feeling of belonging.

Giving an individual the opportunity to pick the persons with whom he or she will work on some discussion project is a good way to develop belongingness. We refer the reader to the material on sociometrics in Chapter 4.

3. *Feeling of accomplishment:* Success builds success. Children are motivated to try more difficult tasks if they have succeeded in the past. Adults, however, frequently lose hope if they do not feel that anything they have done is worthwhile. All of us want to feel that we can make and are making useful contributions to a group task; we also like to feel that we are "in the right," and that others realize this.

All group members should have a sense of accomplishment in discussion. This means that the progress the group is making must be clear to everyone, that the group's activities must not be misdirected, and that individuals must feel they are contributing to the achievement of the group's goals. It is an ideal situation when other group members point out the value of an individual's contribution.

Maintaining a Critical Attitude toward the Quality of Discussion

Discussion as a tool in problem solving and learning is only as effective as its users make it. Hence, it is important to the discussion group as well as to its individual members to check on the process periodically and to modify performance and activity accordingly.

We should demand high standards of individual performance in a group, and of the progress made. Obviously, we cannot expect perfection at first; it may take some time before the members will feel that they are performing somewhere near par. But if they seek excellence, the end product will be that much better.

In the classroom, it is generally the instructor who instigates or directs discussion evaluation until the practice takes hold and spreads of its own accord. But a discussion outside the classroom rarely has—or requests—such expert direction as part of its everyday functioning. Nevertheless, much that happens in the classroom might prove helpful in the meeting room, conference room, or living room. The operating rules of any discussion group might well provide for continual feedback through individual reaction sheets, occasional "where-are-we-going-and-where-have-we-been?" sessions, critiques by an outside expert or by a member of the group delegated to the job, or by a combination of these methods.

Using Conflict Constructively in Problem-Solving Discussion

One form of interaction that occurs in almost every problem-solving discussion is conflict. And it can vary in proportion from minor to major. The statements: "I can't

see much difference between our views," and, "I could never accept that idea. It is illogical, the result of biased, emotional inferences, and would have nothing but negative results" reflect these extremes. The first extreme may indicate either a casual approach to decision-making or an honest belief. In any event progress in the discussion is speeded up. The second extreme is or can be a major block to the discussion.

It is necessary to recognize what the valuable results of conflict are and to try to obtain them. First, conflict results in creativity. One writer[10] puts it his way:

Rather that being undesirable, conflict is desirable from at least two standpoints. It has been demonstrated that through conflict man is creative. Further, a relationship in conflict is a relation—not the absence of one. Such a relationship may result in creativity because of its intensity.

A second valuable result of conflict is that it can serve to increase the amount of information needed to solve a problem most efficiently. As long as the members expressing extreme views do not literally withdraw from the discussion, a skilled leader can elicit the reasons for the posi-

tions they hold. Sometimes a whole new approach to a solution, or a compromise not previously considered, will result.

Third, conflict frequently reveals valuable data about the participants' backgrounds, the power structure within a group, and the strength of expressed beliefs and attitudes. In addition, it can reveal the extent to which a viewpoint is based on fact or fiction, the knowledge of what new facts are needed and the nature of those facts, and an understanding of what agreements and decisions are impossible to reach, thereby saving time and effort on the part of all the group members.

Keep in mind these cautions: Do not let your desire to attain high standards of productivity make you so critical, agressive, and insensitive to the other group members that you destroy a member's security, self-respect, and sense of having made worthwhile contributions to the discussion. You must adapt your procedural standards to the members, their skills in discussion, the goals of the group, the hierarchy within the group, the pressures from some parent or outside organization, and the total resource potential of the group.

---

[10] Fred E. Jandt, *Conflict Resolution through Communication* (Harper & Row, 1973), p. 3.

IMPLICATIONS FOR THE
DISCUSSION GROUP MEMBER

1. The situations or groups in which discussion is used include therapy, commitment, learning, and problem solving. Since the last three are not completely different from one another and since each includes at least a few of the characteristics of the others, study and practice of all three are warranted. Therapy, however, should remain the province of professionals.

2. Following the steps outlined in this chapter for selecting and wording a problem-statement will lessen or eliminate some of the perplexing procedural barriers to effective problem solution.

3. Preparing for a discussion is essential. This includes accurately stating the problem, studying and researching its nature, critically examining any conclusions or hypotheses you may have made or held before the discussion, and preparing a tentative agenda or outline of the topic.

4. Dewey's "steps in thinking," or some adaptation of it, is the usual sequence used in problem-solving discussion. But this pattern cannot and should not be followed to the letter. To do so may stifle creativity, prevent the emergence of what may be the best or most acceptable solution, dampen free, open communication, and result in a decision that cannot be supported by group members.

5. The attitudes, beliefs, experiences, and knowledge of each discussant is a part of his or her discussion input. Approaches essential to effective problem-solving discussion include developing and maintaining a reflective and objective attitude, recognizing the ego needs of other discussants, and creating a critical yet understanding attitude.

A SUMMARY AND LOOK AHEAD

Most people participate in problem-solving discussion many times throughout their lives. The problems may be questions of value, questions of fact, or ones calling for action. The amount and nature of reflective thinking that takes place on any discussion topic is a function of how it has been selected and worded and how well-prepared the discussants are. Effectiveness in problem-solving discussion increases when the participants attempt to follow a logical sequence and when their attitudes contribute to good interpersonal relations.

In Chapter 8, we consider role-playing, a technique that has a wide variety of uses in discussion.

SUGGESTED READINGS

Bonner, Hubert, *Group Dynamics: Principles and Applications* (New York: Ronald Press, 1959), Ch. 7.

Bormann, Ernest G., *Discussion and Group Methods,* 2nd ed. (New York: Harper & Row, 1975), Chs. 4–6, 14.

Brembeck, Winston L., and William S. **Howell,** *Persuasion: A Means of Social Control* (Englewood Cliffs, N.J.: Prentice-Hall, 1952), Chs. 11–12.

Brilhart, John K., *Effective Group Discussion,* 2nd ed., (Dubuque, Iowa: Wm. C. Brown, 1974), Ch. 5.

Burgoon, Michael, Judee K. **Heston,** and James **McCroskey,** *Small Group Communication: A Functional Approach* (New York: Holt, Rinehart and Winston, 1974), Ch. 8–9.

Deutsch, Morton, "An Experimental Study of the Effects of Cooperation and Competition upon Group Process," *Human Relations,* Vol. 2, No. 3 (1949), pp. 199–231.

Fisher, B. Aubrey, *Small Group Decision Making* (New York: McGraw-Hill, 1974), Ch. 7.

Galvin, Kathleen, and Cassandra **Book,** *Person to Person: An Introduction to Speech Communication* (Skokie, Ill.: National Textbook, 1974), Ch. 5.

Gouran, Dennis S., *The Process of Group Decision-Making* (New York: Harper & Row, 1974), Ch. 4.

Gouran, Dennis S., and John E. **Baird,** Jr., "An Analysis of Distributional and Sequential Structure in Problem-Solving and Informal Group Discussions," *Speech Monographs,* Vol. 39 (March 1972), pp. 16–22.

Haiman, Franklyn S., *Group Leadership and Democratic Action* (Boston: Houghton Mifflin, 1951), Chs. 7–8.

Harnack, R. Victor, and Thorrel B. **Fest,** *Group Discussion: Theory and Technique* (New York: Appleton-Century-Crofts, 1964), Chs. 4–6, 15–16.

Jandt, Fred E., *Conflict Resolution Through Communication* (New York: Harper & Row, 1973), Part IV.

Kelly, Harold H., and John W. **Thibaut,** "Group Problem Solving," in Gardner Lindzey and Elliot Aronson, eds., *The Handbook of Social Psychology,* 2nd ed., Vol. 4 (Cambridge, Mass.: Addison-Wesley, 1969), Ch. 9.

Larson, Carl E., "Forms of Analysis and Small Group Problem Solving," *Speech Monographs,* Vol. 36 (November 1969), pp. 452–455.

Magoon, F. Alexander, *The Teaching of Human Relations* (Boston: Beacon Press, 1959), Ch. 2.

Maier, Norman R. F., *Problem-Solving Discussions and Conferences* (New York: McGraw-Hill, 1963).

Patton, Bobby R., and Kim **Giffin,** *Problem-Solving Group Interaction* (New York: Harper & Row, 1973), Chs. 8–11.

Phillips, Gerald M., *Communication and the Small Group,* 2nd ed. (Indianapolis: Bobbs-Merrill, 1973), Ch. 4.

Schutz, William C., "What Makes Groups Productive?" *Human Relations,* Vol. 8, No. 4 (1956), pp. 429–465.

Shaw, Marvin E., and William T. **Penrod,** Jr., "Does More Information Available to a Group Improve Group Performance?" *Sociometry,* Vol. 25 (December 1962), pp. 377–390.

Smith, William S., *Group Problem-Solving through Discussion,* rev. ed. (Indianapolis: Bobbs-Merrill, 1965), Chs. 2, 4, 5–6.

EXERCISES

1. In the last two decades, it has seemed that the number of serious problems facing this nation is multiplying rather than decreasing. This apparent increase may have resulted because the mass media have focused attention on the problems and because more people are becoming increasingly involved in social, political, and economic affairs. Under these three categories — social, political, and economic — make a list of problems suitable for class discussion. Include in your lists only those topics with which you are personally concerned. Keep in mind what we have said in this chapter about the nature of discussion topics.

2. Select any two of the general subject areas listed below and, for each, phrase three problem-questions for discussion. Make one a problem-question of fact, one of value, and one of policy.

Adult education
Agriculture and federal subsidies
Airplane hijacking
Air traffic
America's foreign aid program
Amnesty
Black community problems
Brown community problems
Building school–community relations
College education costs
Community Chest drives
Conservation
Credibility gaps
Cuba and the United States
Culture in America
Dangers in do-it-yourself repairs
Drug addiction
Drug use in America
Ecology

Federal tax structure
Foreign tax structure
Foreign policy
Freedom for young people
Government spending
Hard-core movies
Housing for low-income families
Keeping within the family budget
Labor–management relations
Leadership in the Democratic party
Leadership in the Republican party
Mass media in communication
Medical care for the aged
New developments in religious education
Peace Corps
Population movements in the United States
Professional sports
Professionalism in college sports
Racism
Railroads and federal subsidies
Sexuality and sexual freedom
Stock market and the American public
Student participation in college administration
Suburbia
Thirty-hour week
United States–Canada relations
United States–Mexico relations
Vietnam: past and future
Volunteers for the armed forces
The Women's Rights Amendment

3. On the basis of your study and experiences in actual discussions, write out what you consider to be the best sequence in problem solving.

4. Divide the class into subgroups of five or six persons and decide as a group which of the following abilities and characteristics are most important for effective participation in problem-solving discussion.

Accuracy

Creativity

Critical listening

Forcefulness

Friendliness

Humility

Intimate knowledge of group members

Joviality

Knowledge of topic

Lively imagination

Objectivity

Patience

Reasoning ability

Sense of humor

Sensitivity to interpersonal relations

Skepticism

Skill in language use

Thoroughness

Submit your list to the instructor for his comments.

5. Each of the following references contains excellent sections on reasoning fallacies. Read one of the references and be prepared to discuss in class the fallacies most likely to occur in discussion.

Beardsley, Monroe C., *Thinking Straight* (Englewood Cliffs, N.J.: Prentice-Hall, 1956).

Chase, Stuart, *Guides to Straight Thinking* (New York: Harper & Row, 1956).

Ewbank, Henry Lee, and J. Jeffery Auer, *Discussion and Debate*, 2nd ed. (New York: Appleton-Century-Crofts, 1961).

Fearnside, W. Ward, and William B. Holther, *Fallacy: The Counterfeit of Argument* (Englewood Cliffs, N.J.: Prentice-Hall, 1959).

Kahane, Howard, *Logic and Contemporary Rhetoric: The Use of Reason in Everyday Life* (Belmont, Calif.: Wadsworth, 1971).

6. Following are phrases that are used to describe various fallacies in reasoning. In your next problem-solving discussion in class, try to note which fallacies are used. Which are used most? Look up the meaning of the phrases you do not understand.

Appeal to sympathy

Arguing in a circle

Argumentum ad hominen

False cause and effect

False dilemma

Generalization from too few specific instances

Irrelevant conclusion

Loaded words

Name-calling

Obscure language

Sarcasm or ridicule

Straw man

Suggestion by repeated affirmation

Universal appeal

Use of glittering generalities

Use of nonexpert prestige and status

7. Prepare a tentative outline for a problem-solving panel-forum on one of the following topics, or on another assigned by your instructor.

a. How can television better serve the public interest?

b. How can slum clearance and reconstruction be speeded up in our large cities?

c. How can a college education be made available to all?

d. How can students make a more meaningful contribution to the administration of college affairs?

e. How can the automobile be made safer?

f. How can nonviolence be made a more effective form of protest?

g. What can be done to ensure greater participation of the Black and Brown communities in government?

h. What is the proper function of governmental and private foundation grants in promoting research in industry?

i. What changes in governmental administrative procedures are needed? How can they be achieved?

8. The following list includes a number of general topic areas. Working in subgroups of five or six, have each person in your group add three or four more topic areas. From the topics thus accumulated, your subgroup should pick one. Then, prepare and present a discussion before the class on this subject. It will be necessary to word a problem-question, prepare a group discussion agenda (outline), do the necessary study, and make detailed plans for the discussion presentation.

College Students

Black and Brown college problems
Improving college counseling
Increasing students' control over their educations
Integration in the schools
Making education relevant to student needs
Racism
Rising costs of college education
Shortening the time necessary for an education
Students in college administration
Teacher-student relations

Labor and Industry

Automation and the worker
Corruption in labor unions
Corruption in management
Data processing in industry
Farm workers and unionization
Growing power of unions
Outlawing of strikes
Retraining the war veterans
Roles of labor and industry in city planning
Spiraling costs of living

Home and the Family

Changing home standards
Divorce increases
Freedom and the child
Increase in the generation gap
Inner-city living
Militants in the family
Mobility and the family
Moral standards among adults
Population explosion
Suburbia's problems
Television in the home
Use of alcohol by adults

National Defense

Defense and the home front

Defense costs and inflation

Disunion in the armed forces

Increasing defense costs

Keeping the peace with Russia

Increasing defense costs

Nationalist China and the United States

Nuclear defenses

Space technology developments

Values of foreign aid to Afro-Asian countries

Voluntary military forces

9. How would you change the following items to make them conform to the criteria for wording a discussion problem given in this chapter?

a. New forms of rapid transportation.

b. Do we need changes in the ways public officials are elected or selected?

c. Should we drop out of the United Nations, stop giving to foreign countries, or stay in NATO?

d. Should we support the well-intentioned aims of Southern states to maintain at all costs their inalienable right to self-government?

e. What about soil erosion?

f. Is it easy for a married college student to live on a budget?

10. On the following pages of this chapter are two different analysis forms. Plan to use each form for self-analysis or for analyzing at least one discussion you observe or participate in during the semester. In addition to the reports that you submit to your instructor on the data secured by using the forms, comment on how the forms might be improved to reveal meaningful data about problem-solving discussion.

**EVALUATION OF
DISCUSSION: GOAL ACHIEVEMENT**

Topic _____

Date _____

Seating arrangement (diagram)

1. What was the announced purpose of the discussion?

2. How suitable was the topic for:

a) The discussion group?

b) The audience (if any)?

c) The time allotted?

d) In the light of the above factors, how might the topic have been reworded?

3. What hidden purposes appeared during the discussion? If any, to what extent did they act as barriers to goal achievement?

4. How did the group reconcile these hidden purposes?

5. Did the group follow a systematic series of steps in moving toward its goals? If not, why not? Did the group make repeated attempts to solve the entire problem, as frequently occurs in "decision emergence" problem solving? Describe the successive decisions. How were these successive decisions related to the final decision made?

6. If the group did not completely reach its goal, how much did it accomplish?

7. What specific skills and attitudes seemed to assist the group in its functioning?

What attitudes, conflicting purposes, and failures in leadership stood in the way of the group achieving its announced purpose?

8. What group maintenance and/or task functions—initiating discussion, bringing up new or unpopular ideas for consideration, giving and testing information and opinion, clarifying, summarizing, coordinating, relieving tension, seeking consensus, and so on—did the group members assume?

9. If certain individuals had assumed specific roles at various stages of the discussion, would this have aided the group in reaching its announced goal? Give illustrations.

10. What suggestions can you offer for improving the group's procedures and performance?

EVALUATION OF DISCUSSION:
PROBLEM-SOLVING EFFECTIVENESS

Discussion leader _____

Topic _____

Date _____

Check the point on each scale that represents your considered opinion. Briefly support your opinion in the space marked "Explanation."

1. How suitable for discussion was the topic selected?

_____
  Very   Moderately   Poorly

Explanation:

2. How effectively was the topic introduced and defined?

_____
  Very well   Adequately   Poorly

Explanation:

3. What evidence was there of careful problem study and analysis?

_____
  Ample   Some   Little

Explanation:

4. What was the caliber of the evidence and reasoning employed?

_____
  High   Average   Poor

Explanation:

5. Did the group follow systematic steps in solving the problem?

_____
  Very much so Somewhat   Not at all

Explanation:

6. How did the communication pattern contribute to effective discussion?

_____
  Outstanding   Average   Poor

Explanation:

7. Were the discussants' attitudes conducive to effective discussion?

_____
  Very   Moderately   Not at all

Explanation:

8. How did the group treat important if unpopular viewpoints?

_____
  Carefully   Summarily   Not at all

Explanation:

9. How were interpersonal conflicts, if any, resolved?

_____
  Skillfully   Fairly well   Poorly

Explanation:

10. How was the progress toward the group's goals noted and implemented?

_____
  Very effectively Adequately   Poorly

Explanation:

EVALUATION OF DISCUSSION: PROBLEM-SOLVING EFFECTIVENESS

Discussion leader _____

Topic _____

Date _____

Check the point on each scale that represents your considered opinion. Briefly support your opinion in the space marked "Explanation."

1. How suitable for discussion was the topic selected?

_____

Very   Moderately   Poorly

Explanation:

2. How effectively was the topic introduced and defined?

_____

Very well   Adequately   Poorly

Explanation:

3. What evidence was there of careful problem study and analysis?

_____

Ample   Some   Little

Explanation:

4. What was the caliber of the evidence and reasoning employed?

_____

High   Average   Poor

Explanation:

5. Did the group follow systematic steps in solving the problem?

_____

Very much so   Somewhat   Not at all

Explanation:

6. How did the communication pattern contribute to effective discussion?

_____

Outstanding   Average   Poor

Explanation:

7. Were the discussants' attitudes conducive to effective discussion?

_____

Very   Moderately   Not at all

Explanation:

8. How did the group treat important if unpopular viewpoints?

_____

Carefully   Summarily   Not at all

Explanation:

9. How were interpersonal conflicts, if any, resolved?

_____

Skillfully   Fairly well   Poorly

Explanation:

10. How was the progress toward the group's goals noted and implemented?

_____

Very effectively Adequately   Poorly

Explanation:

Few conferences, workshops, training sessions, or human-relations institutes take place in the United States today without using the technique of role-playing to a degree. Role-playing is an offshoot of a group therapeutic technique introduced in the early 1920s by J. L. Moreno. In this chapter, we describe the nature of role-playing, why it is used or might be used, and how the technique is employed. We also talk about some variations and about how role-playing can improve participation and leadership in discussion and in the analysis of problems. As with most techniques, there are some things to avoid and other things to be aware of, so we also include a few cautions.

DESCRIPTION OF ROLE-PLAYING

As the term is generally used, role-playing refers to a technique of group and personal involvement. In this situation, people act out problems containing human conflicts and then analyze their actions and reactions with the help of the other role-players and observers. Usually role-playing includes:

1. Selecting a problem that approaches reality as closely as possible—one that is steeped in meaning for the individuals portraying the roles or witnessing the unfolding of the action. Generally, the situation or plot is constructed in barest outline and is simply and clearly stated.

2. Structuring a problem only to the point where the problem is clear and the players have a mental picture of the roles that they are to portray. Usually no lines are written or memorized.

3. Choosing the role-players from within the group.

4. Instructing and, on occasion, "warming up" the players.

5. Instructing the observers.

6. Role-playing the problem situation; cutting or stopping the role-playing when the issues of the problem have been delineated.

7. Analyzing the role-playing in order to explore further the insights revealed and in order to put the behavior modifications suggested into practice.

USES OF ROLE-PLAYING

Role-playing is a popular and flexible technique to apply in learning, training, and situation analysis. Its extensive use stems partly from the fact that it gets participants and observers totally involved on physical, intellectual, and psychological levels. No other technique engages as much of the whole individual as this one does. Why? The reason is because individuals see, hear, experience, and describe their responses as well as the reactions of the other players. Few techniques have been so successful in dramatizing the wants and fears that members bring to their groups. And for groups to function effectively, the needs and fears of group members must be understood. Further, role-playing is a good technique because it reinforces other learning and teaching procedures and devices. Thus, for example, it can be used to supplement the photo-situation, described in Chapter 9.

The technique of role-playing is used widely in business and industry for training in supervision, counseling, interviewing, and problem-analysis, and for improving industrial relations and bargaining skills. It has been successful in training situations because the participants have many different and sometimes conflicting opinions as to how a problem may be resolved. The wide variety of solutions that are role-played will usually provide some helpful suggestions that each participant can use in his job. Role-playing has similar practical training values when it is used in education.

One major value of the role-playing technique is that it helps many important emotional currents to surface. Such currents run deep and hidden through every group, and the group must control them if it is to realize its full potential. When the problem situation is well suited to the needs and interests of the group and is well directed, it tends to dissolve the vocal and emotional blocks of the players. And when the players are permitted or asked to assume a variety of roles, they practice looking into the thoughts and emotions of others, and, equally important, they practice communicating those thoughts and feelings. The end result is often a greater appreciation and understanding of the problems of the other people and a noteworthy improvement in communicative skills.

Persons who are not skilled in handling situations in which others can become emotionally aroused should be cautioned against trying to use this technique as a therapeutic device. Role-playing—sometimes called sociodrama—does aim at achieving changes in attitudes and behavior, but such changes are primarily on the intellectual level. The director of role-playing, unless he or she is properly qualified, should not attempt to perform the functions of a psychologist or psychiatrist. The changes sought through role-playing come from a heightened mental awareness and sensitivity to one's own and to another's feelings, attitudes, and need-value systems.

When role-players have the ability to project themselves into the position of the assigned role, another advantage of this technique becomes apparent. It can be used in pretesting a problem situation. Thus, a management representative in preparation for a bargaining session might engage in a mock session with a colleague cast in the role of the labor representative. Perhaps, in addition to anticipating opposition arguments and stratagems, the players might also gain greater understanding of labor's position—and of their own as well.

Just as the player comes to appreciate the position and emotions of the character he portrays, the group comes to realize the impact of particular modes of behavior because of the evaluation session that concludes role-playing. This rivalry makes role-playing a useful tool when the group is plagued by an uncooperative member or members. A problem situation can be constructed in which the focus of attention is on a "dogmatic" member or an "authoritarian" moderator. A relatively objective discussion following the role-playing can

ROLE-PLAYING PROCEDURE

help the guilty parties realize the results of their actions. It might also indicate to the group that it should not be too hasty in stereotyping roles and members! (It is quite possible that the "playboy" has reasons for his actions that appear good to him.) It can also indicate where it might benefit individuals to assume new or desirable roles.

Perhaps most important of all, role-playing is a relatively safe way of practicing certain skills and modes of behavior, developing sensitivity, and modifying behavior. One's co-workers and fellow seekers should not punish failure in a situation by dismissal or withdrawal, as so frequently happens in real life, but should give understanding and encouragement.

Procedure is, of course, a key problem — one that we cannot solve easily. The very mention of role-playing will often arouse much resistance from some members of the group. They may anticipate feeling self-conscious or perhaps they have seen the technique poorly handled. It is important to remember that role-playing, like any other procedure, must not be forced on anyone. Introduce it gradually if there is even the slightest resistance. When possible, try using it with other techniques so that role assumption follows naturally. And make certain that the preliminary problems are ones that will not offend the participants.

The following steps are usually followed in the application of role-playing. Of course, they must often be modified to suit the membership of the group and its acquaintance with the method.

Selecting a Problem and Warm-up

We have already indicated that the problem for role-playing should be a real-life situation, full of meaning for both actors and observers. There are different ways of constructing or selecting a meaningful problem situation.

First, the members of a group may all assist in creating the problem situation, structuring the initial stages of the action, suggesting the characters and their patterns of behavior, and giving the characters the instructions they may need for their portrayals. A director or leader then will guide the development or refinement of the plot and characterizations. Second, after a group has had some experience in role-playing, a selected team, directed by a trainer, may plan a role-playing situation and perform before the rest. Third, the director may plan the problem and the characterizations. Fourth, the director, a committee, or the entire group may select a problem from prepared cases available in the many books on human relations, management problems, or the like. However the problem situation is chosen, it should have real meaning to the players and observers.

When there are several problems to choose from, it is wise to let the group decide which one it prefers. Most groups arrive readily at this decision. Many times it stems easily from the question under discussion. Thus, at an interracial summer youth camp, a discussion group was considering the question of racial prejudice. The leader asked if any of the group members knew of or had seen instances of prejudice. Several hands were raised and many role-playing situations were soon available to the group. A problem-census quickly determined a priority order. Similarly, a group of supervisors at a training conference were discussing problems of enforcing company rules. One foreman in the group commented on worker resistance to a change in his plant's safety regulations. Others agreed on the prevalence of this unwillingness to adopt new practices. The group quickly decided that a good way to gain insight into the problem would be to portray two workers talking about new rules during their coffee break.

Structuring the Problem and Characterizations

The role-playing situation should only be structured to the point where the issue or problem becomes clear and the players have a mental picture of the characters they are to represent. The following examples, which we have used in our classes, indicate how little structuring is needed for both plot and characters.

Supervision

A manager in a plant making children's toys felt that two workers were taking too much time during a coffee break. Both were good workers; the manager was new on the job. How should he handle the situation?

A supervisor in a plant dates several women in his division because this allows him to talk about his job. One woman has boasted that she will soon receive a proposal "from the boss." The supervisor hears a report of this. What should he do?

Sales Training

A door-to-door salesperson of cooking ware is making a scheduled demonstration at a prospective purchaser's house. A second salesperson representing a competing product calls at the same time, and the housewife invites her in as well. What does the first salesperson do?

A salesperson in the hat department of a large store has made a courteous but unsuccessful attempt to find a hat that will please a customer. The customer angrily states: "Well, you certainly don't seem to know much about hat styles." What should be the reaction of the salesperson?

Instructor-Student Relations

A young teaching assistant, who is brilliant but conceited, has openly criticized a mature, conscientious student, who has returned to college after military service, for failing to follow instructions on a written assignment. What does the student do?

An able, amiable, elderly instructor conducts a lecture class of about 150 students. A group of four or five students frequently comes in late and usually carries on disturbing conversations during much of the lecture. What does the instructor do?

A very conscientious student has loaned his term-paper notes to a classmate. After the term papers are turned in, the teacher calls the first student into her office and accuses him of plagiarism. How can the student resolve the problem without implicating his classmate?

At times the plot for a role-playing situation is no more than a statement of an issue. For example, the following questions illustrate issues in industrial and personnel situations:

On what basis can management allocate new office space?

How does a new, fast worker on a piecework job adjust to the slower rate of the older workers?

On what basis should a supervisor allocate overtime work?

What does a manager do when he has to enforce a company rule that presents a hardship to certain workers?

What can the members of a work team do about a co-worker who is frequently late, or who takes excessive time off because of home problems?

What member of a work crew gets a new truck?

In a case that developed the plot and characters for this last issue, we can see the extreme of great detail that can be used in constructing a role-playing situation. We present below the general problem and role descriptions given by Maier.[1]

[1] Norman R. F. Maier and others, *Supervisory and Executive Development: A Manual for Role Playing* (New York: Wiley, 1957), pp. 26–32.

General Instruction
(Given to role-players)

You work for the telephone company and one of you will be the foreman while the others will be the repairmen. The job of a repairman is to fix phones that are out of order, and this requires knowledge and diagnostic skills as well as muscular skills. Repairmen must climb telephone poles, work with small tools, and meet customers. The foreman of a crew is usually an ex-repairman and this happens to be true in this case. He has an office at the garage location but spends a good deal of time making the rounds, visiting the places where the men are working. Each repairman works alone and ordinarily does several jobs in a day. The foreman gives such help and instruction as are needed.

The repairmen drive to the various locations in the city to do repair work. Each of them drives a small truck and takes pride in keeping it looking good. The repairmen have a possessive feeling about their trucks and like to keep them in good running order. Naturally, the men like to have new trucks too, because a new truck gives them a feeling of pride.

Here are some facts about the trucks and the men in the crew who reported to Walt Marshall, the supervisor of repairs:

George,	17 years on crew, has	2-year old	Ford
Bill,	11	5	Dodge
John,	10	4	Ford
Charlie,	5	3	Ford
Hank,	3	5	Chevrolet

Most of the men do all of their driving in the city, but John and Charlie cover the jobs in the suburbs.

In acting your part in role-playing, accept the facts as given as well as assuming the attitude supplied in your specific rule. From this point on, let your feelings develop in accordance with the events that transpire in the role-playing process. When facts or events arise that are not covered by the roles, make up things which are consistent with the way it might be in a real-life situation.

Role for Walt Marshall, Foreman: You are the foreman of a crew of repairmen, each of whom drives a small service truck to and from his various jobs. Every so often you get a new truck to exchange for an old one, and you have the problem of deciding to which of your men you should give the new truck. Often there are hard feelings because each man seems to feel he is entitled to the new truck, so you have a tough time being fair. As a matter of fact, it usually turns out that whatever you do decide, most of the men consider it wrong. You now have to face the same issue again because a new truck has just been allocated to you for distribution. The new truck is a Chevrolet.

In order to handle this problem, you have decided to put the decision to the men themselves. You will tell them about the new truck and will put the problem in terms of what would be the most fair way to distribute the truck. Don't take a position yourself because you want to do what the men think is most fair.

Role for George: When a new Chevrolet truck becomes available, you think you should get it because you have most seniority and don't like your present truck. Your own car is a Chevrolet, and you prefer a Chevrolet truck such as you drove before you got the Ford.

Role for Bill: You feel you deserve a new truck and it is certainly your turn. Your present truck is old, and since the more senior man has a fairly new truck, you should get the next one. You have taken excellent care of your present Dodge, and have kept it looking like new. A man deserves to be rewarded if he treats a commany truck like his own.

Role for John: You have to do more driving than most of the other men because you work in the suburbs. You have a fairly old truck and you feel you should have the new one because you do so much driving.

Role for Charlie: The heater in your present truck is inadequate. Since Hank backed into the door of your truck it has never been repaired to fit right. The door lets in too much cold air, and you attribute your frequent colds to this. You want to have a warm truck since you have a good deal of driving to do. As long as it has good tires, brakes, and is comfortable you don't care about its make.

Role for Hank: You have the poorest truck in the crew. It is five years old, and before you got it, it had been in a bad wreck. It has never been good, and you've put up with it for three years. It's about time you got a good truck to drive, and it only seems fair the next one should be yours. You have a good accident record. The only accident you had was when you sprung the door of Charlie's truck when he opened it as you backed out of the garage. You hope the new truck is a Ford since you prefer to drive one.

OK, TIMOTHY— —YOU CAN BE THE NEW CHEVROLET TRUCK......

Choosing the Role-Players

There are several ways of choosing which individuals will play which roles. In general, directors may ask the group for volunteers for specific roles, or they may assign those who volunteer to the roles they feel, on the basis of brief observation, are most appropriate. They may also ask group members to suggest the persons they think would best suit the various parts. A fourth, and perhaps the best, method is for directors to study the members of their groups carefully and determine the one whose interests in and sensitivity to a particular role would enable her or him to enact it with a high degree of perception. In selecting the characters you should observe these rules: (1) Do not force a person to play a role. (2) Do not make the selection at random. (3) Try to select people who will participate seriously in the role-playing. (4) Do not select persons for roles in which they are deeply involved emotionally. (5) Do not carry out the selection as if it were a try-out for parts in a play. (6) Choose the characters as quickly as possible.

Instructing the Players

This step should also be brief. You should say a word or two about the roles to be portrayed, such as:

A man who hates his boss and has been trying to get another job without letting the boss find out about it.

A father who believes that children must be obedient and respectful to their elders at all times.

A workman whose wife nags him, whose children are a disappointment to him, and who feels he is not a success at his job.

You should also stress the fact that the actors are to play the roles as if they were the persons involved. They should try to feel the part, take the role-playing seriously, and make up lines and action consistent with the character description. Depending on the purpose of the role-playing, you will either give these instructions privately to each participant or announce them to the assembled group.

Instructing the Observers

Since only a few persons can participate in any role-playing scene, directors must also prepare the observers for what will follow. Again, they adapt their instructions to the purpose and nature of the training situation. Usually they advise the observers to do the following: (1) Note what actually takes place. (2) Try to determine the feelings of the role-players as they enact their roles. (3) Note actions that aid in resolving the problem situation or blocking its resolution. (4) Note how a specific role-player handles his part. (5) Determine motivations for the actions of the role-players. (6) Try to imagine how the role-players might have acted to resolve the problem more quickly. And (7), note whether the problem situation as enacted was similar to human-relations problems in other areas of life.

Setting the Stage

The staging instructions are usually concise. They may be no longer than the following, which might be used in a parent-child-teacher role-playing situation.

"The scene is the family living room. These two chairs are easy chairs in which the parents are seated as they watch a favorite TV show. This desk is the TV set. The child is in a nearby bedroom studying. The entrance door is between these two chairs. The teacher is knocking at the door as the scene opens."

With such a brief description of the scene, the role-playing begins. Occasionally a scene can be set by asking the role-players to specify physical conditions as they see them.

Carrying Out the Role-Playing

As soon as the director says, "Begin," the improvisation gets underway. Through action and speech the participants show how they think the problem situation would develop. Each player does his or her best to reflect the personality of the protagonist being represented. Role-playing lasts only long enough to point up key issues, develop a climax, and permit all players to participate at least minimally. Scenes are usually short, or at least do not extend beyond the climactic point in the problem or beyond the point at which a particular character has been adequately portrayed. A simple "Stop," or "That's enough," from the director brings the role-playing to a halt.

Groups skilled in role-playing may modify the above "straight" technique. A role-player may use a *soliloquy* (a dramatic monologue) to reveal hidden thoughts and feelings that do not fit into the role situation. By some prearranged signals the individual may stop and start the action, thus gaining time for these inserted comments about his or her private feelings, attitudes toward other role-players, or reactions to the total situation.

In the technique of the *double,* a second person or *auxiliary ego,* takes a position in back of the role-player. This ego exists only for the role-player, and presumably it only talks to and can be heard by the player. The double breaks into the situation at will, and during the dialogue between him and the role-player all action stops, as in the soliloquy. The comments of the double may be instructions to the role-player, reactions to what he has said, or expressions of the player's conscience.

The technique of the *revealer* also uses an auxiliary ego. Instead of talking to the player only, the ego expresses to the audience thoughts it presumes to be in the player's mind. This technique helps show the reason for the behavior of the role-player.

Analyzing the Performance

Because the major purposes of role-playing are to promote an understanding of a human-relations problem and to develop skill in handling such a problem, the analysis stage of the procedure is vital. It is here that the observers and the participants refine their insights into the feelings, motivations, pressures, and attitudes that operate during interpersonal relations. And it is here that follow-up action and procedure are usually determined.

Although the specific questions considered in analyzing a scene must relate directly to the problem portrayed, the following general questions may serve as a guide:

1. What things actually took place during the role-playing? (This descriptive, who-did-what type of analysis aids in answering later questions.)

2. What were the feelings of the role-players as the plot unfolded? (This question focuses on the various players in turn, beginning with the player the audience is most interested in.)

3. In what ways could the players have acted to bring about a quicker or better resolution of the problem?

4. What problem situations in other areas of life are similar to the one portrayed? (The purpose of this is to force the audience and players to begin seeing relationships and applying what they have learned from the analysis discussion.)

5. What insights have been gained that might aid in resolving a problem situation such as that portrayed?

We have found that this sequence, when used with the same group over a period of time with necessary modifications to suit each training session, forces group members to become more and more penetrating in their analyses.

VARIATIONS OF ROLE-PLAYING

At all times, directors of role-playing situations will attempt to fit technique and procedure to what they consider the best advantage of their groups and players. We describe two variations of role-playing that have been used under certain circumstances that might indicate other modifications to you.

Multiple Role-Playing

Developed by Norman Maier and popularized by the National Training Laboratory in Group Development at Bethel, Maine, and in industrial training situations, the technique of multiple role-playing is particularly useful in large-audience situations. Let us say that we have an audience of a hundred or more persons who are concerned with such a problem as the new-truck dilemma described earlier in this chapter. Because there are six characters in the problem situation, the audience divides itself into groups of six. Those left over may act as observers. All persons receive the general instructions. Each group then decides who will play the six roles, and these persons receive the appropriate role descriptions. As soon as players feel that they understand their parts, they indicate to the group that they are ready

Replaying the Scene

Role-playing scenes are frequently replayed. The same individuals may take different roles or may take the same roles but play them differently. Other actors may take the roles. There may be major or minor changes in the plot or characterizations. The scene may be stopped either before or after the previous stopping point. Soliloquies may be added. With practice, a group can develop other interesting and pointed ways of replaying a scene. Its main purpose, of course, is to broaden the basis of understanding, learning, and skill practice.

to begin. The role-playing may start simultaneously at a signal from the director and continue for an appropriate period of time.

There are different ways of handling the analysis of multiple role-playing. Each subgroup might receive a uniform set of questions for analysis and then discuss them, keeping a record that will later be reported to the larger group. Where the problem calls for a decision (for example, "Who is to get the new truck?"), the director may ask each subgroup to report its decision; then, other members of the subgroup may indicate their satisfaction or dissatisfaction with it. The subgroups may write reports and submit them to the director so that he or she can summarize and report them to the larger audience.

The multiple role-playing method involves all members of the audience in actual role-playing situations, provides the opportunity for comparisons between groups, and demonstrates that a single problem may be solved in many different ways.

CAUTIONS IN ROLE-PLAYING

Scripted Role-Playing

Role-playing in the classroom or in training situations need not be completely spontaneous. Scripts are useful when the group is particularly reserved and fearful of the role-playing process. They are especially helpful in focusing on specific characterizations, language usage, and problems that catalyze discussion of a particular approach, issue, or behavior. By confining the role-players to carefully structured verbal and action patterns, the instructor can, to a greater degree, channel the interaction he desires. But he must always remember to select or write a script that is within the capabilities of his players and is related to the intimate interests of the group. And he must be careful to keep his script short enough to fit the attention span of the players and their auditors.

We have employed role-playing techniques profitably as a teaching device in classrooms, for improving communication in large audiences, and for training purposes in industrial concerns, community groups, and religious organizations. And, we have also been parties to role-playing situations that have not been completely successful. From our own experience and that of others, we suggest that you keep in mind the following limitations of the method as a safeguard:

1.   Select a situation closely related to the interests and problems of the group members. If the problem is meaningful to the group, motivation for involvement is likely.

2.   Do not force the technique on a group. Break down resistance to new ways of problem analysis gradually. Prepare the group for role-playing before they try it.

3.   Be sure the problems are practical and clearly defined. In structuring the plot and characterizations, give enough information to reveal clear-cut issues.

4.   Do not use role-playing as a means of entertainment. Present it as a method for analysis and study of real human-relations problems.

5.   Remember that role-playing consumes time. Sessions should rarely be less than an hour, and then only if a group has had a great deal of experience with the method.

6.   Remember that problem analysis is the main step in a role-playing sequence. Don't be seduced by the desires of role-players to perfect a scene. Polished acting is neither necessary nor desirable.

7.   Well-trained directors are essential for successful role-playing. The errors that most untrained directors commit are the failure to keep the role-players from hamming up the scene and a tendency to let the analysis take on characteristics of therapy. Role-playing for therapeutic purposes should be used only by well-trained group therapists.

8.   Success in role-playing also depends on the participants. If they are receptive to the use of the method, are serious, have some dramatic imagination, and are cooperative, role-playing can be an extremely effective tool in training and in improving large-group communication.

IMPLICATIONS FOR THE DISCUSSION GROUP MEMBER

1. Role-playing is a form of "dramatized discussion" in which people act out problems emphasizing human conflicts. Analyzing why a certain role was played in a certain way broadens a person's understanding of the interpersonal relations involved. It helps to sensitize role-players when they can see how they have acted and how others have perceived them to act.

2. In any discussion involving human relations, role-playing enables participants to look briefly at the motivations that cause people to act the way they do.

3. Role-reversal enables the player to see how another person or persons would handle a conflict situation.

4. Unless they are professionally trained, the directors of role-playing situations should avoid using the technique as a therapeutic device.

5. Role-playing is a relatively safe way of practicing skills and behavior, developing sensitivity to human relations, and dramatizing the need for changes in person-to-person situations.

6. Role-playing situations should be real-life situations.

7. The procedures for role-playing situations are described in the text. These should be followed carefully to achieve the greatest benefit from a role-playing session.

8. Modifying role-playing techniques gives variety to this training tool. Variations might include role-reversal, the *soliloquy* (in which the player stops his role-playing and gives expression to his feelings or attitudes), the *double* (who may stop the role-playing at any moment and converse with player whom he represents), and the *revealer* (who also stops the interaction and reveals to the audience thoughts he presumes to be in the player's mind).

9. Perhaps the most important part of a role-playing session is the analysis.

10. Scripts for role-playing are sometimes used. These give the director or teacher an opportunity to channel the interaction.

11. It is particularly important to understand that role-playing is a helpful, serious educational tool—not a vehicle for class entertainment.

A SUMMARY AND LOOK AHEAD

Role-playing is a dramatized discussion in which individuals portray their reactions to a problem situation. It is a technique widely used for training, analyzing and resolving problems, and communication.

To provide further practice in the materials already covered in this text-workbook, the next two chapters present forms and techniques of discussion.

SUGGESTED READINGS

Bonner, Hubert, *Group Dynamics: Principles and Applications* (New York: Ronald Press, 1959), Ch. 12.

Davis, Keith, *Human Relations at Work,* 2nd ed. (New York: McGraw-Hill, 1962), Ch. 9.

Kane, Peter E., "Role Playing for Educational Use," *The Speech Teacher,* Vol. 13 (November 1964), pp. 320–323.

Keltner, John W., *Group Discussion Process* (New York: David McKay, 1957), Ch. 23.

Klein, Alan F., *Role Playing* (New York: Association Press, 1956).

Levy, Ronald B., *Human Relations: A Conceptual Approach* (Scranton, Pa.: International Textbook, 1969), Ch. 8.

Maier, Norman R. F. *et al., Supervisory and Executive Development: A Manual for Role Playing* (New York: Wiley, 1957).

Shaftel, George, and Fannie R. **Shaftel,** *Role Playing the Problem Story* (New York: National Conference of Christians and Jews, 1952).

Sheats, Paul H., "Sociodrama as an Aid to Large Group Communication," *Sociatry,* Vol. 1 (March 1948), pp. 431–435.

EXERCISES

1.   What are some of the roles we play in real life (such as father, daughter, friend, salesperson)? In what ways does real-life role-playing help us to understand others better? How do these real-life roles affect the way we role-play in a discussion situation? Comment on your answers to these questions in a class discussion.

2.   One of the primary uses of role-playing is for training. It has been profitably used in the situations listed below. Select two of these situations; think about how you would set up a role-playing training scene; pick the roles, decide on the instructions you would give the role-players and the observers; and decide on how you would act as the director.

In interviewing

In management training

In vocational guidance

In the military

In marriage counseling

In vocational guidance

In sensitivity training

In supervisory training

In religious education

In improving interpersonal relations

If you wish, you may select a situation that you know better than any of the above. In collaboration with your instructor, arrange for the presentation and analysis of your role-playing session.

3.   How can role-playing be used in secondary schools or college classes in these subjects?

American government

History

Sociology

Education

English

Ethnic studies

Psychology

ROTC courses

Driver education

Journalism

Sensitivity training

Management

Prepare to discuss your suggestions in class. Has this exercise broadened your understanding of the possible uses of role-playing? How?

4. Working with a group of five or six people, plan a multiple role-playing problem situation that deals with some minority group problem. Write out the problem statement, the descriptions of the characters, and needed instructions for carrying out a role-playing sequence. Involve the entire class and conduct an analysis along the lines suggested earlier in this chapter.

5. Select any one of the following problem situations and develop a role-playing scene around it. Modify the problem in any way that you desire. Now use the developed problem situation for classroom role-playing practice.

a. A teacher unjustly accuses a student of cheating in an examination.

b. A teenager comes home two hours after his parents have said he should.

c. A graduate is applying for his first job.

d. A clerk has overcharged you for a purchase at a department store, and you are discussing the matter with him or her.

e. A classmate to whom you lent some lecture notes has told you that he never received the notes from you.

f. You are a supervisor in a manufacturing plant and find it necessary to explain a new management regulation to the workers in your group.

g. You believe that an examination grade should be changed and are talking to your instructor about the matter.

h. You are a union steward and have to present a grievance to management.

i. You are a parent and are having difficulty persuading your two teenage children to take their share of responsibility for housework and yardwork.

j. You have just paid the bill for a dinner at a restaurant and have been shortchanged ten dollars. The waiter claims you gave him a ten-dollar bill, not a twenty.

k. You are a teenager and have been stopped by a policeman for being on the street after the curfew.

l. You are a father who is trying to convince his son not to drop out of school.

m. You are a member of a militant student protest group. You are trying to explain your beliefs to a member of the "establishment."

n. You are a young girl who has been sent home from school for wearing clothes which do not conform to the school's accepted standards. You and your mother (who approves of your clothing) are talking to the principal.

o. You are a policeman on a beat in an inner-city ghetto area. You meet the leader of a street gang. You are talking about the accusation made by business men in the area that the gang is responsible for much of the recent petty theft and vandalism.

p. You are a housewife who enjoys watching several television shows. The set is relatively new but has broken down three times in two weeks. The television repairperson is making a third visit to your home.

q. You are a parent who has just learned that one of your teenage children has been using drugs for some time. The high school principal has called you into his office to talk about the situation.

r. A large corporation conducts an elaborate training program for all employees who will be given supervisory responsibilities. A training staff member is conducting a session for newly appointed production line supervisors. The problem is "how to handle a grievance made by one of the workers." Two persons are involved, the line worker and the supervisor.

s. An instructor in English has a reputation for being "tough" on athletes. A football player in the instructor's class has failed a mid-term exam, making him ineligible for the homecoming game. The scene is in the instructor's office. The athlete is asking to take the exam a second time.

t. A family problem about a teenage daughter's dating has arisen. The daughter wants greater freedom from rules laid down by the father. The mother, daughter, and father are involved in a discussion.

u. A recent college graduate is being interviewed for a job. The interviewer for the company is strictly "establishment." The applicant for the job is somewhat anti-establishment in attitudes, dress, and experience.

v. A college student likes rock music, is a member of a student combo that plays occasionally in dance halls in the college community area, and has a large collection of rock records. He lives in a small apartment building and frequently plays his records with the volume so high that other tenants complain. The apartment manager is having a talk with the student.

THE PANEL-FORUM

We described private discussions in Chapter 4 as more or less complete within themselves. The participants are their own auditors; they frequently determine their own goals and procedures; and the interaction is confined to the group itself. But discussion is not only useful in private and informal situations, it is also a valuable tool in more public and formal instances. In this chapter, we consider some of the forms and techniques associated with public discussions.

As early as 1929, Harry A. Overstreet[1] experimented with the panel-forum, which is essentially a small round-table (private) discussion staged for a predetermined period of time before an audience. It is followed by audience participation in the form of questions or comments. The function of the panel is to provide expert analysis of a problem—besides raising significant issues and presenting pertinent facts and opinions—prior to the forum period, so that the listeners' understanding will be increased and their thinking will be focused on the problem. The forum period after the panel discussion provides the audience an opportunity to call attention to points overlooked by the panelists, raise questions about matters already considered, present needed facts, suggest applications, and even express individual feelings.

As Overstreet and thousands of others have discovered since 1929, the panel-forum is an extremely versatile and yet problematic form of discussion. Its versatility is indicated by its widespread use and abuse on radio, television, and public platforms. It has been used—not always successfully—in the classroom, at conventions, as well as a medium for information-

gathering, problem-analysis, value-determining, and even entertainment. When a group is at the initial stages of its analysis, it is a valuable tool in exploring a problem. It can focus one or more viewpoints on that problem to help form and crystallize the opinions of audience members. It is an effective tool for learning and it frequently serves to demonstrate informal, face-to-face discussion at its best. The essence of a panel is its give-and-take nature, but sometimes it keeps the panel from developing an orderly, logic-tight line of thought. Symposiums, debates, or public speeches are better suited to the presentation of a case or cases. Nevertheless, few methods of communication do more to stimulate the mind and furnish a goal to emulate than a well-moderated panel.

We have referred to the panel as problem-laden as well as versatile. The problems stem from the fact that panelists must be top-notch stimulators. If they are not, the performance will be less than top-notch. It simply is not enough to select a topic of inherent audience interest. Nor

[1] Morse A. Cartwright, "Panel," *Journal of Adult Education*, Vol. 5 (January 1933), pp. 37–42.

is it enough to select a moderator who knows how to start the panel off right and to stop its discussion before inertia takes over. It is vital that the panelists be authorities, or at least to have considerable background in the topic area. Second, the panelists—and this is perhaps of greater importance—must have the ability to use their knowledge and background in such a way as to transmit the stimulation they feel to the audience. Once a panel is assembled, the moderator can do relatively little about providing information on the topic. However, she or he can do something about the way the panelists use the information at their disposal. The moderator can, and usually should, arrange a warm-up period before the scheduled

performance. By "warm-up" we do not mean rehearsing a script; spontaneity, of course, is the lifeblood of a panel discussion. We do mean that an agenda may be set up or, if time and inclination permit, a discussion outline may be prepared. The viewpoints of the panelists can be determined and made known to all, and the issues may be tentatively explored. But the warm-up should stop short of actually discussing the issues. Too frequently, panelists make their best contributions in the rehearsal, or else they cannot remember if they have already dealt with an important issue.

A second caution: Even if we assume that the panelists are well selected, carefully prepared, and warmed up, that the moderator is competent, and that the topic is carefully chosen and succinctly phrased, we cannot conclude that success will necessarily follow. We must still overcome the bugaboo of poor physical arrangements. Too often the panelists must sit side-by-side behind a straight table quite distant from the audience. And too often it harbors but one centrally placed microphone. Such conditions result in poor amplification and a loss of the visual and vocal intimacy so necessary for good audience reaction.

An inflexible seating arrangement and inadequate amplification are also barriers to good panel interaction. The straight-line effect tends to create what we call *dyadic* islands—splinter discussion groups of two—within the panel. The moderator thus becomes a relay station for exchanges between panelists on his or her right and left. We suggest, therefore, that before every panel-forum begins, the moderator carefully check the acoustics and the size of the meeting room, the possible seating arrangements for his panel, and the operating efficiency of available amplifying systems.

An ideal physical setup would be one in which the panelists maintain maximum face-to-face contact with each other, while

WELL, WE'VE FORMED A SEMICIRCLE — SO LET'S BEGIN.........

THE SYMPOSIUM-FORUM

the audience can see and hear the resulting interaction to the largest degree possible. To be specific, if a thirty- or forty-minute panel-forum with five or six panelists is to take place in a classroom, the chairperson should arrange the chairs in as deep a semicircle as visibility to the audience permits. The moderator may occupy a seat near the middle of the group, or—if the panelists are articulate and knowledgeable and she or he does not need to exert ostensible control over the situation—the position may be on one of the extreme wings. But the moderator should still be able to see all the panelists as well as the audience. Panel groups with six to nine members should also sit in a semicircle. A group of three to five panelists might occupy seats on three sides of a *small* rectangular table. When the meeting room contains movable chairs or is arranged so that the audience is at a level above the panel group, eight or even fifteen panelists can sit in a circle surrounded by the audience—a discussion in the round, as it were—and the result can be as stimulating as the intellectual and emotional make-up of the panel group permits.

A second type of staged discussion is the symposium-forum, in which two or more speakers talk from ten to twenty minutes. In the process, they develop individual approaches or solutions to a problem, or present different aspects of a policy, process, or program. The speeches are followed by questions or comments from the audience, as in the panel-forum. The speeches may be persuasive, argumentative, informative, or evocative. Each speech proceeds without interruption. The chairperson of the symposium introduces the topic, suggests something of its importance, sometimes indicates the general approaches the speakers will take, introduces each speaker, and moderates the forum session. The symposium-forum serves as an excellent device for informing an audience and crystallizing opinion. And, it generally provides the listeners with the information needed to arrive at decisions, policies, value judgments, or understanding.

Since careful listening is the major requirement for symposium interaction (unless the symposium members are to discuss the topic after the delivery of the speeches), all members of the performing group can sit in a straight line behind a table or on adjoining chairs, with the chairperson in the middle or to one side of the speakers. Or, if the symposium is to present two conflicting points of view, the seating arrangement can separate the speakers on the platform in order to indicate difference in opinion—or in order to preserve peace.

We suggest three cautions in the use of the symposium-forum. First, if you are the moderator, be sure to prepare your speakers or see that they are prepared. They should know the rules of procedure, the speaking sequence, and the way in which the forum will be conducted. Further, they should be aware of the ideas and background of the other performers. Like panelists, they might benefit from a brief warm-up. Second, the chairperson, or whoever is responsible for preparing the agenda, should not omit or ignore vital phases of the problem as speakers are selected or delegated. It is bad enough to face up to an inadvertent misinterpretation or omission. To distort or omit an important viewpoint deliberately is to invite disaster. And, third, the chairperson in all forum situations must plan the questioning period that follows the prepared speeches very carefully, unless he or she is willing to risk boredom or bedlam.

THE LECTURE-FORUM

Often, more extensive treatment is desired. In this case, the thoughtful program chairperson will invite a single speaker to explore a topic, present information, crystallize opinion, argue for a certain viewpoint, and answer questions.

A challenging speaker can stimulate a group and generate more reactions in the ensuing forum than one might imagine. But the single-speaker situation is capable of backfiring—even more so than the panel and the symposium-forum. If the speaker is unable to communicate his message,[2] or—worse still—if the message is unworthy of delivery, the consequence can be a painful silence or an emotional explosion taxing the resources of even experienced moderators. As in all types of forums, someone or some group within the sponsoring organization must be responsible for selecting and priming the speaker for her or his audience. And, again, as in all forum types, no one should assume that responsibility casually.

[2] In this situation, the skilled chairperson will often resort to an interview, which we consider later in this chapter.

THE DIALOGUE

As the name implies, the dialogue is a form of public discussion featuring two persons. Although scarcely considered a basic type of discussion today, it is an ancient form of public discourse. Its popularity in America dates back to colonial times. On commencement platforms, for example, it demonstrated academic accomplishments. In literary-society halls, it substituted for prohibited theatricals. Today the dialogue survives primarily on radio and television—media that still exploit ancient facets of education and entertainment. Typical topics discussed are best sellers, outstanding plays, foreign policy, taxation and government spending, and the merits of professional sports. When the participants are equally well informed and verbally or visually stimulating and when the moderator introduces the subject well, makes transitions smoothly, and concludes before subject and audience are exhausted, the chances are high that the audience will enjoy and learn from the dialogue. Usually the dialogue is carefully plotted but not rehearsed. Speeches, of course, are outlawed, while spontaneity and wit are cultivated. Although the dialogue is well adapted for large audiences, it infrequently appears in that form. When it does, it generally features well-known personalities or authorities who wittily and/or learnedly explore aspects of a vital problem, a contentious issue, or a pressing course of action. After many brief dialogues, forums usually follow. Thus, the audience has another chance to tune in on the knowledge and experience of the performers.

On occasion, a dialogue may take place between two speakers of a symposium following all of the speeches. Or, the chairman and a single speaker in a lecture-forum, or even two members of a panel, may engage in dialogue when they need to explore a particularly knotty problem in the discussion.

Stimulating dialogues can be dynamic, but the ordinary variety can be horribly dull. Success will more likely result when the participants know the subject well, are articulate, and are able to and willing to capitalize on the dramatic elements of the situation.

THE INTERVIEW

The interview differs from the dialogue chiefly in its manner of procedure. In the dialogue, both participants share responsibility for presenting content material. In the interview, the answers are the responsibility of the guest or celebrity; the interviewer (preferably quick-witted and fluent) is responsible for the questions. When the celebrity is a newsworthy source of information or opinion (or possesses strong video attraction) and when the interviewer is reasonably adept, an enjoyable short learning or entertainment period is possible. Indeed, a good interview can, in the space of thirty minutes or even less, produce more revealing information than most speakers and panels can in an hour. In addition, an air of suspense is often engendered by audience anticipation of clashes or unintentional slips.

The interview is sometimes impromptu in nature. But usually the interview is planned, and the line of questioning is blocked out in advance. Many interviewers have a stock of basic questions on hand, although they must always be prepared to improvise. Many interviewees know the specific questions they will be asked—especially on political campaign shows. But usually only a basic understanding of the line of questioning is provided, for this aids spontaneity and motivates audience response.

THE FILM-FORUM

In all public forms of discussion, the program planners must try to present information on the topic in the best way possible before the forum period begins. Sometimes the film-forum—showing a film followed by a forum—is decided on. But this decision presumes that necessary precautions in film selection, manner of audience introduction, and conduct of the forum are taken.

Film-Forum Adaptations

How can a film be used in combination with a forum? Let us consider two examples. Suppose that the purpose of your meeting is to find ways to improve job safety habits, and your audience consists solely of newly employed workers. Since you are responsible for orientating these workers, you select a twenty-minute film specifically designed to introduce new workers to approved safety methods in your plant. The film presents a complete story of what happens when a worker fails to follow safety regulations. It dramatizes unfortunate physical and economic consequences. Then, it demonstrates that proper

and safe procedures take no more and usually less time on the part of the worker. It emphasizes the benefits—economic and physical—from correct work habits. You can play the film in slow motion to repeat certain vital procedures, or replay it entirely, or in part, for added emphasis. Afterwards, the audience can go to the shop to witness an actual demonstration of the practice advocated. If the film is well-written, well-directed, and well-acted and produced, you should have a most useful tool at your command.

Consider another example: Suppose you are a member of a committee planning to use a film in a class concerned with teenage dating problems. Your purpose in using a film is to stimulate discussion, not to gain acceptance of a particular viewpoint. You might select a twenty-five-minute film that tells a more or less complete story, but you would do so only if you had a great deal of time. By stopping the film at various points to check group reactions, and then using the film's solution as the springboard for continued group discussion and evaluation, you could promote considerable individual and group thinking. But usually a film longer than ten or fifteen minutes will not allow sufficient discussion time in a single class period. Consequently, you would probably select a shorter film that vividly presents prime issues or basic problems. Then, in introducing the film, you would suggest the purpose of the meeting and the ways in which the film is to be used. You might even point out specific facets of the problem for the audience to consider as it watches—thus creating an agenda for the ensuing forum. You might select groups to serve as question-and-answer or critique panels. The possibilities of adaptation are almost limitless.

Cautions in Using Film-Forums

There are four major cautions to consider. The first has to do with selecting the film. Not only should the film be technically perfect (or nearly so) in script, direction, and action, it should also be adaptable to a discussion situation.[3] You should keep in mind certain criteria: (1) Does it clearly state a human problem bearing directly on the discussion topic? (2) Does the film provide evidence and background on the problem presented? (3) Does the film give suggestions on how to handle the problem? (4) Is the content of the film reasonably fair and accurate? (5) Is the film timely? (6) Is it short enough to allow sufficient time for discussion? If all these questions can be answered in the affirmative, so much the better. If you must answer "No" to three or more, you would do well to select another film.

[3] Most university audio-visual departments publish film catalogues and are generous with their previewing facilities. We suggest that you read the descriptions in the catalogues and preview every film before showing it. Helpful manuals written specifically for the film-forum user frequently accompany the films.

Prepare adequately for showing the film. Preview it so you will know what it's about. Be certain the projection facilities are in order. You will usually have a projectionist to handle this task, but you must check to see that everything is in order—that the projector works, electric outlets are available, the film is wound for immediate showing, a screen is on hand, and the room is suitable for film-showing. Otherwise, you may find yourself in the position of having to give a talk on the topic or improvise in some other way.

Just prior to the actual showing of the film, you will need to introduce the film, perhaps by describing the film or its high-lights, suggesting some of the problems it raises, and noting parts that should be observed closely.

After the film is over, you will need to observe all the rules that contribute to effective forum discussions. Try to keep the discussion focused on the *issues* raised by the film, not the film's inadequacies or adequacies.

THE PHOTO-SITUATION

Related in method and application to the film-forum is a still-picture discussion stimulus that we call the photo-situation. As the name implies, a still picture is the focal point. In setting up the photo-situation, the initiator of the discussion shows or projects to the audience a single picture which freezes—at the height of its intensity or, conversely, at its most subtle moment—some situation involving a problem pertinent to the viewers. He or she then asks the viewers to examine what is happening, has happened, or might happen, what clues support each hypothesis, possible causes for the difficulties, and how such situations might be prevented or ameliorated.

Photo-situation discussions place a premium on keen and undistorted perception and reporting ability. In preparing a class for such discussions, we often use a modification of the rumor-clinic technique first described by Allport and Postman.[4]

In this technique, we use a slide based on a classic drawing that shows a subway or elevated-car incident. In it, among other interesting and easy-to-confuse happenings, a white workman with a straight-edged razor confronts a neatly attired black. First, however, we ask all but five or six class members to leave the room. Then we show the slide and request that one viewer tell a member outside the room all the pertinent information he or she can recall. The person who has been told what the slide contains in turn relates what she or he can remember to the next nonviewer, who relates to the next, and so forth. When the cycle is complete, we show the slide to everybody—usually to the mixed amusement and consternation of the individuals who have created or added to the "rumor." Then we stress the importance of seeing and reporting without prejudice or stereotypes, as well as the necessity of developing increased perceptivity, more accurate reporting, and ways these desirable skills can be attained.

Following this introduction, we often pass out a picture like that on page 167 and ask our students to jot down answers to questions such as those accompanying the photo.

Although photo-situations often require little equipment and, in our experience, can assist in developing keen evaluative, perceptive, and reporting skills, the method is not without its problems. First, it is difficult to obtain good and stimulating pictures. Unless one zealously scans newspapers and periodicals, has easy access to a good photographer, or has a picture-taking budget, he might find the stock of pictures very inadequate. Second, the photo-situation often elicits a strong emotional response, one that even careful preparation cannot avoid. The result can be emotional upset rather than immediate learning. But greater sensitivity to the needs and wants of the group, as well as excellent practice in the analysis of nonverbal communication, can result.

[4] Gordon W. Allport and Leo F. Postman, "The Basic Psychology of Rumor," in Theodore M. Newcomb and Eugene L. Hartley, eds., *Readings in Social Psychology* (New York: Holt, Rinehart and Winston, 1947), pp. 547–558.

A SUMMARY AND LOOK AHEAD

The public discussion is one medium through which citizens in a democracy can gain information on problems affecting their welfare. The most important types of public discussion are the panel-forum, symposium-forum, lecture-forum, public interview, and film-forum. Each is a valuable tool in increasing an audience's understanding of issues that have widespread ramifications or of more specialized subjects.

The next chapter deals with special discussion techniques that can be used in both public and private discussions.

SUGGESTED READINGS

Brilhart, John K., *Effective Group Discussion,* 2nd ed. (Dubuque, Iowa: Wm. C. Brown, 1974), Ch. 7.

Cortright, Rupert L., and George L. **Hinds,** *Creative Discussion* (New York: Macmillan, 1959), Ch. 2.

Howell, William S., and Donald K. **Smith,** *Discussion* (New York: Macmillan, 1956), Ch. 11.

Scheidel, Thomas M., *Speech Communication and Human Interaction* (Glenview, Ill.: Scott, Foresman, 1972), Ch. 10.

Zelko, Harold P., *Successful Conference and Discussion Techniques* (New York: McGraw-Hill, 1957), Chs. 4, 9.

EXERCISES

1. On the basis of your present understanding, what are the essential differences between private and public forms of discussion? What similarities do they have, if any? Submit a brief written statement of your conclusions to your instructor.

2. From your experience with different discussion forms and techniques, what do you consider to be the five greatest barriers to effective private discussion? To effective panel-forums? Submit a written list of these barriers to your instructor.

3. Assume that you have been asked to serve as chairperson (or moderator) of a panel-forum. Make a list of things you would do to prepare for the discussion. At the next panel-forum you attend, use this list as a guideline to see if the chairman has followed most of the steps that you thought important.

4. In a previous chapter, we indicated that much research has been conducted on different leadership climates in discussion: democratic, autocratic, and laissez-faire. Which ones of these climates seem especially applicable to the panel-forum, the symposium-forum, or the lecture-forum? Why?

5. You have been asked to serve as moderator for three public discussions on the subject, "How we can best serve the youth in our community." One of the meetings will be a panel-forum, one a symposium, and one a lecture-forum. Your community is quite small and the city council has agreed to take some positive action based on discussion results. You have complete responsibility for selecting all the participants, helping with any preparation needed, and chairing the sessions. Write out what you would do. In what sequence would the forums be held? What recommendations would you make to the panel members, to the symposium speakers, and to the speaker at the lecture-forum? Be prepared to comment on your conclusions in a general class discussion.

6. A number of television programs are labeled as discussions. Pick two or three that might be described as "small group" discussions. Why are they successful, if they are? How do they differ from "live" discussions, such as those held in your class? What are the goals of these TV shows? Study and think about these television programs as a guide for changes you might make in your discussion behavior.

7. Preparation and presentation of a panel-forum:

Part A, Selecting the Topic: On the basis of what you have learned from class discussion about panel-forums, you now have a good picture how to prepare for and present one. An important factor in the success of a panel-forum is the topic selected. When it is delimited and can be handled in the time allotted, is of interest to the group, is one on which the group could possibly act, and is one on which information is available, then success is more nearly assured. It is not wise to select a topic just because it is interesting to one or a few vocal group members. A discussion topic should reflect the interests, needs, and wishes of all members of a group.

Your instructor will assist you in forming subgroups of five to seven. Each group will select a topic suitable for presentation in a fifty-minute panel-forum. In Chapter 6, you will find a large number of subject areas and many specific topics. After selecting one of these, or some other one that your group is interested in, indicate the problem-statement and give your reasons for selecting this particular topic.

Part B, Outlining and Studying the Topic: Success in discussion partly depends on how carefully the topic is delimited and outlined. Each member of a discussion group should have a general outline of the overall topic and specific information on the phase of the topic for which he is responsible.

After you have selected a topic for your panel-forum, answer the following questions:

a. How would you define any terms in the problem-statement that might not be understood?

b. What is the significance of the topic for the class members or other audience?

c. Why should something be done about the problem with which the topic deals?

d. What are the probable causes of the problem?

e. What criteria must be used in judging the effectiveness of possible solutions?

f. What are the possible solutions to the problem?

g. What facts or evidence support the conclusion that you advocate?

h. What sources of material have you drawn on in answering the above questions?

i. After having studied the problem and answered the above questions, what changes in the problem-statement could be made?

j. Indicate the persons who have responsibility for the various phases of the topic.

Part C, Presentation and Evaluation: In presenting the panel-forum that you have planned, you may wish to review some of the suggestions given in preceding chapters on participation, leadership, and the problem-solving sequence. The following suggestions are also valuable:

a. Remember that a panel-forum is a staged discussion. Try to capture the spontaneous intimacy of lively, informal discussion while speaking loudly enough so that the audience can hear.

b. Look alert! Listen carefully! Follow the discussion progress. If you are interested in the discussion, your audience will be too.

c. Make the discussion a happy affair. Discussion does not need to be dull.

d. Let the audience get acquainted with you. Use large name tags or placecards to identify each panelist. Be sure the audience can see every panel member.

You should evaluate your panel-forum presentation so that your next one will be better. You may use either or both of the analysis forms given in this chapter, or some of those in other chapters. Study the results of the evaluations yourself and, if possible, report to the group at your next meeting.

8. What basic discussion type do you think is best suited for each of the situations described below? Indicate the reasons for your selection.

a. A small group of research scientists need to discover why a missile failed on its first flight test.

b. Twenty-five members of the League of Women Voters are holding a regular meeting, and the topic is: "What is the best form of government for our city?"

c. A public meeting is to take place in a city of 25,000 on the topic of industrial expansion.

d. Only fifty to sixty people, out of a membership of about 200 persons, regularly attend the meetings of a PTA group. The topic for the next meeting deals with the location of a new grade-school building. The topic has a great deal of public interest.

e. A large corporation is holding its annual shareholders meeting.

f. A small luncheon club has invited a guest speaker.

g. A Congressional investigating committee is holding a hearing in a large industrial center.

h. A student protest group is meeting with a group of school administrators to resolve an important issue.

i. A subgroup in a discussion class is planning to present a panel-forum in the classroom.

j. A large professional organization is having its annual convention, and about 800 persons are expected to attend. The convention will last for two days, with four half-day sessions. The planners want to ensure the maximum amount of delegate participation, as well as opportunities to hear keynote speakers.

9. A photo-situation:

a. What do you think is taking place?

b. What cues do you detect to support your hypothesis?

c. What do you think will happen? Why?

d. How might this situation have been avoided? How could it be alleviated?

Photo courtesy of Hap Stewart/Jeroboam Inc.

EVALUATION OF A GROUP MEETING

Check one column on the right for each item on the left.

	Superior	Good	Average	Passable	Poor
Meeting Characteristics					
1. Did the meeting show careful planning?					
2. Were materials and equipment ready?					
3. Were seating arrangements adequate?					
4. Had consideration been given to lighting and ventilation?					
5. Was timing considered? Did the meeting start and stop on time?					
6. Was the goal or problem clearly defined at the outset?					
7. Was the atmosphere congenial and friendly?					
8. Was the audience interested in the topic? Was the topic appropriate?					
9. Was needed information presented? Were facts properly documented?					
10. Were needed opinions presented?					
11. Were facts and opinions presented clearly?					
12. Did all (panelists) have a chance to participate in the discussion?					
13. Was the discussion logical and orderly? Hasty decisions avoided?					

	Superior	Good	Average	Passable	Poor
Meeting Characteristics					
14. Was the goal kept clearly in mind throughout?					
15. Were there frequent and adequate summaries?					
16. Was the discussion lively throughout?					
17. Was the meeting generally effective?					

POST-MEETING REACTION FORM

Give your reactions to the questions listed here. Your evaluation will lead to improvement of future discussions. Please check *directly above the appropriate expression* in each question. Use the reverse side of this form for any comments you may wish to make about the eight items below, such as your reactions to the contributions of particular members.

1. What is your overall rating of this discussion?

Very satisfactory	Satisfactory	Average	Unimpressive	Very unsatisfactory

2. Did you feel the goals of the meeting were clear to everyone?

Very clear	Reasonably clear	Clear	Unclear	Muddled

3. What progress do you think the group made toward its goal?

Achieved goal	Much progress	Some progress	Very little progress	No progress

4. How effective was the planning for this session?

Every detail planned for (outstanding)	Most details considered (superior)	Planning seemed adequate (average)	Some details not considered (poor)	Very poor planning (unsatisfactory)

5. Did the members of the group seem to contribute to the extent of their ability?

Outstanding participation by all	Superior participation by most	Adequate participation	Poor participation by some	Ineffective participation by most

6. How effective was the leadership of this meeting?

Outstanding	Superior	Average	Poor	Very poor

7. Did the chairperson effectively guide the session?

Outstanding throughout	Effective most of the time	Adequate	Effective occasionally	Unsatisfactory: lost control of the group

8. Did the atmosphere contribute to effective discussion?

Outstanding	Superior	Average	Poor	Very poor

POST-MEETING REACTION FORM

Give your reactions to the questions listed here. Your evaluation will lead to improvement of future discussions. Please check *directly above the appropriate expression* in each question. Use the reverse side of this form for any comments you may wish to make about the eight items below, such as your reactions to the contributions of particular members.

1. What is your overall rating of this discussion?

Very satisfactory	Satisfactory	Average	Unimpressive	Very unsatisfactory

2. Did you feel the goals of the meeting were clear to everyone?

Very clear	Reasonably clear	Clear	Unclear	Muddled

3. What progress do you think the group made toward its goal?

Achieved goal	Much progress	Some progress	Very little progress	No progress

4. How effective was the planning for this session?

Every detail planned for (outstanding)	Most details considered (superior)	Planning seemed adequate (average)	Some details not considered (poor)	Very poor planning (unsatisfactory)

5. Did the members of the group seem to contribute to the extent of their ability?

Outstanding participation by all	Superior participation by most	Adequate participation	Poor participation by some	Ineffective participation by most

6. How effective was the leadership of this meeting?

Outstanding	Superior	Average	Poor	Very poor

7. Did the chairperson effectively guide the session?

Outstanding throughout	Effective most of the time	Adequate	Effective occasionally	Unsatisfactory: lost control of the group

8. Did the atmosphere contribute to effective discussion?

Outstanding	Superior	Average	Poor	Very poor

TECHNIQUES FOR
INCREASING PARTICIPATION

It would be difficult to select a single criterion, or even three or four criteria, that would always ensure the success of any discussion. We can be certain, however, that maximum achievement will more nearly be realized if the group members are interested in the topic, participate actively in its consideration, and are committed to decisions made. In other words, the participants must be completely involved in a discussion in order to make it a success.

In this chapter, we present a number of special techniques, some commonly employed and others less widely used, that increase discussion involvement. For convenience, we divide them into three categories: (1) those that increase participation, (2) those that improve content presentation, and (3) those that increase understanding of, and skill in, communication.

These techniques cut across the private–public classification of discussion forms. Although some techniques are better suited to private or public types of discussion, all can be adapted for use in either. They may be used in combination in both large- and small-group discussion situations. We discuss combinations at the end of the chapter.

Most people participate actively and readily in small private discussions but hesitate to do so in large public ones. When small group conditions can be simulated in a large audience, and when individual contributions can be anonymous, participation is frequently increased.

The Discussion Cluster

In large groups, the discussion cluster is a sure-fire method of capturing the sense of personal involvement and active participation found in small face-to-face groups. It is also known as the buzz group or Phillips 66. (The last name comes from the fact that Phillips,[1] one of the early users of the method, often followed the practice of dividing audiences into groups of six, each group having six minutes in which to conduct its assigned business.)

The procedure for a discussion cluster or buzz session is followed whether the clusters are held immediately before a speech, panel, or symposium; during a panel discussion when some quick reaction from the audience is wanted; or after a speech or panel when audience

[1] J. Donald Phillips, "Report on Discussion 66," *Adult Education Journal*, Vol. 7 (October 1948), pp. 181–182.

participation is desired. The main steps of the procedure follow:

1. The general chairperson of the meeting divides the audience into small groups of five to eight persons by having the groups arrange themselves in circles (if the chairs are movable and if space permits), or by having the persons in every other row turn and face the people seated immediately behind them. The diagram below shows the arrangement of the clusters in a room with fixed chairs.

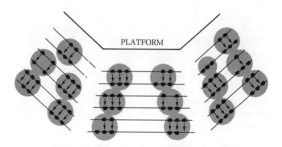

2. The members of each group introduce themselves if they are not already known to one another.

3. Each group selects a group leader and a recording secretary. To avoid having the most loquacious person as moderator, the group might make both selections by chance, choosing the persons whose last names start with letters closest to the beginning and end of the alphabet; or the general chairperson might appoint persons to these tasks.

4. The general chairperson then gives each group a single, specific question to consider or a task to perform. This task may be to suggest answers to a question, problems to be considered, objections to a proposition, nominations, or the like. Subgroups may perform the same or different tasks. The task should call for simple answers, such as the listing of points, rather than for reactions to some involved concept or idea.

5. The next step may proceed in one of two ways: (a) The members of each subgroup write down their answers or reactions to the task assigned, and each individual reads his or hers prior to discussion within the subgroup. (b) There is no writing of reactions, and discussion on the task assigned begins at once.

6. The small groups have from six to fifteen minutes to consider the assigned question. The moderator of each group should try to get every member to participate. The recorder keeps a record of the discussion.

7. When a minute or two remains of the allotted time, the recorder has the chance to check on the report he she is to make. What that person has written is compared with the group's recollection of its conclusions.

8. The recorder (or the moderator) of the subgroup then gives a brief report to the entire assembly. These reports may be oral, written, or shown on a blackboard.

9. Writing the content of the reports on a blackboard will often reveal a lot of duplication. When this occurs, the general chairperson should suggest that only items differing significantly from those already submitted will be presented. To be sure that later groups still have something to say, it is sometimes preferable to have each subgroup report only one item at a time, before calling for the second item on any subgroup's list.

10. If adequate blackboard space is available, it is desirable to group all suggestions from the reports under general headings so that the ensuing general discussion will be more efficient.

The value of the discussion cluster lies chiefly in its flexibility. It is useful at the beginning of a meeting for determining what a group wants to discuss (here it is comparable to a problem-census) and at the end of a meeting to determine what action a group desires to take. It can be used once or several times during a given meeting, in conjunction with any public-discussion form or with any topic under consideration. The more specific values of the method are these:

1. It encourages participation from everyone no matter what the audience size is.

2. It elicits immediate audience reaction to a point brought out by a speaker or panel group.

3. It focuses attention on a specific, limited aspect of a topic under discussion.

4. It creates a small group discussion climate in a large audience.

5. It provides variety to the procedures that usually characterize large meetings.

As might be deduced, "buzzing" rapidly involves each individual in the group's activities. The ice is broken in a matter of moments. Further, muscles tired from being in one position get temporary relief, especially when furniture must be moved or clusters arranged. This brief emotional, physical, and intellectual respite can result in good thinking, good speaking, and worthwhile contributions. *But this method is not and should not be considered a substitute for a well-planned and carefully prepared small group discussion.* To repeat, it is most useful in situations calling for quick reactions to a relatively simple assignment. It is much better at raising problems than in solving them, more useful in indicating symptoms than in discovering underlying causes. The reasons are that (a) sufficient time for considering weighty matters simply is not available; (b) many meeting places do not have adequate acoustics, sufficient space, and movable chairs; and (c) speaking in competition with a hundred other persons while seated in an uncomfortable position can be most disconcerting.

We have discovered that a brief set of instructions given to each subgroup leader makes the cluster technique more effective. The following list may be modified to suit your purposes.

Your Responsibilities in Chairing a Discussion Cluster

1. Make sure that each member of your group is introduced to every other member. Try to create an atmosphere in which it will be easy for everyone to participate.

2. Be sure that you and your group members understand the assigned task. Ask the general chairperson to repeat the question if it is unclear.

3. Give each group member a moment to write the assignment or to think about it, if the general chairperson has not requested written reactions.

4. Give each person an opportunity to read or state her or his reaction or answer.

5. See that everyone has an opportunity to express an opinion before the group reaches a conclusion. If you are sure it will not embarrass them, call on those who do not join in the discussion.

6. Before the recorder must submit his report, check what he or she has written against what the group members have said.

Listening Teams

Experts in the field of listening tell us that most people do not listen as well as they could, and that we can train ourselves to be better listeners. We can improve our listening skills through the use of a number of simple techniques. Some of these are: (1) concentrating on what is being said, (2) noting main ideas and their relationships, (3) noting the relationship of supporting materials to the idea they elaborate, (4) determining the speaker's frame of reference, (5) relating what is said to what you know about the subject, and (6) determining what you want to listen for before the speaker begins. All of these suggestions call for active involvement in the speaking–listening exchange. And this is just what we have said is essential for effective discussion. Besides taking an active part by speaking, the discussant must be active in his listening.

Too frequently, people do not listen well because no one has asked them to do so. To make sure everyone in a large group, as well as sometimes in small groups, is actively listening, the listening team is a useful technique. It works in the following fashion. Prior to a lecture, panel, or symposium, the audience is divided into three or four listening sections, each with a specific listening task. For example, you are at a symposium-forum considering the problem of vandalism in community school buildings. The symposium speakers reflect county and statewide viewpoints. It is anticipated that the speakers are only somewhat familiar with local conditions—although they have been briefed in ad-

vance—and will use illustrations mainly "from other communities." The listening teams, therefore, have been asked to try to relate the broader picture presented by the speakers to the local situation. One section listens in terms of causes; a second section concentrates on financial implications; a third searches for solutions that might be applicable in the local situation.

The listening-team procedure, when used in connection with a single speech or when there is more time for audience participation, aids understanding. One section may be asked to listen for terms or concepts that need further clarification, another to think of possible applications of a speaker's points, and a third to think of illustrations of his or her comments. After the presentation, the chairperson calls on several persons from each listening team to report their questions, which the speaker then answers. There is a psychological value in this technique, apart from the information given by the speaker in response to the questions. It lies in the fact that the audience feels it has been given some "control"[2] over the content of the speaker's remarks.

[2] See the remarks in Chapter 2 on the concepts of "affection, inclusion, and control."

The method can backfire, however. The audience may not be sufficiently aroused to think of questions in the categories suggested; the listening instructions may not have been clear; the speech or symposium presentation may not warrant critical analysis. Under ideal conditions—stimulating speakers and a competent chairperson—this technique can do much to stimulate audience participation.

Audience Panels

With this technique, a small number of audience members are selected to "talk for" the larger audience that they represent. These panels may enliven and improve large group discussion situations in numerous ways. In an interview, panel members representing the various interest groups in the audience—such as parents, students, government workers, or union members—are selected and asked to come to the platform. This audience panel is then responsible for interviewing the lecturer, questioning symposium speakers, or commenting on the points made by members of the main panel. The audience panel may participate prior to a speech in a lecture-forum or before the forum period begins. The audience panel may also be permitted to ask questions during

the presentation. However, their questions should be ones that they think members of the large audience would like to have answered.

Multiple-Choice Case Problems

This method was developed and popularized by Utterback of Ohio State University.[3] This section describes a modification of the method.

A briefly stated case problem is typed on a sheet of paper, together with five possible solutions or actions that might be taken. One of these actions is the best, according to experts in the field, but the participants aren't told which one is. A copy of the "case problem and solutions" is given to each student previously assigned to a small discussion group of six or seven members. Each participant is then asked to read the case problem and decide which of the five possible actions suggested she or he considers to be the best. A pre-discussion ballot is used for recording votes, which are then picked up by a group secretary. After all members of a given small group

[3] For a full description of the method and procedures for evaluating student performance, see William E. Utterback, *Group Thinking and Conference Leadership*, rev. ed. (New York: Holt, Rinehart and Winston, 1964).

have voted individually on the case problem, that group is asked to discuss the problem and to decide which is the best solution. The group decision is recorded and collected by the secretary. Next, each member of the small group is asked to record on a post-discussion ballot what he or she now considers the best solution. These ballots are also collected for subsequent recording. Depending on the amount of time needed for small group discussion, four or five case problems may be discussed in a single hour.

From the above steps, a record is available of each person's pre- and post-discussion voting. When you have participated in ten or fifteen case-problem discussions, you will have some indication of your overall performance. Since the correct solution is known, an analysis of your record will reveal information such as the following:

1. How correct was your pre-discussion judgment?

2. How correct was your post-discussion judgment?

3. How much did your judgment improve over time?

4. How frequently did you adhere to a correct (incorrect) judgment after group discussion when the group selected the incorrect (correct) solution?

5. In your own self-analysis, be concerned with the role you played in contributing to group consensus that chose the correct solution.

This technique is an excellent way to get an audience involved at all levels — physical, intellectual, and psychological. It is also valuable because of its flexibility. Case problems may be short or long; they may be prepared in advance or, depending on circumstances, developed "on the spot"; one case problem or a number may be used; they may be prepared so that they draw on both the general and specific knowledge of the participants; and correct answers may be selected by the participants. Frequently, the discussion on a given case problem will continue well after the close of the planned session, especially if participants disagree with the solution picked by the experts. Several sample case problems are given here:

Case 1: The mayor of a large middle-western city appoints all members of city commissions, and the appointments must be approved by the city council. Sometime after his appointment, one appointee was convicted of accepting a bribe because he voted a certain way when a large city contract was granted. In a subsequent mayoralty contest, the mayor was charged with having a corrupt administration.

What action seems most appropriate for the mayor in his campaign?

1. He should blame the city council for the corruption because it approved the appointment of the commissioner.

2. He should ignore the charges.

3. He should ignore the charges and point to the large number of his appointees against whom no charges had been made.

4. He should point out that when he made the appointment he thought the appointee was an honorable man.

5. He should point out that, when he learned of the bribe situation, he started the investigation which led to the commissioner's conviction.

Case 2: A college committee composed of faculty and students has met to consider a series of demands made by a group of militants, which includes some nonstudents. No member of the militants is present, although they all have been invited.

Which one of the following comments seems to you most sound?

1. No meeting should be held until the militants are present.

2. It is best to have at least a preliminary meeting when the militants are not present.

3. Decision on action to be taken should be made by administrative officers.

4.   The militant group should be informed that its demands cannot be considered because the group has nonstudents in its membership.

5.   The meeting should be held; decisions should be made; the militant group should be advised.

Case 3: Income for the last fiscal year in a large manufacturing plant decreased by six million. This decrease might have been the result of a sharp decrease in sales. The heads of several sales division departments were called to a meeting by an executive vice-president immediately after the income loss was announced. The purpose of the meeting ostensibly was to explore the reasons for the sales drop, but the presiding executive vice-president planned to use the meeting publicly to blame the sales division head, possibly to build a case to have him fired. The heads of all other company divisions, such as production, personnel, and finance, were also to be present.

Which of the following statements on the situation seems most sound to you?

1.   The presiding officer was premature in placing the blame for the sales decrease on the person in charge of that division without studying the facts.

2.   The censure of a subordinate should always take place in private.

3.   The heads of the other departments should not be present at this first meeting.

4.   The sales division head should be willing to accept all responsibility for the decline in sales.

5.   The sales division head should be primed to point out that the decrease in income could have resulted from a number of other causes, such as higher operating or production costs, outside competition, and so on.

Case 4: During the 1960s and 1970s, a large number of individuals—both blacks and whites—have gained national attention as leaders of minority group programs that have focused on attaining the rights of "first class citizens" for all. The programs advocated by these leaders and carried out by their followers have run the gamut from nonviolent to violent, legal to illegal or extralegal, largely supported to minimally supported, and from extremely successful to complete failure. During the latter years of the period, the Chicanos (or Mexican-Americans as some prefer to be called) and the American Indians have begun to speak out for their rights.

On the basis of the experiences of the blacks, which course do you consider best for the Chicanos and the American Indians to follow?

1.   Stage large group protest activities, such as "sit-ins," marches to Washington, demonstrations, and so on.

2.   Try to get elected or appointed to positions within the government as mayors, police chiefs, legislators, or as important governmental committee members—persons who will support their causes.

3.   Carry out only what might be called a "low-profile" approach. Depend on educational programs; try to increase the sensitivity and support of whites to minority needs and causes.

4.   Recognize that the wheels of "justice" grind slowly and that their lives will eventually be bettered.

5.   Select or develop within the minority group individual leaders who are astute, creative, unafraid of the "establishment," and are willing to sacrifice themselves, if need be, to aid their compatriots.

TECHNIQUES FOR
IMPROVING CONTENT PRESENTATION

One of the important elements of discussion is its content—the facts and opinions necessary for wise decision making. At times, you may find it desirable or necessary to vary the manner of presenting the content in a discussion. In this section, we describe a number of special methods for content presentation.

The Agree–Disagree Discussion Guide[4]

An extremely useful way to present a carefully selected amount of content and to stimulate dynamic participation is the agree–disagree guide. It is a one- or two-page printed or typed statement that contains the following: (1) The title or discussion topic. (2) A limited amount of content material on the topic. (If it follows assigned readings or a lecture, symposium, panel, or film, this content material may be omitted.) (3) Brief instructions for using the guide.

[4] Martin P. Andersen, "The Agree–Disagree Discussion Guide," *The Speech Teacher,* Vol. 8 (January 1959), pp. 41–48.

And (4), a series of statements with which the discussant indicates his agreement, disagreement, or indecision.

Since it must be prepared in advance, this special discussion technique is not quite as flexible as those previously described in this chapter. It can, however, apply to any topic under consideration. The sequence of steps in actual use are these:

1. Prepare the audience for using the guide. Indicate the importance of the topic, the planned use of the guide, and the existence of no absolute right-or-wrong answers.

2. Hand out the guides. In a large group, it is best to have assistance.

3. Ask the discussants to read the content material and instructions, then check their agreement, disagreement, or lack of commitment for each statement. With ten statements or less, this step need take no more than three to five minutes.

4. When using small discussion clusters, you may have each group discuss those questions it is most interested in or on which there is considerable disagreement. The reasons for disagreement (or agreement) become the basis for the discussion. Each cluster may later give a report of its findings to the larger audience.

5. When buzz groups are not in use, follow the same procedure, seeking individual rather than group reactions.

Used at the outset of a discussion program, this technique serves a number of purposes. First, it provides at least some content material on the discussion topic. Although it in no way replaces a speaker, panel, or symposium, it can come in handy when resources for these methods are not available. Second, it stimulates immediate thinking on the problem. An individual must first marshal facts and opinions on each statement before a position can be indicated. A third, and perhaps the most valuable aspect of this method, is that it establishes, in effect, the boundaries of the ensuing discussion. If selected to deal with the important issues in any topic, the statements constitute an agenda for discussion. Fourth, an individual who checks an agree–disagree guide becomes both intellectually and psychologically involved; he recalls facts and beliefs, arranges or rearranges his ideas, raises questions about word meanings, discovers inadequacies in his own store of knowledge, and in many ways engages in reflective thinking. A fifth value is that the following discussion uncovers significant reasons for differences of opinion. A final positive result may be that overdue changes of opinion are effected.

There are major cautions to observe when using this technique. The first involves preparing the guide. Obviously, you must give considerable care to selecting the statements. They should be clear and simply worded, deal only with significant issues, not be too numerous or lengthy, and not emphasize one side of a topic or issue at the expense of another side. This introduces the second caution. The moderator must be wary of the occasional participant who, in the process of checking his or her belief, becomes so committed that revising the belief is impossible. To prevent such over-commitment, an alert moderator will utilize the statements in the guide—and the answers

—to raise such questions as, "Why do some people believe that . . . ?" or, "I wonder if we can discover the reasons for a non-committal answer to Statement 1?" Nor will he attempt to saddle a discussant with the task of defending his viewpoint, or of saving face. Here is one example of an agree–disagree guide. You should be able to adapt it to your own purposes.

How do you talk about people?[5]

Human evaluation is not easy. ". . . Sometimes a man misevaluates by his haphazard, superficial or eccentric mode of approach. . . ." (p. 6)

"In a survey of 10,000 Lutheran congregations . . . it was discovered that congregations having no contact with Jews show, on the average, more undesirable attitudes than congregations which do have such contact." (p. 7)

"It seems that attitudes toward Negroes are now chiefly determined not by contacts with Negroes, but by contact with the prevalent attitude toward Negores." (p. 7)

We should know the difference between Observation Statements (about things with which we are acquainted) and Inference Statements (about things we imply are true although not in the range of our acquaintance). (pp. 10–12)

[5] From Irving J. Lee, *How Do You Talk about People* (New York: Anti-Defamation League of B'nai B'rith, 1950).

Questions for Discussion: Read these statements once. Check whether you agree (A) or disagree (D) with each statement. Don't take over five minutes. Then discuss each statement and try to arrive at a group consensus. Try to discover reasons for disagreement. The secretary of your group will be called upon later to report the group's thinking.

A D

1. __ __ Since desirable attitudes on the part of Protestants toward Jews are developed through direct contacts, it is our responsibility to become more completely involved in general community affairs.

2. __ __ If a person is described as "good citizen," "lodge member," "church member," "union member," "taxpayer," "businessperson," it reveals how that person thinks and acts in most situations.

3. __ __ People always believe good things about people they want to believe good things about.

4. __ __ Sometimes it is helpful to say bad things about other people because it makes us feel better.

5. — — The reason most of us are prejudiced is that our prejudices help us keep our self-respect.

6. — — Mexicans would make good American citizens if they would mix more with other people.

The "agree–disagree discussion guide" technique may also be employed when the subject matter deals with discussion principles and methods. The following one may be used in connection with outside reading assignments or exercises on the nature or effective use of questions considered in Chapter 3.

What is your "questioning" IQ?

In the appropriate column to the left of each statement, check whether you agree with the statement (A), disagree with it (D), or cannot tell (CT).

A D CT

1. — — — The use of questions is the least important of the discussion leader's skills.

2. — — — When a question is asked of a specific person, it is usually best to name the person after the question is asked.

3. — — — Most discussion participants pay little attention to the need for effective questioning in discussion.

4. — — — A probe question may be either overhead or directed.

5. — — — The power of a question lies in its power to elicit a well-considered answer.

6. — — — The proper use of questions is an aid in most situations in which communication occurs.

7. — — — In a small-group discussion of five to twelve people, the leader is the only one who should ask questions.

8. — — — The phrasing of questions is of minor importance.

9. — — — The effect (content) dimension of a question is more important than its affect (feeling) dimension.

10. — — — Closed-end questions are the best type to use in problem-solving discussions.

11. — — — The effective discussion leader uses questions to involve all members of the group.

12. — — — It is "right and proper" in discussion to phrase questions so that they commend some group member.

13. — — — Questions asked by discussion group members of the leader should always be answered by the leader.

14. — — — Questions that seek to elicit a "yes" or "no" answer are never proper in a discussion.

Quiz Techniques

One of the reasons for the great popularity of radio and television quiz programs is the chance they give members of the viewing audience to test their own knowledge and skill. We all like to see how many of the prizes we might have won. The challenge of a quiz can have the same stimulating and involving effect when used with a discussion program. We shall describe two types of quizzes. It should take but a little ingenuity to develop others.

1. **The multiple-choice discussion quiz:**
All of us are familiar, much to the sorrow of many, with the multiple-choice test. To take such tests and be graded on our knowledge may intensify the dislike we have for them. However, if we take a test and keep the results to ourselves, it may be a rather enjoyable game. This is the basis for using a multiple-choice test in connection with a discussion.

The multiple-choice discussion quiz is similar to the agree–disagree discussion guide in certain ways. It must be prepared in advance for each different topic. On one or two typed or printed pages, it states the topic, gives a short set of instructions, and asks five or six multiple-choice questions. The questions deal with significant aspects of the topic and have only one correct answer. The technique may be used in connection with the discussion cluster or other selected methods.

Several years ago, a group of students prepared and used the sample below before a classroom presentation of a panel-forum. Needless to say, the quiz aroused considerable interest in the topic for discussion.

How Barren is the Vast Wasteland?

This short quiz is designed to give you a chance to test your general knowledge of the subject that will be considered in our panel-forum, "How Barren is the Vast Wasteland?" Please read each question and place a checkmark before the answer you consider to be the correct one. We will give the right answers during the panel discussion.

1. Newton Minow was:

____ President of NBC-TV

____ Chairman of the FCC

____ Chairman of the AEC

____ Chief of the TVA

2. Of the three major networks, which telecasts the most violent-action shows?

____ NBC

____ ABC

____ CBS

3. The type of television show that has increased most rapidly in recent years has been:

____ Soap operas

____ All black shows

____ Newscasts

____ Reruns of old movies

4. "Vast Wasteland" is a term referring to:

____ Conservation

____ Mass communication media

____ Radar space control

____ Khrushchev's denunciation of capitalism

5. Current surveys prove that the proportion of young children actually affected in any degree by violence on television is:

____ Over 50%

____ 30%

____ 20%

____ 10%

____ Less than 3%

6. Newton Minow's major objection to current TV programming lies in the area of:

____ Westerns

____ Gangster shows

____ Public information shows

____ Trite situation comedies

7. The demise of many TV shows during recent years has resulted primarily from:

_____ Increased costs of production

_____ Basic differences between the networks and a show's headliners (stars)

_____ Too many shows dealing with the same subject, such as crime and law enforcement

_____ Lack of educational values

Because the quiz is so effective as an involvement technique, it has been increasingly used as a training tool. For example, the following quiz was used to develop interest at a training program for credit union personnel held in California.[6]

[6] Conducted at an "officials' seminar" of the Los Angeles County Employees No. 1 Federal Credit Union, held in March 1968.

What is Your Credit Union IQ?

Today, we want to talk about your credit union and how it can serve you better. But first, let us see what you now know about the credit union movement and the credit union services. For each of the questions below, check the answer that you consider to be the correct one. You will not be graded on how well you do. Please keep this form after you have answered the questions. We will talk about your answers later.

1. The first credit union of the type we have in America today was started:

_____ In Denmark in 1866

_____ In Canada in 1900

_____ In Germany in 1864

_____ In England in 1844

2. Which of the following persons has *not* been active in the credit union movement in America?

_____ Alphonse Desjardins

_____ Roy F. Bergengren

_____ J. Deane Gannon

_____ Mannes Baruch

3. Which of the following is *not* a correct statement?

_____ Credit union members have a remarkable record for repayment of loans—only between 6.5 percent and 7 percent prove uncollectable.

_____ Credit unions are required to set aside a portion of their earnings, usually 20% of net, in a reserve fund to pay off loans that a borrower cannot repay.

_____ CUNA provides training programs to teach credit union employees improved procedures and internal security measures.

_____ All of the credit union employees who handle money are required by law to have surety bond coverage. However, only 85% of all U.S. credit unions are bonded against losses up to a million dollars.

4. Which of the following is the primary security for a credit union loan?

_____ The record of repayment of previous loans.

_____ The number and character of the co-signers.

_____ The character of the applicant.

_____ The availability of money to make the loan.

The procedure for using this type of quiz is essentially the same as for the agree–disagree guide. The moderator first prepares the audience for the quiz, by emphasizing that the results are confidential. The quizzes are handed out, read by members of the audience, and checked and retained by them. If discussion clusters are used, each group is asked to agree on what its members consider to be the right answer. The moderator may give the correct answers immediately or may withhold them until sometime during the panel presentation, as was the case with the quiz on "How Barren Is the Vast Wasteland?" Sometimes questions do not lend themselves to further discussion, as is true of questions 1, 4, and 5 of this quiz. However, question 6 could serve as the basis for extended discussion on how to improve the four types of shows mentioned.

In the quiz dealing with credit unions, the correct answers were given at the appropriate time in the speaker's talk.

You can use this technique in connection with any other discussion method and at any time during a program—before, during, or after a lecture, panel, or symposium. After checking the answers, each participant has an outline of the discussion or presentation to follow. We strongly recommend that you practice this technique.

2. The key organizations list: A second type of quiz for priming a discussion can be used in much the same way. The "Key Organizations List" is a single typed or printed page containing the title of the discussion topic, a brief set of instructions for its use, and a list of the initials of selected key organizations. The quiz itself consists of having each member of the audience name as many as possible of the organizations or agencies represented by the initials. The sample given below was prepared for a class discussion on how schools can cooperate with public and private agencies in meeting the problems of minority groups. The student-planners wished to make the discussion following the quiz primarily a learning situation that would also call attention to the wide number of agencies concerned with minority group problems, to the nature of the programs sponsored by these agencies, and to avenues of cooperative effort.

How Can the Resources of Public and Private Agencies be Used More Effectively in the Solution of Minority Group Problems?

Maximum school-agency cooperation in solving minority group problems can be achieved when available resources are used effectively. But first we must know what these resources are. Do you know what services the public and private agencies listed below can provide? Do you know what their programs are? Let's find out.

After each acronym, write out the complete title of all the organizations with which you are familiar.

Place a check in front of those with which you feel the schools should work more closely.

NAACP _____

LULAC _____

AFT _____

LVW _____

SCA _____

ADA _____

WASP _____

CORE _____

LAPD _____

ACLU _____

ABA _____

FBI _____

ALA _____

ADL _____

ASHA _____

CASE _____

UMAS _____

CIA _____

AFL-CIO _____

GSA _____

YWCA _____

OEO _____

SNCC _____

PTA _____

BSA _____

HUAC _____

SCLC _____

The Case Study

In this technique, a brief written statement of a problem situation, or a case, is presented to the discussants. Discussion follows after the case is studied. This method is particularly useful in many law, business, and adult classes where it may be necessary to reroute students' minds from automatically accepting oracular best answers to developing individual thinking and research.

The procedure is similar to the following: First a case or series of cases, drawn with utmost fidelity from actual occurrences, is made available to the persons who will participate in the discussion. As a general rule, only relatively simple cases are used at the outset. Next, the discussants, after carefully studying the case, assemble in a group. The leader opens the discussion. At the first meeting, this opening might consist of a question like, "Do you see a problem in this case?" or, "What is the problem or problems, if any?" After they have discussed a number of cases, the group will respond readily to, "Who would like to start?"

During the discussion, the leader will frequently restate a member's contribution and ask if the restatement represents the idea adequately. This tactic helps to sharpen the thinking of contributors and, because it gives them a chance to retract, clarify, or augment their original stands, it helps prevent many emotional blocks or blowups. More pointed questions—such as "How can you support . . . ? or "Where do you find this evidence?"—can wait until the group members are more familiar with each other and the method. Sharper and more exhilarating give-and-take may then occur. As we have indicated, the leader will find it necessary during the opening sessions to request clarification, support, and elaboration. Later, the group members will take over the policing of analysis. From then on, the questioning will not differ markedly from that in a good informal discussion or panel. As in any other discussion, the moderator should keep the group on a given issue or point until the majority of the group appear to understand what is being studied. Then, by question or by transition-summary, he or she will prod the group to consider another issue or phase of the problem.

When the cases are well-chosen and well-written, and when the leader encourages the group by his example to engage in friendly but challenging discussion, a productive intellectual climate can be established. Such a climate stresses the importance of careful reading, accurate reporting, reliable interpretation, clear communication, and an awareness of many differing but equally valid points of view.

One function of the case study in an academic situation is to develop critical thinking on the part of the students. *But weaning students from the traditional lecture-notebook-examination method of learning does not take place without some traumatic experiences.* Frequently, the student spends the first few weeks in a case-oriented course getting more and more frustrated. An enormous increase in private student-teacher consultation may result. In addition, the person who has not experienced a case-study teaching method will find that his or her preparation for this "new" method is frequently more exacting and time-consuming than preparing for the traditional lecture was. And

finally, it is possible, as many students have discovered, to learn how to analyze a case, prescribe a sound and workable conclusion, and understand the basic problems involved in the case but still fail to carry all that excellent training into an actual on-the-job situation. Why? Because on-the-job decision making is not usually based on a carefully prepared and succinctly written case made available to the executive at his request. He must often find his own information, determine the vital issues involved in the problem, and analyze the case without the aid of other critical minds.

Cases need not be exceedingly long but should contain enough information so that meaningful discussion is possible. Frequently, a case is followed by a number of possible solutions. In that case, the discussion focuses on the solution that is the correct or most nearly correct one. Cases presented orally must be relatively short.

The Incident Technique

The necessity of training a student to discover vital information, to analyze it, and to draw and implement reasonable conclusions from it is the basis for an interesting variation of the case method

called the "Incident Process Variation" by the Pigors.[7] Essentially, the method involves five steps:

1. *Setting the stage:* To begin with, the group members spend a few minutes reading a short statement of a problem given them by the leader. The case presents only a few facts about the problem. The group members are then in the position of having to make some decision about the problem or incident. They are asked: "What would you do about this—now or later?" If the situation involves an arbitrator, the question might be: "How would you prepare yourself for giving the necessary decision?"

2. *Locating the facts:* In this step, the leader—who has access to the complete case and hence has the desired information—is interviewed by the group members, who seek to draw out the necessary facts. During this period, no one expresses an opinion until the facts are known.

3. *Determining key points:* After a half hour of interviewing, the group usually has the essential information and must next determine and agree on the main issues and subordinate points crucial to a decision.

[7] See Paul Pigors and Faith Pigors, "The Incident Process . . . ," *Management Methods* (February 1956), pp. 15–20.

4. *Making the decision:* This step is divided into four stages: (a) All members write down their decision and their reasons for making it. (b) The entire class or group breaks up into smaller groups of persons who have arrived at similar decisions. Each group elects its spokesperson and helps her or him prepare a case to support the particular viewpoint. (c) The spokesperson of each group briefly argues the case. (d) The discussion or group leader, who originally propounded the problem, now steps into the discussion. If arbitration is involved, he or she presents the arbiter's decision and gives the reasons for it.

5. *Analysis of the case:* The entire group now considers the case as a whole in the light of the known solution. This enables the group to determine what may be learned from the case and to consider how the problem might have been avoided in the first place.

Here is a modification of the above procedure: from the entire audience, select a team of four or five persons who will interview the leader, determine the key points, and make the decision. When desirable, the audience can be brought into the process at any time.

In some instances, an observer-reporter assists the leader in preparing the case and in observing and recording the written and oral comments. His or her report, distributed to the group for study and discussion, furnishes additional experience in analysis and evaluation.

Obviously, the incident process requires a number of consecutive sessions if everyone is to serve as a member of an interviewing team—if that procedure is followed—and to develop effective skills in interviewing and decision making. As a teaching device in a discussion course, it can be used only a few times at the most. But even this will give training in a valuable technique and will enliven group and classroom procedures. Problems considered by this method become challenging and real.

We should mention in passing that the case method has many variants that can be improved through practice. It helps to focus attention on specific problems that must be resolved by a group. In some courses, instructors draw cases from everyday campus problems to initiate discussion. In other courses, particularly in the various areas of communication, instructors take cases from related areas where additional study is necessary. Sometimes instructors use a case as a way to test the student's understanding and analytical skills against norms established by experts.

TECHNIQUES FOR IMPROVING SKILL IN COMMUNICATION

In many cases, the failure to achieve a group's goals results from communication breakdowns. Because communication is the primary mode of exchanging ideas, getting consensus, and determining action in groups ranging from dyads (two persons) to large audiences, skill in communication is important. In this section, we describe a number of techniques that will contribute to more effective communication in discussion.

One-way versus Two-way Communication Demonstration

This demonstration is easy to conduct, involves all class members, and is enjoyable. It shows clearly the values of two-way versus one-way communication and, at the same time, indicates how nonverbal aspects enhance the meaning of verbal communication.

A volunteer is asked to come to the front of the room and is given a single sheet of paper—8½" by 11"—on which there is a configuration of six similar geometrical figures, usually rectangles. The figures appear in random positions and touch one another at different points. The six figures cover almost the entire sheet. The volunteer is then asked to describe the configuration of rectangles, and the class members, in turn, are asked to draw on a blank sheet what is described. The aim is to have what is seen and described by the volunteer and what is drawn by the class members completely coincide. Certain rules are imposed on the speaker and the class members.

1.   The speaker is limited to verbal communication only.

2.   The speaker cannot use hand or body movement to show relationships, directions, or positions of any part of the configuration he is describing.

3.   He or she cannot answer questions from the audience (the class).

4.   The speaker cannot use the blackboard.

5.   If the speaker feels that any part of what she or he is saying is not understood, the comments may be repeated or changed. This must reflect his or her own decision and not the request of a class member.

6.   The class members, besides being barred from asking questions, are urged to give no verbal or nonverbal indication as to whether they do or do not understand the directions given.

7.   The speaker may stand in the back of the classroom to heighten the effect of the one-way communication.

A second part of the experiment calls for a second person to volunteer as communicator. The task of this person is to describe a second set of geometrical figures of the same type, size, and number as used in the first set, but placed in a different configuration. All of the rules imposed in the first half of the experiment are lifted. That is, the speaker may accept and answer questions, may use hand or body movements to describe relative positions of the figures, and may ask the class members if they understand a certain part of the description. If not, the person may repeat or restate until she or he is understood.

We have used this technique frequently and have discovered that when communication is one-way, less than 10 percent of the listeners are able to draw a pattern of figures that have even a "reasonable approximation" to those being described by the communicator. In the second part of the experiment, when communication is two-

way, over 90 percent of the listeners draw almost exactly what the communicator has described. Two-way communication may take longer, but it achieves much better results.

An important part of the experiment is to analyze, after each presentation, what the first speaker might have done, or did do, to increase understanding.

The Rumor Clinic

The rumor clinic is a variation of the Allport and Postman procedure described on page 163. Its purpose is to illustrate the changes made in a message when it is passed from one individual through several others and then to a final destination, the audience. Although we recognize that this is not the way comments flow in discussion, it does show that breakdowns may occur even between two people when one is asked to recall what another has said.

Select a small number of students as "chain" communicators and ask them to leave the classroom. The teacher then gives the remaining students a brief statement containing a few figures, possibly one or two dates, some action taken, some inferences, and opinions by one or more persons. Following are two sample messages:

1. McGovern and Ford, Inc., is a small manufacturing concern engaged in the research, development, and production of electronic and computerized medical equipment. Last year their sales totalled about $5 million, with a net profit of $250,000 after taxes. A bitter struggle is taking place within the management. One group wishes to go public, sell shares, and use the new money for expansion, while the other management members on the board of directors wish to retain the present policy of slow, but certain growth. The leader of the first group is Frank Verdugo, a "gung-ho" young and forceful vice-president in charge of sales. The second group, with a minority of board members, is Dr. Fen McCollum, vice-president in charge of production. Both are gearing for a struggle they are sure will occur at the next board meeting.

2. Bellvue College in Bellvue, Indiana, is a small coeducational school of 1,200 students, 450 of whom are women. For the past ten years the men's competitive program has been extremely successful, winning league championships each year in at least three of the following sports: football, basketball, soccer, track, baseball, and swimming. Success has been due to several factors: excellent and well-paid coaching, a large number of full-ride athletic scholarships financed by gifts from alumni, and an unusually efficient recruiting and public relations program. The athletic program has netted at least $100,000 over expenses for nine of the past ten years.

Although the women's athletic program has not been ignored, it has received much less attention and still less support. This year the women/students and the women coaches have organized a group called "Women for Equality in Sports." Representatives from the WES have met with the men in the Athletic Department and intend to present their case to the Faculty Council, the President of the College, and the Student Senate. They demand equality in budget, facilities, and publicity *now*.

The class is instructed to list the names of the six volunteers on paper. Then, when each volunteer relays the messages to a second person, the class notes which of the six modified the message in any way—by deletion, additions, or changes in names, dates, and numbers.

The instructor reads the message to the first volunteer brought back into the classroom. The second volunteer then is brought back, and is given the message orally by the first volunteer; the second communicator then gives the message orally to the third; the third to the fourth, and so on until the last of the six receives the message and tells it to the entire class. Although success in passing a message intact to a second person is partly a matter of memory, this exercise does reveal causes for breakdowns in communication. Class analysis of the changes in the message could reveal ways in which to ensure greater accuracy in the future.

A SUMMARY AND LOOK AHEAD

The success of a discussion is more nearly assured when the group members are physically, intellectually, and psychologically involved. To achieve this involvement, three kinds of special techniques are useful: (1) those that increase participation, (2) those that provide means of improving content presentation, and (3) those that improve understanding and skill in communication.

In Chapter 11 we consider selected aspects of discussion evaluation.

SUGGESTED READINGS

Andersen, Martin P., "The Agree–Disagree Discussion Guide," *The Speech Teacher,* Vol. 8 (Autumn 1957), pp. 111–114.

Andrews, Kenneth R., ed., *The Case Method of Teaching Human Relations and Administration* (Cambridge, Mass.: Harvard University Press, 1953).

Applbaum, Ronald L., *et al., The Process of Group Communication* (Chicago: Science Research Associates, 1974), Ch. 11.

Barnlund, Dean C., "The Use of Group Observers," *Speech Teacher,* Vol. 4 (January 1955), pp. 46–48.

Bass, Bernard M. "The Leaderless Group Discussion Technique," *Personal Psychology,* Vol. 3 (Spring 1950), pp. 17–32.

Bergen, Garret L., and William V. **Haney,** eds., *Organizational Relations and Management Action: Cases and Issues* (New York: McGraw-Hill, 1966).

Bradford, Leland P., "Leading the Large Meeting," *Adult Education Bulletin,* Vol. 14 (December 1949), pp. 38–50.

Levy, Ronald B., *Human Relations: A Conceptual Approach* (Scranton, Pa., International Textbook, 1969), Ch. 6.

Moreno, Jacob L., and Helen H. **Jennings.** "Sociometric Methods of Grouping and Re-Grouping," *Sociometry,* Vol. 7 (November 1944), pp. 397–414.

Utterback, William E., *Group Thinking and Conference Leadership,* rev. ed. (New York: Holt, Rinehart and Winston, 1964), Appendices A, B.

EXERCISES

1. Which of the special techniques presented in this chapter are best suited to problem-solving discussion? To discussion in learning situations? Give reasons for your answer.

2. Of the special techniques presented, which are best suited for use in large groups? Why?

3. Under what conditions or circumstances would you consider it inadvisable to use the following techniques?

a. Film-forum

b. Quiz technique

c. Brainstorming

d. Dialogue

e. Agree–disagree discussion guide

4. Interview several teachers or other professional persons who frequently attend professional conventions. Try to determine how often the lecture-forum is used as the primary presentation method. Determine the extent to which some of the special discussion techniques presented in this chapter and in earlier chapters are used. Find out which methods are preferred by your respondent, and why.

5. Problems in teaching discussion:* A few weeks ago, a new semester began in the University High School. Mr. K., the speech instructor, greeted twenty-two new students in his sophomore speech class. He knew something about the group from having studied their personal records, from having checked their performances in other classes, and from talking to other members of the sophomore class.

He discovered that the class might be considered very average in intelligence, with no single outstanding scholar in the group. Most of the students had engaged in some extracurricular activities, largely athletic, musical, and scientific. There was an even distribution between boys and girls. There were no recognized class leaders in the group. Very few of the students had been exposed to previous formal speech training. Several of the students were reputed to be very vocal in several of their classes. However, at least half the students had the dubious reputation of being nonvocal members of their various classes.

As a result of this information (and the pressure of one of his graduate professors), Mr. K. elected to begin the semester with the project, "Learning to Solve Problems through Group Discussion." He set his plan in action at the first meeting of the class. And, immediately, he encountered a number of annoying problems. Basically, the problems concerned the utilization of discussion processes, forms, and techniques. Essentially, the problems are similar to those that many beginning and even some experienced teachers will encounter while attempting to teach a unit in discussion.

On the next few pages you will find brief descriptions of the situations that seemed to engender the specific problems as the instructor interpreted them. Following each problem or situation is a list of various methods, procedures, or techniques he used or might have used to "solve" what he considered to be his problem. *How would you have used each of these teaching tools were you in his position?* Please be specific as you make your adaptations. If you would not use a specific technique, indicate the reasons for your decision.

After you have finished these problems, you might want to try your hand at another problem. If you were Mr. K. and if you faced a class like this, how would you go about planning and introducing a unit on discussion? We will let you choose the number of class meetings you might want for the unit.

* Prepared by Prof. Marvin Kleinau, Southern Illinois University.

Problem 1: On the very first day of the class, the teacher opened the meeting by saying, "Let's just sit around and discuss some of the problems that interest us. In that way I can get to know something about the way you think. Now, what topics would you like to discuss?" No response came from the class. The teacher continued, "Come on, what topics concerning your school or your environment would you like to talk about?" Still the class maintained its silence. The teacher was upset. He had hoped that eventually the class would discuss some school problems, teenage problems, and even national and international problems that had a bearing on their lives. But the continued silence indicated that first he would have to find a method of getting them to react vocally. He attempted to solve his problem by using some of these "ice" or "silence" breakers:

a. A buzz session
b. Scripted "role plays"
c. An agree–disagree guide
d. A problem census
e. A film-forum

Problem 2: The class finally agreed to discuss a topic concerning teenagers and their responsibilities in the school community. But they didn't really seem interested in the subject and the following discussion fell flat on its face. How could the instructor motivate the students? How could he arouse interest in their topic? He tried his hand at utilizing one of the following "interest catchers:"

a. A case study
b. The Pigors' incident process variation of the case method
c. Role-playing (impromptu and scripted)
d. Picture stimuli

Problem 3: Midway through the second discussion, which involved the entire class of twenty-two students, the teacher-chairperson noticed that six of the students took very little part in what was going on. He asked one student if he had anything to add. The student said, "Nothing." However, two other students, when asked direct questions, gave brief but useful replies. Why, wondered the instructor, did he get that negative answer? Why did the other two contribute when asked? Perhaps, he concluded to himself, he'd better study various techniques of asking questions. And definitely, he'd employ some of the following procedures to ensure greater participation:

a. A panel discussion
b. A symposium-forum
c. A written question outline for the next discussion
d. Role-playing
e. Outside classroom conferences with the quiet ones
f. Requiring the nonparticipants to act as critics or evaluators of discussion

Problem 4: Eventually various subgroups in the class began to enjoy discussing school problems and their performances encouraged the teacher to ask the groups to tackle a problem of greater scope. The first group to discuss an expanded topic decided to examine "all points of view;" they equated "all" with their opinions or the opinions of their parents. In reply to the teacher's question, "Why haven't you gathered sufficient information to enable you to discuss this subject intelligently?" the students said, "We don't know what to look for or where to go to find it." The instructor's main problem then became one of finding good ways to teach his students how to gather information. He decided to utilize the following:

a. An adaptation of the question analysis sheet
b. A class discussion on the topic "How does one get information for a discussion?"
c. Readings and assignments in various texts on debate and discussion

Problem 5: It was obvious that the work done in class to aid the students in gathering information was helpful. As a matter of fact, it was too helpful! At the next class meeting, the group members had "tons" of factual material and opinionated evidence ready to be tossed into the discussion that followed. It seemed that they had determined that if someone said or thought something and put it in print, it was automatically true. That is, if the student agreed with it. How could the teacher show the students the importance of intelligently using material? He finally came up with the following possible solutions to his problem:

a. A lecture on how to use evidence
b. A film-forum
c. A transcription of a taped discussion and an evaluation of that discussion
d. Readings and written assignments in available textbooks

Problem 6: To the instructor's delight, the students seemed to be warming up to topics of interest and importance. And now the groups demonstrated that they knew where to locate pertinent supporting material. But a number of students seemed more intent upon taking and maintaining positions than in solving problems through concerted or collective action. The instructor's new problem appeared to be one of convincing the students that objectivity, good human relations, and reflectiveness were basic to group productivity and morale. To demonstrate to his charges that objectivity and reflective pattern, the instructor developed a variety of approaches involving the following:

a. Role-playing—scripted and spontaneous
b. An agree–disagree guide
c. Class analysis of various readings

Problem 7: Up to this time, the teacher had been acting as the discussion chairperson most of the time. On a few occasions he had allowed the group to proceed without a designated leader. Now he felt that it was time for a member of the group to serve as his officially designated discussion leader. His first chairperson, however, was so dictatorial and controlled the discussion to such an extent that the "discussion" actually was a recitation revolving about the chairman's questions and statements. The instructor tried a second chairman, this time a very kind and permissive young person. But this person was overwhelmed by the group and mass confusion was the result. The instructor sensed that his new problem involved teaching or demonstrating good leadership techniques and the responsibilities of both the moderators and the discussants. He drew his teaching materials and methods from:

a. Role-playing
b. An agree–disagree guide
c. A class discussion on the nature and responsibilities of leadership
d. A film-forum
e. A class evaluation of a taped discussion

Problem 8: One of the most perplexing problems the teacher faced in his discussion unit involved the failure of many students to listen to what others were saying. Often a student would make a comment completely irrelevant to the subject being discussed. Frequently, discussants would misinterpret the comments of others or repeat what had already been said. The teacher attempted to meet this serious problem of listening and understanding by utilizing some of the following procedures:

a. An interview with a specialist on listening
b. Role-playing
c. A film-forum
d. A listening test, to be taken by the entire class

6. Working in subgroups of five or six, plan a discussion on some topic of your choice. Plan to use at least three different discussion methods (including all that have been presented to this point in the book). In addition, develop your own analysis forms for evaluation. Here are three sample combinations:

Topic: *Human Relations*

Show the ten-minute film *Boundary Lines.*

Use discussion clusters to determine issues raised by the film.

Have a panel of experts discuss the issues selected.

Topic: *How to Improve Counseling in Our College*

Use an agree–disagree guide to determine degree of consensus in the group on major issues.

Interview a faculty counselor on these issues.

Use role-playing to clarify issues unresolved by counselor.

Topic: *The Role of the Militant in College Education Today*

Use the discussion cluster method to determine what the participants consider the major issue to be.

Get a representative from the college faculty, from BSU, and from LULAC to lecture (ten minutes maximum) on the issues raised in the clusters.

Use discussion clusters to reach agreement as to how militants can contribute to improving higher education without disrupting campus life and programs.

METHODS OF MEASUREMENT AND EVALUATION

Evaluating a discussion involves two steps: (1) collecting, by observation or other methods, data about individual participation and group interaction, and (2) interpreting these data. When we evaluate discussion, we are making inferences from available data as to the success or failure of a discussion, or some aspect of it.

We believe that the discussion process and discussion skills cannot be improved unless they are evaluated—judged against some standard. That standard should be the achievement of the goals of discussion, assuming the method has been used for ethical purposes, and the optimum satisfaction of the discussants ego needs.

You have probably used some of the Analysis Forms in previous chapters, so the idea of evaluation is not new to you. And you may have already recognized that some of these forms do not fit every evaluation situation. Let us emphasize again that the content and questions in the forms should not be considered restrictive. Although the Analysis Forms included here have been used extensively by many teachers of discussion, there is frequently a need to make changes. In this chapter, we present additional suggestions on how to analyze and evaluate discussion. The suggestions are general in nature and may well help you to develop your own forms.

Methods of discussion analysis cover a wide range from the actual counting of discrete occurrences of an event—such as the number of times a person talked—to the subjective interpretation of what a person intended when he talked. Some of these methods are completely objective. Some give numerical indices of subjective judgment. Others are highly subjective. In the following description of analysis methods, we consider two types: (1) those giving a quantitative index, based either on objective or subjective data, and (2) those dealing primarily with feelings, which in turn may or may not have some basis in objective fact.

Quantitative Measures of Discussion

There are four general quantitative measures that we may use in the discussion analysis.

1. *Enumeration:* This refers to simply counting the number of times an event occurs. Included might be how often a person speaks, the length of his contributions, and the names of the persons to whom he speaks. Also included might be notes as to whether a contribution is a question or a statement, whether the contribution deals with fact or opinion, and so on. Once we have gathered data by enumeration, we usually make some subjective interpretation.

2. *Scale measures:* The simplest form of scale measure is the *linear scale*. It is merely a linear continuum, and an individual is asked to indicate his position on a certain matter. For example: What is your overall rating of this discussion session?

Very satisfactory	Satisfactory	Average	Unimpressive	Very poor

Sometimes we use a simple ballot and obtain an indication of extreme position on an issue. Here the individual votes "Yes" or "No." A shift-of-opinion ballot permits choices, such as "Very much in favor," "Neutral," or "Opposed."

A final type of scale measure is the *attitude test.* This test consists of several questions that an individual is supposed to agree or disagree with. By a complicated process of scale construction, each statement has been given an index number falling on a linear continuum from "In favor" to "Opposed." By averaging the indices of all the questions a person agrees with, it is possible to get a numerical index of his or her attitude on a given subject.

3. *Information tests:* In learning situations, we may use information tests to check on the effectiveness of discussion as a teaching device, on the relative effectiveness of discussion in comparison with other teaching techniques, or on the differences between working alone or together on some learning task.

4. *Skill tests:* Tests for measuring different skills may be a way to gauge the effectiveness of discussion. For example, tests of critical thinking may be useful after a group of students have participated in several problem-solving discussions. We may test other mental faculties after a group of persons have participated in a discussion and after they have listened to a speech to compare the effectiveness of the two methods in developing a particular ability. We may also test manual skills following discussion participation.

Qualitative Appraisals of Discussion

Under this heading, we include all the forms, check sheets, and questions that call for a relatively subjective answer. These methods seek out feelings of satisfaction or dissatisfaction, estimates of relative merit, interpretations, opinions, judgments, and comparisons. Most of the evaluation forms in this text-workbook call for some subjective replies.

Individual or Group Appraisal

Measuring and evaluating discussions may focus either on the individual or on the group. In the latter case, we try to determine how well the members worked as a group. Or, we try to get group indices of productivity or satisfaction. Individual appraisal seeks to determine the effectiveness of one person alone—how he performs, how his knowledge and personality affect the discussion, and whether his ego needs are met. You will find a sample self-appraisal sheet on pages 209–210.

CONDITIONS FOR EFFECTIVE USE OF ANALYSIS METHODS

Preparing for an evaluation situation is extremely important in determining the effectiveness of discussion. Essential to the preparation stage are: (1) making certain that the group accepts the idea of evaluation, and (2) using methods that are related to what precedes and follows the discussion.

We must remember that most of us become disturbed when we realize that someone is observing our actions critically. Some people cannot face the reality of self-evaluation or will not accept what they see when they do look at themselves. It often takes a long time before a group is mature enough to look critically at how it functions. Frequently, it is even longer before the group is ready to take the steps necessary to improve that functioning. Therefore, in the first evaluation of a discussion group, the focus should be descriptive rather than prescriptive. We should allow the individual members of the group to draw their own conclusions and make changes in their behavior if they desire. Later on, the group can specify ways in which group functioning and individual behavior should change. At no time should evaluation be so critical that it destroys or weakens the self-confidence and security of the group members.

You should focus, therefore, on only a few evaluation aspects at a time. To try to cure all things at one time may result in remedying none of the faults. It is better to concentrate on one or two discussion aspects at one meeting and on others at the next. Or, perhaps it would be better to continue the analysis of a few selected facets over several meetings. Some exceptions to this caution are acceptable in a classroom situation where the students are primarily interested in learning how to use the evaluation techniques.

In addition, be sure to design the analysis forms to extract the information you want. Plan them carefully for each discussion.

Analyzing the discussion effectiveness must always take into account the goals of that discussion. The reason is fairly obvious: there is no point in measurement and evaluation unless the resulting data offer suggestions for improving the discussion or for indicating progress toward specific goals.

OPEN-END
QUESTIONS IN EVALUATION

Most evaluation forms rely on the question, and a basic question is the type we call *open-end*. It is phrased in such a way that the respondent is encouraged to comment on whatever aspects of the query he or she deems significant. Thus, if the question is of the "How did you like . . . ?" type, the person answering might make a reply of commendation or condemnation. An individual might couch his or her answer in general or specific terms. The reply might emphasize process, content, or persons. Or, the response might be personal or impersonal.

Open-end questions may be *broad* or *focused*. A broad question permits the respondent to reply in a variety of ways. Focused questions allow freedom in answering, but they are directed toward specific aspects of the discussion.

When combined with short-answer questions, open-end ones are especially valuable in analysis. Most post-meeting reaction forms contain some focused, open-end questions. The broad type reveals what discussion aspects the respondent actually feels are significant because they disclose faults or strengths. These questions also reveal much more about the respondent than just his reactions to a discussion. Consequently, their use provides discussion planners with additional information about the group members.

POST-MEETING REACTION-FORMS

The *post-meeting reaction-form* (PMRF) most commonly used is rather short. It consists of a linear scale and a selected number of broad and focused open-end questions. The participants must complete it in writing after the discussion is over, and their comments guide preparations for subsequent discussions. The form also helps to determine how satisfied the participants are with the discussion; it gives them a chance to praise or criticize.

The form is usually only a half page in length and contains (1) the title of the discussion topic, (2) a brief set of instructions, (3) a linear scale on which the participants may check their overall reaction to the discussion, and (4) four or five open-end questions requesting reactions to certain facets of the discussion. It is preferable to prepare the PMRF's for each discussion, although the same form may be used in a series of discussion meetings, as at a convention or workshop. Below is a commonly used format of PMRF. Note that it asks the person completing the form *not* to sign his name. This request usually ensures candor in replying.

Post-Meeting Reaction-Form

What Is the Future in Data Processing Methods? We need your help in planning the next session of this conference. Please answer all the questions and give as complete an answer as you can. Your replies will be considered in preparing for our next discussion session. Your cooperation is appreciated. *Please do not sign your name.*

1. What is your overall opinion of this session?

   |_____|_____|_____|_____|_____|

   Outstanding Excellent Good Mediocre Very poor

2. The thing(s) I liked best about the meeting was (were):

3. The thing(s) I liked least about the meeting was (were):

4. To improve our next meeting I would suggest:

When no further meetings are planned, the PMRF may serve to elicit reactions to a single discussion session. Since the participants have cooperated in giving their reactions to the meeting, they deserve at least a brief summary report of the PMRF's. This means that they must complete the forms before the actual close of the meeting. It takes only a few moments to tabulate the results of Question 1 and see some indication of general satisfaction or dissatisfaction. In any event, the participants have had the opportunity for one form of catharsis. When it includes the last question, the PMRF guides planners in adapting succeeding meetings to the needs and interests of the participants.

A single numerical index that reflects the overall degree of satisfaction to the meeting can be determined from the reaction to Question 1. Each category is weighted from 5 for "Outstanding" to 1 for "Very poor." Let us now assume that there were twenty participants and that five checked "Outstanding," seven checked "Excellent," five checked "Good," two checked "Mediocre," and one checked "Very poor." The weight for all categories would be determined as follows:

Category	Weight	Number checking	Product	
Outstanding	5	5	5 × 5	25
Excellent	4	7	4 × 7	28
Good	3	5	3 × 5	15
Mediocre	2	2	2 × 2	4
Very poor	1	1	1 × 1	1
				73

The sum of Column 4, 73, is then divided by the total number of persons completing the PMRF—in this case 20. The quotient of 3.65 indicates that the general reaction to the session was close to excellent. When this overall index is determined for a series of discussion meetings, it is possible to chart numerically the increase, decrease, or other variations in the participants' satisfaction.

The most important value of a PMRF is that it gives the planners and moderator of a meeting some idea of what they must do to improve the next discussion. And, even when there is no follow-up discussion, the PMRF will tell a moderator how his or her moderating can be improved in other groups.

THE PROCESS-OBSERVER

Most of us are familiar with the function performed by the secretary who records the action a group takes. We are not as familiar, however, with that of the *process-observer*, whose job it is to observe the way a group functions. She or he is concerned with process. In contrast, the secretary or the recorder is concerned only with content. The main purpose of the process-observer is to assist the group to assess its own behavior in such areas as productivity, leadership, participation patterns, communication, atmosphere, and problem-solving. He or she seeks to make the group more critical of its performance so that it will improve in successive meetings.

How this evaluator reports his or her interpretations of what has been observed depends largely on the group's familiarity with a process-observer. It also depends on her or his own skill to do more than just describe observations. However, simple description may suffice when a group has not previously used a process-observer or when it is meeting for a single time only. What the observer reports to the group also depends on the stage of the group's development, the extent to which it can take objective criticism, and the particular process problems that may be of primary interest to it, as well as on what the observer actually does observe (he or she cannot see everything that happens in a group) and what the group asks him or her to observe.

The process-observer must remember that his or her task is to help the group improve its functioning. Contributions must be constructive yet critical. She or he must be aware of how sensitive others are to criticism. Hence, remarks must be objective and based on fact; they must be suggestions or queries rather than dogmatic statements; they must lead the group as fast as it will go to a point where it can take over its own process-policing.

Below we list a number of questions pertaining to certain major areas in which the discussion process may be impeded. Remember, skill in process-observation comes largely through practice. And, with practice, a refinement and extension of the criteria for evaluation also results.

1. *Observations on productivity:*
Is the group aware of its goals?

How does the group go about choosing its goals?

Does the group plan successive steps in achieving its goals?

Are these successive steps well defined?

Do all of the members contribute equally in achieving the goals?

Does the group agree as to what its goals should be?

Does the group effectively employ all available resources in achieving its goals?

2. *Observations on leadership:*
In what ways does the leadership contribute to the achievement of the group's goals?

What is the general pattern of leadership behavior: democratic, authoritarian, or laissez-faire?

How sensitive is the leader to the group's needs and interests?

What does the leader do to avoid internal conflicts? To make effective use of internal conflicts?

Is the leadership function shared by many or carried out by the chairperson only?

Are the group members being trained to take over the leadership tasks?

3. *Observations on participation patterns:*
Are the knowledge, skills, and understandings of the individual members utilized maximally in the discussion?

Is there overparticipation by some and under-participation by others? What is being done to prevent these dangers?

Does the group seem to be working as a team? In what way(s)?

Do the group members seem interested in the discussion? Do they take responsibility for participation?

Do the group members assume responsibility for improving the participation patterns? How?

4. *Observations on communication:*
How effective are the members in expressing their ideas? Can they improve on this score? How?

Does everyone understand what is going on? If not, why not?

What are the barriers to communication? What is being done to remove them?

What specific words, phrases, or concepts have been misunderstood?

Do the members feel free to express their ideas? If not, why not?

Are subgroup communication networks developing?

Does the leader involve all or just a few members in the communication pattern?

5. *Observations on atmosphere:*
Does the atmosphere seem informal and permissive?

Do the members seem willing to share personal feelings? If not, why not?

How flexible is the group in adapting to changing needs?

Does the conflict that occurs concern issues or personalities?

Do the members of the group seem sensitive to the interpersonal needs of others?

Does the chairperson have this sensitivity?

6. *Observations on problem solving:*
Is the group aware of the steps in a problem-solving sequence?

Does the group know where it is in the sequence at any given time?

Does the group recognize when it needs new facts and opinions? What does it do to acquire this information?

Are the members of the group willing to hold decisions in abeyance until all the facts are in, or do they want to make decisions hastily?

What behavior within the group creates barriers to effective problem solving?

7. *Observations on nonverbal communication:*
Do the nonverbal aspects of an individual's contributions coincide with and enhance the understanding of what she or he says?

Does the way a person acts lend credibility to his or her statements?

Do the discussants' physical actions reflect interest in the discussion, friendliness toward others, willingness to let others talk, approval of what is said and how it is said, and apparent intensive listening—or the opposites of these perceptions?

Are the discussants' actions formal or informal, do they indicate understanding or lack of it, and do they reflect concern for others or disregard for them?

What is the general nature of the physical actions of each discussant? Do they add to or detract from the productivity of the discussion?

When the process-observer is skilled in observation, in interpreting objectively what he or she sees, and in reporting what will be of greatest value to the group for improving its own functioning, he or she should be a regular member of the leadership team in discussion. When a person does not have these skills, that individual should be used less frequently or not at all. Or, such a person should know what part of his or her own perception is objective fact and what part is subjective interpretation. If this awareness exists, the process-observer can contribute much to improving the group's functioning.

FEEDBACK

The term *feedback*, taken from the field of electronics, refers to feeding back information into a communication system so that system may modify and improve its functioning. Thus, a PMRF provides a group with information that can be used by the planners to improve subsequent meetings.

We mention feedback at this point because we wish to stress that this principle should be incorporated in every discussion situation.

"The difference between 'intended' and 'perceived' meanings can have disastrous effects on discussion . . ."

PERCEPTUAL MEANING– COINCIDENCE TESTING

Throughout this text, we have emphasized a proposition—supported by researchers and practitioners alike—that the real meaning of a message lies in the listener. Because understanding is a perceptual process, and because no two perceptual fields are identical, a speaker can never be sure his listeners have interpreted his meaning correctly. The difference between "intended" and "perceived" meanings can have disastrous effects on discussion, where one misinterpretation builds on another. The perceptual meaning–coincidence technique helps to decrease some misunderstanding.

The procedure is simple. All participants are told about the test before the discussion starts. Whenever two succeeding contributions seem to be explicitly or implicitly in conflict, the discussion is halted by the leader. The second speaker is asked to rephrase her or his contribution so that it reflects a coherent understanding of what the first speaker said. The discussion then continues.

Although this procedure does interrupt the flow of a discussion and may at first be time-consuming, we have discovered that it is productive in the long run. After the first four or five times a discussion has been stopped for a "rephrasing," all of the discussants become more aware that they need to accurately interpret what is said. Their subsequent statements must reflect this awareness.

A SUMMARY AND A LOOK AHEAD

Evaluating a discussion is essential if you are to improve it. Quantitative and qualitative methods may be employed. The post-meeting reaction-form and process-observation are the most commonly used methods. Evaluation may focus on either the individual or the group, or both. Measurement and evaluation may deal with productivity, leadership, participation patterns, communication (both verbal and nonverbal), discussion climate, and problem solving.

In the next chapter, we consider the planning and conduct of large group meetings, in which both private and public discussion forms may be used.

SUGGESTED READINGS

Bales, Robert F., "A Set of Categories for the Analysis of Small Groups' Interaction," *American Sociological Review*, Vol. 15 (April 1950), pp. 257–263.

Bane, C. Laverne, "Evaluation of Training in Discussion," *Western Speech*, Vol. 22 (Summer 1958), pp. 148–153.

Barnlund, Dean C., and Franklyn S. **Haiman,** *The Dynamics of Discussion* (Boston: Houghton Mifflin, 1960), Ch. 8.

Beal, George M., Joe M. **Bohlen,** and J. Neil **Raudabaugh,** *Leadership and Dynamic Group Action* (Ames, Iowa: Iowa State University Press, 1962), Part 3.

Bradford, Leland, D. **Stock,** and M. **Horwitz,** "Improving Group Efficiency," in *Understanding How Groups Work* (Chicago: Adult Education Association of the U.S.A., 1955), pp. 41–48.

Brandenburg, Ernest, and Philip A. **Neal,** "Graphic Techniques for Evaluating Discussion and Conference Techniques," *Quarterly Journal of Speech*, Vol. 39 (April 1953), pp. 201–208.

Egan, Gerard, *Face to Face* (Monterey, Calif.: Brooks/Cole, 1973), pp. 154–158.

EXERCISES

Galvin, Kathleen, and Cassandra **Book,** *Person to Person: An Introduction to Speech Communication* (Skokie, Ill.: National Textbook, 1974), Ch. 5.

Grove, Theodore G., "Abstracted Feedback in Teaching Discussion," *The Speech Teacher,* Vol. 16 (March 1967), pp. 103–108.

Johnson, F. Craig, and George R. **Klare,** "Feedback: Principles and Analogies," *Journal of Communication,* Vol. 12 (September 1962), pp. 150–159.

Keltner, John, "Symposium: Problems in the Measurement of Discussion," *Journal of Communication,* Vol. 3 (May 1953), pp. 9–33.

Patton, Bobby R., and Kim **Giffin,** *Problem-Solving Group Interaction* (New York: Harper & Row, 1973), Chs. 12–14.

Scheidel, Thomas M., and Laura **Crowell,** "Feedback in Small Group Communication," *Quarterly Journal of Speech,* Vol. 52 (October 1966), pp. 273–278.

Wilhelms, Fred T., ed., *Evaluation as Feedback and Guide* (Washington: Association for Supervision and Curriculum Development, NEA, 1967).

1. Plan to observe at least three discussions of some on- or off-campus organization. Make a critical analysis of each discussion using the PMRF form given in the chapter. Try to determine if the practice helps you refine and extend your observations. Arrange to discuss your findings with your instructor.

2. In the opening of this chapter, we stressed that the discussion process and one's individual skills in discussion will not improve greatly unless they are continuously evaluated. The purpose of this exercise is to obtain some idea of the extent to which persons in charge of out-of-the-classroom discussions concern themselves with process evaluation:

Arrange to interview the people in charge of several organizations that hold regular discussion sessions. Included might be the chairman of the faculty council or senate, the chairman of the student body association, the president of a fraternity or sorority, or the leader of some off-campus group. Find out if process-observers are employed. Does the leader evaluate his own conduct of the discussion sessions? Does the leader discuss "process" with the members of the group? What "measurements" are taken of the progress made by the group toward its goals? Ask the person being interviewed if he believes some consideration of process would have improved the functioning of his group. In what ways?

In a class discussion, share your findings with the other members.

3. In this chapter, we have talked about seven different aspects of discussion that may become the focus of a process-observer's attention. Select one of these aspects, then prepare an Analysis Form suitable for analyzing it in class. The following method may be used to select a certain aspect. Begin with one class member and count from "one" through "seven." Repeat until all class members have a number. All number "ones" will prepare an Analysis Form dealing with productivity, all "twos" will focus on leadership, "threes" with participation patterns, and so on through all the aspects of discussion process given in this chapter.

After preparing your own Analysis Form, meet with the other persons dealing with the same aspect. Prepare a group Analysis Form, and plan to use it in some class discussion.

4. As you have noted, this text contains several analysis forms that can be used to evaluate different aspects of the discussion process. Turn back to a number of these forms and study them thoroughly. Now, select any three and revise them in the light of your study. The following questions may help to guide your thinking:

a. Does the analysis form focus on an aspect limited enough to make the form useful?

b. What are the values of having a broad focus in evaluation? What is the function of a broad-focus analysis form for groups that meet regularly over a period of time?

c. In forms containing a large number of different categories for observation, are the categories mutually exclusive? Should they be?

d. What are your reactions to the physical format of the forms? Too small? Arranged for handy use?

e. What type of analysis form do you prefer, and why? The type that requires counting or checking only? The type that employs closed-end questions only? The type that employs open-end questions only? Some combination of these types?

f. What problems do you believe exist in training persons to use discussion analysis forms? What additions should be made to the instructions in order to eliminate these problems? When they are included with the forms in the text, are the instructions clear and adequate? Do you believe that long instructions are needed?

g. What changes in the sequence of questions would you make in the analysis forms you are planning to revise?

h. What facets of the discussion process have we overlooked in the forms included in this text?

REACTION TO GROUP DISCUSSION

Please check the point on the scale that represents your considered opinion. If you wish to clarify or explain your decision, please do so on the reverse side of this sheet. *Do not sign your name.*

1. Are you satisfied with the conclusions (if any) reached in the discussion?

Very much so	Moderately	Not at all

2. Were the attitudes of the discussants conducive to cooperative action?

Very much so	Moderately	Not at all

3. Did the group adopt and follow an orderly or systematic approach toward solving the problem confronting it?

Very much so	Somewhat	Not at all

4. As a consequence of the discussion, have you gained any new insights or new and useful information and understanding?

A great deal	Some	Very little

5. Were you given opportunities to express your opinions and present facts?

Often	Occasionally	Infrequently

6. Did the nonverbal aspects of the communication in the group affect in any way the outcomes of the discussion?

A great deal	Some	Very little

7. Would you suggest any changes in the leadership of the discussion?

Many	A few	None at all

8. Could the members have contributed more effectively to the group's leadership?

_____

Very much more   Slightly   Not at all

9. Which of the following changes would benefit the group? (Check as many as you wish.)

_____ a. Better definition of problems discussed.

_____ b. Better individual preparation.

_____ c. More responsible leadership.

_____ d. More carefully planned agenda.

_____ e. More democratic leadership.

_____ f. More consideration for members of the group.

_____ g. Greater sharing of leadership responsibilities.

_____ h. More orderly procedures.

_____ i. Friendlier atmosphere.

_____ j. Wider spread of participation.

_____ k. Greater adherence to the discussion topic.

_____ l. Greater concern for the feelings of the discussants.

_____ m. More effective presentation of facts and opinions.

_____ n. More constructive use of conflict.

_____ o. Greater sensitivity to the nonverbal aspects of communication.

_____ p. Fewer tangential statements.

_____ q. Greater control of the discussion by the leader.

SELF-ANALYSIS FORM

The effective discussion participant is one who recognizes his or her defects, does not feel defensive about them, and is willing to do something about them. How do you score on the following items? Indicate in the first two columns your self-rating early in the semester; check your rating later in the semester in the last two columns. Have you improved?

	Early		Later	
(Check one)	yes	no	yes	no
Criteria for Determining Individual Growth:				
1. Have you substituted adequate practices for inadequate ones?				
2. Do you try to understand and accept others' viewpoints?				
3. Do you have few feelings of inferiority and superiority toward others in the group?				
4. Are your feelings of resistance to disagreement relatively infrequent?				
5. Can you express your convictions without excessive emotional involvement?				
6. Can you work harmoniously with others who differ with you?				
7. Are you interested in assuming leadership functions as well as being a follower?				
8. Do you try to support others in discussion?				
9. Do you internalize private concerns in discussion?				
10. Do you try to be cooperative rather than competitive in discussion?				

(Check one)	Early		Later	
	yes	no	yes	no
Criteria Reflecting Proper Attitudes and Procedures:				
1. Do you make thorough preparation for each discussion?				
2. Do you try to be a good team member?				
3. Do you make maximum use of your own experience and knowledge in discussion?				
4. Do you concentrate on the group's goal above your own ego needs?				
5. Do you make flexible adaptations to the needs of the discussion situation?				
6. Do you have few feelings of defensiveness?				
7. Do you try to complete as best you can all tasks that may be assigned to you?				
8. Do you know what your faults are and do you do something about them?				
9. Do you try to focus on issues rather than on personalities in discussion?				
10. Do you try to provide opportunities for others to participate effectively in discussion?				
11. Do you assume responsibility for your actions?				
12. Are you more concerned about getting a job done than about getting credit for it?				

GENERAL CONSIDERATIONS
FOR GOOD PLANNING

Conventions, conferences, workshops, public forums, training sessions — the meetings that take place annually in this country are innumerable. Unfortunately, the number of poorly conducted meetings is so great that many national and community organizations, business and industrial concerns, governmental agencies, religious groups, and educational institutions carry on regular training programs to improve the skills of their members in conducting large meetings. Such training programs usually cover materials discussed in this text, and specifically, the content of this chapter.

We focus here on planning meetings that are to last longer than a single discussion session — a full day to several weeks. Many different techniques and modes of presentation will necessarily be employed at such sessions.

There are at least eleven major considerations that underlie every planning activity.

Goals

Planning must always be related to the goals of a group. You decide on your destination before you plan the route to get there. Goals may be classified in a number of different ways, and each classification must be given some consideration. In terms of scope, goals may serve the individual, the group of which he is a member, the community of which the group is a part, the state, the region or nation, and the still larger world community. Goals may be put into effect immediately or at some later time, have only temporary or lasting values, and be easy or difficult to implement. Goals may seek to provide training, get commitment to action, or resolve some issue of concern to the planning group. Whatever the goals, they constitute the guidelines to planning.

Sponsorship

Closely related to the goals of any conference is the sponsorship — the organizations, groups, and agencies that will aid in planning and/or whose members will participate. In recent years, multiple sponsorship of institutes and conferences has increased. Many of these programs are co-sponsored by educational institutions, branches of the government, or private foundations. Sometimes, the latter provide financial support only. More and more frequently, however, they are also involved in the planning. Planning is thus made more complex because arrangements must be made by correspondence, by phone, or at infrequent planning meetings.

Procedures

Procedure relates to all the tools that a group uses to achieve its goals: discussion methods and types, human resources, business procedures, socializing, promotion, evaluation methods, membership activities, training programs, and so on. Usually, the procedures followed at a convention conform to the advance plans. However, the procedures for training programs must have a built-in flexibility that will permit on-the-spot modifications.

Personnel

Someone must perform the tasks of a group before it can achieve its goals. Sometimes, high status people are needed to give an organization and its activities needed publicity. Resource persons of many types are needed: discussion leaders are essential; organization officers must give continuity to the group's work; technicians help on specific tasks; committees must have active personnel; and, sometimes, a group needs persons who do no more than to goad it into action.

Program Aids

We include here all of the physical-video-audio-visual aids that any group personnel may use in performing their respective tasks. Video-tape recorders, tape recorders, visual-aid equipment, printed materials, discussion primers such as guides or quizzes, evaluation forms, record forms of

all sorts, posters, displays, and materials group members can study after a meeting are some types of program aids.

Promotion and Publicity

This topic includes all the techniques and materials used to encourage people to become members of a group, to attend a single meeting, or to serve the organization in various capacities. News stories, telephone campaigns, radio and television spot announcements, advertisements, interviews, and printed brochures are some of these methods. For a single discussion, the purpose of promotion is to get an interested, motivated audience to attend.

Financing

There usually is some cost involved in every meeting or discussion. Publicity may sometimes be a large item. Honoraria for speakers or panel members, entertainment, printed materials, and film and equipment rentals are just a few of the often necessary expenses. Sources of financing

must also be considered — will the costs be borne by fees for attendance, organization support, or governmental or foundation grant. Or, will other resources be tapped?

Facilities and Equipment

These, too, are factors to consider for every discussion and meeting. They include providing video-audio-visual and public-address equipment, securing accessories for showing visual aids, making seating arrangements for both panel members and the audience, assuring adequate lighting and ventilation, making plans for meeting-breaks, and considering how the group's activities will be recorded.

Timing

Under the heading of timing, we consider specifics such as planning for the specific day and time of day when an event is to take place. Someone should think out the projected sequence of activities at a given meeting and the amount of time to be given to each activity. Also, consider the starting and stopping times of the meeting, the amount of time for the forum period in a forum type of discussion, the length of contributions, the order of speakers, and the time needed for evaluation.

Timing also includes the scheduling of all pre-meeting activities, such as deadlines for selecting speakers, distributing publicity, preparing materials, making physical arrangements, and securing financing.

Evaluation

Plans must be made to obtain the data necessary for evaluating a meeting. Sometimes the group members and sometimes an outside observer may do the evaluating.

Members must be made aware of the need for evaluation and must consent to participate in evaluation activities. Evaluation is especially useful in getting improvement suggestions when a series of meetings are being held.

Follow-up

Once plans for a discussion or meeting are complete, the necessary steps must then be carried out. Follow-up also involves implementing the action decisions the group has made, as well as planning for any future meetings.

Interrelationships among the Goals

It is obvious that planning considerations are not and cannot be carried out on a mutually exclusive basis. Each is related to and affects the others. For example, the money available to conduct a convention program will, in part, determine the goals. In turn, the achievement of goals will partially depend on the procedures and the personnel.

DEVELOPING CHECKLISTS FOR CONDUCTING LARGE GROUP MEETINGS

College students are not frequently involved in planning and conducting large conferences. If such occasions do arise, enough information is given in the previous sections so that the student can make his or her own checklists. Most hotels and convention centers in the larger cities employ at least one specialist who helps to plan and conduct large meetings and conferences. But even with such a person's aid, you will still need to determine goals, decide on the program—including personnel and procedures, handle the publicity and promotion, decide on what financing is needed, and plan for evaluation and follow-up.

Since we are concerned in part with procedural matters in this chapter, we include an exercise for illustrative purposes: a Planning Worksheet on procedures. Your instructor may ask you to prepare checklists on some of the other general considerations in planning and conducting large meetings.

A SUMMARY AND LOOK AHEAD

Most adults lack the skills needed for planning large group meetings. Considerations in planning include goals, sponsorship, procedures, personnel, program aids, promotion and publicity, finances, facilities and equipment, time schedules, evaluation, and follow-up. Planning effectiveness increases when carefully prepared checklists that cover the important aspects of each of these general considerations are used.

At this point, looking ahead deals with how you apply what you have learned. We wish you well!

SUGGESTED READINGS

Beal, George M., Joe M. **Bohlen,** and J. Neil **Raudabaugh,** *Leadership and Dynamic Group Action* (Ames: Iowa State University Press 1962), Part 2.

Bradford, Leland P., and Stephen M. **Corey,** "Improving Large Group Meetings," *Adult Education,* Vol. 1 (April 1951), pp. 121–138.

Burke, W. Warner, and Richard **Beckhard,** eds., *Conference Planning,* 2nd ed. (Washington, D.C.: National Training Laboratories, 1970).

Conferences that Work (Chicago: Adult Education Association of the U.S.A., 1960).

Huseman, Richard C., Cal M. **Logue,** and Dwight L. **Freshley,** *Readings in Interpersonal and Organizational Communication* (Boston: Holbrook Press, 1969), Part V.

Jenkins, David H., "Feedback and Group Self-Evaluation," *Journal of Social Issues,* Vol. 4 (Spring 1947), pp. 50–60.

Kindler, Herbert S., *Organizing the Technical Conference* (New York: Reinhold, 1960).

Rice, A. K., *Learning for Leadership* (London: Tavistock Publications, 1965), Chs. 2–4.

Zelko, Harold P., *The Business Conference* (New York: McGraw-Hill, 1969), Ch. 5.

EXERCISES

1. **Planning a professional organization convention:** Assume that the members of your class belong to a local chapter of some national professional organization. You live in a large city that has adequate facilities for holding large conventions. The next annual convention is to take place in your city at some future date that you are to determine. The members of your class, who all live in or near the city, will head all the committees needed to plan the convention. One of your class members is national vice-president of the organization and has the major responsibility for planning the convention program.

The convention is to be two days long. Delegates will come from all over the United States, with the majority coming from the area surrounding the convention city. Many of the delegates will bring their spouses. The convention is to take place on a Thursday and Friday, allowing the delegates to sight-see on the weekend, if they desire. The convention goals are comparable to those of many national conventions held annually in this country. But the convention must also consider and decide on a major policy matter. For other recurring business matters—such as the election of a slate of officers for the ensuing year, committee reports, constitutional changes, and so on—a business session will be held on the last half day of the convention. On the first evening, there will be a convention banquet.

Completing this project will require at least two or more class sessions, plus a number of meetings of the various committees outside of class. The first class session will constitute a preliminary meeting of all the committee moderators and as many of the committee members as can attend. At this meeting, you are to make general plans for the convention, assign additional needed committee members, outline and make clear the responsibilities of the various committees, and—to the extent possible—answer all questions pertaining to the work of the committees.

Consider a second class meeting as the second meeting of the same planning group, taking place about two months before the convention. At this time, finalize your plans for the convention, hear reports from the various committees, and try to see that everything is taken care of.

The person who acts as vice-president in charge of the program will also serve as chairperson of the overall planning committee for the convention.

Each committee working on the project may wish to develop a "checklist." Planning should cover at least the following areas:

Overall goals
Promotion and publicity
Finance
Space and physical requirements
Hospitality
Convention program
Evaluation
Materials and reports
Recreation
Exhibits
Registration
Business sessions

Participants are encouraged to use their initiative in making the planning a realistic project. Plan the format for each of the convention sessions. Find out what outside speakers might be available, get an estimate of how much they would charge to speak at the convention, what travel costs would be, and so forth. Check with your local university or college, or some local representatives of national organizations, to determine the type of publicity that might be desirable. And investigate the problems of having a large convention in your city, such as housing, meals, and recreation. Each committee should decide its own policy matters, and these should be consistent with the instructions or restrictions it has received from the overall planning committee.

You will be able to get valuable help in completing this project from your speech instructor as well as from instructors in other subject areas. You might also contact the convention bureau of your local chamber of commerce for advice and help. As we have already noted, most large hotels and convention centers have a staff that works solely with convention planners. Finally, do not overlook the conference planning departments in the extension divisions of local or nearby universities or colleges.

2. **Planning procedures for a professional organization convention:** The aim of every convention dealing with substantive subject areas is, or should be, to provide delegates with as much information as they can absorb in a short period of time. Many things may occur to prevent this from happening: Sometimes speakers are dull or poorly prepared; too much information is crowded into too short a period of time; no time is allowed for relaxation; physical facilities are inadequate; the presentation techniques lack variety; or little opportunity is given for delegate involvement in the program. To prevent these and other blocks to communication from occurring, a convention program must vary its content presentation, provide for relaxation, maximum involvement of the delegates, adequate and tested physical facilities and equipment, and take-home materials that will cover some of the content presented. The following procedural checklist may be useful in achieving maximum delegate satisfaction.

This checklist includes different techniques and activities that may be used to achieve the objectives of a group meeting or series of meetings, as at a conference or workshop. The numbers after the procedures indicate whether the procedure serves primarily as (1) a presentation method, (2) an audience-participation method, (3) an evaluation method, (4) a socializing activity, or (5) a planning technique. A number of the procedures serve multiple functions.

To use the worksheet, first determine the major functions that must be performed at a given session. Then check which procedures should be used. If several are to be used, you may wish to plan and record the sequence of their use in the space at the bottom of the sheet.

1. After-dinner speeches (4) _____
2. Audience panel (2) _____
3. Audience polls (2) _____
4. Brainstorming (2) _____
5. Case study (1, 2) _____
6. Chalk-talks (1) _____
7. Clarifier (1) _____
8. Coffee breaks (4) _____
9. Colloquy (1, 2) _____
10. Debate forum (1) _____
11. Demonstration (1) _____
12. Dialogue (1) _____
13. Discussion clusters (2) _____
14. Discussion guides (1, 2) _____
15. Discussion models (1) _____
16. Discussion quizzes (1, 2) _____
17. Displays (1, 2) _____
18. Dramatic skit (1) _____
19. Evaluation forms (2, 3) _____
20. Feedback (2, 3) _____
21. Filmstrips (1) _____
22. Forum (2) _____
23. Handouts (1, 2) _____
24. Incident technique (1, 2) _____
25. Informal discussion (2) _____
26. Interaction analysis (3) _____
27. Interview (2) _____
28. Lecture forum (1) _____
29. Listening teams (2) _____
30. Meals (4) _____
31. Measurement methods (2) _____
32. Movies (1) _____
33. Multiple-choice case problems (1) _____
34. Multiple role-playing (1, 2, 3) _____
35. Observers (3) _____
36. Observing teams (3) _____
37. One-way communication demonstration (3) _____
38. Panel forum (1) _____
39. Parliamentary procedures (2) _____
40. PERT* (5) _____
41. Play (1) _____
42. Problem-census (2) _____
43. Problem-solving formats (1, 2) _____
44. Post-Meeting Reaction-Forms (3) _____
45. Question-and-answer periods (1, 2) _____
46. Question cards (2) _____
47. Quiz techniques (1, 2) _____
48. Resource persons (1, 2) _____
49. Role-playing (1, 2, 3) _____
50. Rumor clinic (2, 3) _____
51. Sociometric methods (2, 3) _____
52. Standard agenda (12) _____
53. Symposium forum (1) _____
54. Tape recordings (1, 2) _____
55. Video tape recordings (1, 2, 3) _____
56. Visual aids (1) _____

* For a description of this "quasi-mathematical" process, see Gerald M. Phillips, *Communication and the Small Group,* 2nd ed. (Indianapolis: Bobbs-Merrill, 1973), pp. 114–133.